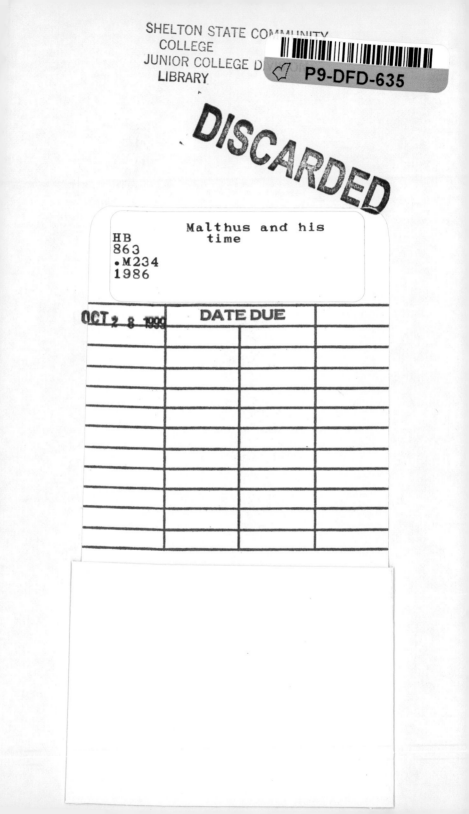

MALTHUS AND HIS TIME

Also by Michael Turner

A DOMESDAY OF ENGLISH ENCLOSURE ACTS AND
AWARDS (*editor*)

ENGLISH PARLIAMENTARY ENCLOSURE

THE HOME OFFICE ACREAGE RETURNS OF 1801
(4 vols; *editor*)

ENCLOSURES IN BRITAIN, 1750–1830

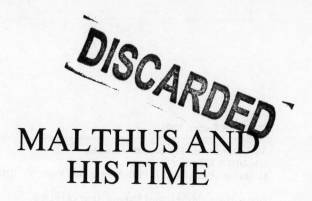

MALTHUS AND HIS TIME

Edited by

Michael Turner

Lecturer in Economic History
University of Hull

St. Martin's Press   New York

First published in the United States of America in 1986

Printed in Hong Kong

ISBN 0–312–50942–1

Library of Congress Cataloging-in-Publication Data
Main entry under title:
Malthus and his time.
    "The origin of this book is an international
conference held in Paris from 27–29 May 1980 entitled
Malthus Hier et Aujourd'hui"—P.
Bibliography: p.
Includes index.
1. Malthus, T. R. (Thomas Robert), 1766–1834—
Congresses. I. Turner, Michael Edward.
HB863.M234 1986   330.15′3   85–25190
ISBN 0–312–50942–1

Contents

List of Figures

Chapter 8 Turner

Chapter 10 Eccleston

List of Tables

List of Appendixes

Preface

The years which are bounded by the birth and death of T. Robert Malthus (1766–1834) were questionably the most momentous for modern British commercial and industrial expansion. Historians' views of the process or processes of industrialisation vary considerably; nevertheless, though we may be uncomfortable with terms such as the 'Industrial Revolution', these six or seven decades figure prominently in most eyes as the genesis of modern industrial society.

Malthus was born and grew up at a time during which many of the major new techniques and inventions which eventually transformed industry from domestic to factory production were developed; he began his academic writing at the end of a century of major British commercial expansion, which took place especially away from traditional trading areas in Europe and more towards the 'New World'; and it was a century during which foreign policy and diplomacy was often subordinated to economic ends in the promotion of this commercial expansion. The century culminated in a war with the traditional enemy, France, which was to last, off and on, for over twenty years. Britain emerged from that war with greater opportunities for further commercial expansion, though at the cost of a spectacularly large National Debt, but it was a war which left her closest eighteenth-century commercial and industrial rival, France, in considerable disarray. Even as the war raged Britain was in the throes of an unprecedented demographic revolution, which neither the war itself nor a food dearth crisis of 'Malthusian' style description could seriously interrupt.

Into this age came Malthus, but his most famous work, his *Essay on Population*, was only one 'chapter' in a considerable writing on political economy. He observed and commented upon the industrial and commercial expansion that surrounded him; he analysed the economic and social ramifications of both population growth and the transformation of industry; and he foretold the economic and social consequences which would arise from the changing requirements of industrial and labour processes. As well as his demographic interests and observations these other concerns of contemporary political economy are also the subject-matter of this book. This is not, however, a volume exclusively about Malthus, but neither is it simply about his age; at times it is both.

Malthus and His Time takes as a central position the observations that this man made about the age in which he lived. Those observations were embodied either in his theoretical exposition of the political economy of his age (and in his debates with contemporaries, especially David Ricardo), or in his writings and observations of specific events, such as his visit to Scandinavia in 1799, his views on the food supply crises of the 1790s, his attitudes to a protected agriculture, or his reflections on the operation of poor relief with his suspicion of the value of local or national social welfare. Some of the chapters linger more on the man than on his time, while others emphasise his time. The book and individual chapters in it are not specifically in praise of Malthus, even though 1984, when they were collated, marked the 150th anniversary of his death. They are critical of him, of his interpretations of contemporary political economy, of his observations, and as often as not they are negatively rather than positively critical.

The origin of this book is an international conference held in Paris from 27–29 May 1980 entitled *Malthus Hier et Aujourd'hui*.[1] It was organised in ten themes of a wide-ranging nature, and these in turn covered many issues from within both the social and biological sciences. The fifth theme, which was organised by the late Professor Michael Flinn, was called 'Malthus and his Time', a title which we now borrow for this book. The organisers of the conference, the Société de Démographie Historique of Paris, fostered the hope that the full collection of conference papers would one day be published in some form. As it turned out this was an overambitious hope for authors and organisers alike – not surprisingly so considering that over 170 papers were originally presented. There is still the possibility that a microform edition may be produced, but at the moment the only full record of the conference is the book of summaries prepared for the conference and distributed to contributors and those in attendance. Ultimately just twenty-nine essays and rapporteurs' summaries were collated and these were presented in the autumn of 1983 under the title *Malthus Past and Present*. The original ten themes were reorganised into six parts, the second of which was called 'Malthus and His Time'. It contains three essays and also Professor Flinn's rapporteur's summary. Two of those essays, by Dr Anne Digby and Professor E. A. Wrigley, formed part of the original theme and are reproduced in revised form below. In addition, Barry Stapleton's revised essay printed below was presented in part one of the book under the subheading 'Malthus'.[2] The remaining twelve chapters in this book, therefore, are those which were not published as part of the conference proceedings. The chapter by Professor J. P. Huzel printed below was originally published independently shortly after the conference in the pages of the *Economic History Review*.[3]

I have organised the chapters into broad themes which seem to me to capture some of the main economic and social forces at play in the emergence of industrial Britain in the late eighteenth century and the first half of the nineteenth. Starting from a pre-Malthusian or pre-Malthus base they illuminate in diverse ways the ongoing revolutions in demography, agriculture and commercialism; they elucidate the circumstances which influenced so-called 'Malthusian' demographic behaviour and demonstrate that behaviour with specific local illustrations from both Britain and the European mainland. The story proceeds to discover an age in which agriculture was still the major single contributor to national income and employment in Britain up to the end of the eighteenth century, but this primary sector was steadily overwhelmed by subsequent industrial and commercial expansion. The processes in play were aided at times, arrested at others, by the long conflict with France. This economic expansion and transformation was not without considerable social reorganisation, whether in terms of the labour process – both labour supply and labour skills – or in terms of the newly acquired agricultural and commercial wealth. This wealth was either conspicuously consumed or ploughed back into commerce, though there were times of course when it was used through local taxation or the endowment of local charity to finance the nascent welfare state – that is, poor relief.

NOTES

1. Congrès International de Démographie Historique, *Malthus Hier et Aujourd-'hui* (Société de Démographie Historique, Paris–UNESCO Building, 27–29 May 1980).
2. J. Dupâquier *et al.* (eds), *Malthus Past and Present* (London: Academic Press, 1983) pp. 97–109, 111–24 and 45–59 respectively. A mainly different selection of essays has been published in a French language edition as A. Fauve- Chamoux (ed.), *Malthus Hier et Aujourd'hui* (Paris: CNRS; 1984).
3. Under the same title in *Economic History Review*, 2nd series, XXXIII (1980) 367–81.

Acknowledgements

There are a number of people to whom I and my fellow contributors are indebted. We would like to thank Academic Press for permission to republish in revised form the essays by Anne Digby, Barry Stapleton and E. A. Wrigley. Our thanks also to Professors Roy Church and A. G. Hopkins, editors of the *Economic History Review*, for their permisssion to republish James Huzel's essay. Our thanks to Alison Turner for her translation into English from the original French of Chapter 5; to Irene Baldwin for retyping edited versions of a number of the original chapter typescripts; to Derek Waite of the Hull University Cartographic Office for drawing the maps and graphs; and to the Hull University Library Photographic Department for rendering those drawings into publishable prints. Finally, we would like to express our thanks to the late Professor Michael Flinn. We all share a great sense of loss of this friend of the theme and of the contributors. In the opening sentences of his rapporteur's summary Professor Flinn wrote:

> The papers presented in this section seek to illustrate the social and economic background against which Malthus thought and wrote. Since his first unpublished essay was written in 1796 and he died in 1834, the period of his intellectual activity – let us say roughly from 1790 to 1834 – spans a distinctive and important period of Britain's social and economic development. It was a period of rapid, if fluctuating economic growth – of war with its inflation, and peace bringing deflation. The simultaneity of the processes of population growth and industrialisation produced problems of adjustment between the agricultural and industrial sectors that were exacerbated by the erratic price movements. In short, rapid and often bewildering change was the order of the day, and it was a stimulating, if not exciting time for the professional economist, which, for all practical purposes, Malthus had become.[1]

As professional economists and historians ourselves, nearly two centuries later, we trust that this book is a stimulating, even exciting

addition to an understanding of the time during which Malthus lived
and to which he so greatly contributed. We trust also that it would have
pleased Michael Flinn to see it appear under the title of his theme,
because we owe him so much.

MICHAEL TURNER
Department of Economic and Social History
University of Hull

NOTE

1. Michael Flinn, Theme 5 Report, 'Malthus and His Time', in Congrès, loc.
   cit., *Summaries of Reports and Papers*, p.75.

Versions of Chapters 1, 2 and 11 first appeared in J. Dupâquier *et al.*
(eds), *Malthus Past and Present* (London: Academic Press, 1983). Our
thanks to the copyright holders of those essays, Academic Press, for
permission to publish revised versions.

A version of Chapter 1 has appeared in French in A. Fauve-Chamoux
(ed.), *Malthus Hier et Aujourd'hui* (Paris: CNRS; 1984). Our thanks to
the editor and to the Centre National de la Recherche Scientifique for
permission to publish a revised version.

A version of Chaper 3 first appeared in *Economic History Review*, 2nd
series, volume XXXIII (no. 3, August 1980) 367–81. Our thanks to the
editors of the *Review*, Professors Roy Church and A. G. Hopkins, for
permission to publish this revised version.

Notes on the Contributors

B. L. Anderson is Senior Lecturer in the Department of Economic History at the University of Liverpool. His main research interest is in the history of financial and capital markets. He is the author of articles in the *Economic History Review* and the *Journal of Economic History*, and co-editor of *Commerce, Industry and Transport: Studies in Economic Change on Merseyside*.

Dr David Cannadine is a Fellow of Christ's College and Lecturer in History at the University of Cambridge. His research interests lie in modern British history. He has published widely on many aspects of nineteenth-century urban history in all of the major journals, and is the author of *Lords and Landlords: The Aristocracy and the Towns, 1774–1967*, editor of *Patricians, Power, and Politics in Nineteenth-Century Towns* and co-editor of *Exploring the Urban Past: Essays in Urban History*.

Edmond Cocks is Assistant Professor of History at Virginia State University, Petersburg, Virginia, USA. His main research interest is in the development of population theory. Recently he has had articles published in *The Virginia Geographer*, and in the *History of European Ideas*.

François Crouzet is Professor of Modern History at the University of Paris-Sorbonne. His main research interests are in British and French economic history in the eighteenth and nineteenth centuries. He is the author of numerous articles in all major journals in his field, and the author or editor of many major monographs and essay collections, most recently *The Victorian Economy* and *The First Industrialists: The Problem of Origins*.

Dr Anne Digby is Research Fellow in the Institute of Research in Social Sciences at the University of York. Her main research interests are in the social history of medicine, particularly in the history of the asylum and

xvii

the relationship between patient and practitioner, and also in unemployment and its historical relationship with benefits and relief. She has published articles in the *Economic History Review* and in *Psychological Medicine*, and is the author of *Pauper Palaces* and *Madness, Morality and Medicine*, and the co-author of *Children, School and Society in Nineteenth-Century England*.

Dr Bernard Eccleston is Staff Tutor in Interdisciplinary Studies with the Open University in their Yorkshire Region. His main research interests are in British labour markets in the eighteenth and nineteenth centuries, and in modern Japanese economic development. He is the author of *The Industrialisation of Britain* and has chapters in *State, Finance and Industry* (edited by A. Cox) and *States and Society* (edited by J. Anderson).

Dr J. P. Huzel is Assistant Professor of History at the University of British Columbia, Canada. His main research interests are in Malthusian population theory, and the demographic implications of welfare policy. He recently had published an article on Malthus in *Historical Methods*, and has a chapter on 'Labour under the Old and New Poor Law' in the forthcoming volume V1 of the *Agrarian History of England and Wales*.

Dr Lars Magnusson is Reader in Economic History in the University of Uppsala, Sweden. His main research interests are in aspects of nineteenth-century proto-industrialisation, and the social consequences arising from the transition from craft skills to factory industry. He has published widely on his research in the *Scandinavian Journal of History*, the *Scandinavian Economic History Review*, and the Uppsala University *Studies in Economic History* series. He is the author of *Industrialismens Röther* (The Roots of Industrialism) of *Vägen till Fabrikerna* (The Road to the Factory), and of the forthcoming *Arbetet vid en Svensk Verstad: Muntells 1900–1920* (Work in a Swedish Workshop: Muntells 1900–1920).

Dr G. E. Mingay is Professor of Agrarian History at the University of Kent, Canterbury. His main research interests are in aspects of agricultural productivity, and the question of rural living standards. He has established an international reputation as a foremost authority on British agrarian history, was formerly Editor of the *Agricultural History*

Review, and has published widely in the major journals. Among his many books we might mention *The Agricultural Revolution 1750–1880* (with J. D. Chambers), and more recently *Rural Life in Victorian England* and *The Victorian Countryside*.

François Pradel de Lamaze is a Statistician at the National Institute of Statistics and Economic Studies (INSEE) in Toulouse, France. His main research interests are in regional demography and regional statistics. He has contributed to chapters in books on various aspects of methodology, and has published articles on local demography and related issues in statistical and regional geographical journals.

B. Stapleton is Senior Lecturer in Economic History at Portsmouth Polytechnic. His main research interests are in the study of population and society in pre-industrial England, and also in English local history from the sixteenth to the nineteenth centuries. He is the author of articles in the *Journal of Regional and Local Studies* and *Local Population Studies*, co-editor of *Odiham Castle 1200–1500: Castle v. Community* and author of *Sources for the Demographic Study of a Local Community*.

Dr Michael Turner is Lecturer in Economic History at the University of Hull. His main research interests are in British agricultural history in the eighteenth and nineteenth centuries, and is currently constructing an agricultural atlas of Ireland from the Famine to Partition. He has published widely in the major journals in his field, is the editor of W. E. Tate's *Domesday of English Enclosure Acts and Awards*, and the author of *English Parliamentary Enclosure* and *Enclosures in Britain 1750–1830*.

Dr Wray Vamplew is Reader in Economic History at the Flinders University of South Australia. His main research interest is in the economic history of British and Australian sport. He is the author of *The Turf: A Social and Economic History of Horse Racing*, and has had articles published in the *Economic History Review*, the *Bulletin of Australian Historical Statistics*, and in the principal sports' history journals of Britain, Canada and Australia.

Annie Vinokur is Professor of Political Economy at the University of Paris X-Nanterre. Her main research interests are economic demography, education and employment, and the economics of human resources. Her publications include an article in the *Revue Française de Finances Publiques*, and the authorship of *Educational Finance in France* and *Decentralised Social Services*.

Dr E. A. Wrigley is Professor of Population Studies at the London School of Economics and Director of the Cambridge Group for the History of Population and Social Structure. His main research interest is in the economic and demographic history of England from 1550–1850. For many years he has been a foremost authority on many aspects of English demographic history, publishing widely in the major journals. Of his many books we might usefully list *Industrial Growth and Population Change*, *Population and History*, and his Cambridge Group collaboration with R. S. Schofield, *The Population History of England 1541–1871: A Reconstruction*.

Part I
Population: On Malthus, Demography and Malthusianism

1 Malthus's Model of a Pre-industrial Economy

E. A. WRIGLEY

When Malthus wrote his first *Essay on the Principle of Population* one of his chief aims was to refute the views expressed by Condorcet and Godwin about the perfectibility of man and of human society. Another was to demonstrate the unfortunate effects of the English Poor Law, not least on those who were intended to benefit most from its operation. About half the book is taken up with these matters. His general purpose in writing the *Essay* is well captured by its full title, *An Essay on the Principle of Population as it Affects the Future Improvements of Society*. Since his arguments were powerful and their influence was very widely felt, it is scarcely surprising that he should have been so frequently discussed and judged as a social prophet. Even in this context he has often failed to receive well-informed or charitable treatment. It was recently remarked of him, indeed, that in the whole development of the social sciences, there has probably never been anyone attacked and defended with so little regard for what he had written as Malthus.[1]

The trenchant prose of the *Essay* and its polemical purpose, however, tended to obscure the analytical strength of the brief sections of the book in which Malthus first set out his understanding of what he termed the Principle of Population. In the later editions of the *Essay* the balance changed. They are heavier reading, containing long passages consisting largely of empirical observations, distinguished neither by wit nor elegance of prose. The emphasis becomes more scholarly, the discussion more historical and the title changes to reflect the new emphasis. The second edition, for example, published in 1803, is entitled, *An Essay on the Principles of Population; or, a View of its Past and Present Effects on Human Happiness: with an Inquiry into our Prospects Respecting the Future Removal or Mitigation of the Evils which it Occasions.*

It is to Malthus's discussion of population history that I wish to draw attention. The passage of time has shown that his forebodings about the limits of future economic growth (and hence real income for the mass of the population) were not justified. In this, however, he was in excellent company since the most penetrating of his near contemporaries, such as Adam Smith and Ricardo, shared the same view. All rejected the possibility of general exponential economic growth because the supply of cultivable land was limited and increasing its productivity tended to require large and larger inputs of other production factors to secure a unit increase in output.[2]

The reason for the general failure to appreciate the possibility of what would now be called an industrial revolution (defined to include comparable parallel changes in agriculture) may be simply expressed. There was no warrant in past experience for the belief that such a radical break could occur, and abundant evidence of the extreme difficulty of securing it. As Malthus put it, when arguing against Godwin's facile belief in overcoming all current obstacles to progress by an appropriate improvement in material technology:

> I expect that great discoveries are yet to take place in all the branches of human science, particularly in physics; but the moment we leave past experience as the foundation of our conjectures concerning the future; and still more, if our conjectures absolutely contradict past experience, we are thrown upon a wide field of uncertainty, and any one supposition is then just as good as another.[3]

As it happened, it was Malthus's fate to frame an analysis of the relationship between population, economy and society during the last generation to which it was applicable. Once the world had changed, the very cogency and clarity of his argument, now that it could be seen to miss the mark, made him an easy prey to those who disliked his conclusions. But the reputation of all social analysts is contingent only. As the world changes, the relevance of their remarks tends to decline *pari passu*.

It is important to judge them, in part at least, on the basis of the evidence available to them when they wrote, for it was on this evidence that they formed their theories and drew their conclusions.[4] Malthus spent much effort in the years following the publication of the *First Essay* in assembling historical evidence, and modified the argument of the *First Essay* substantially as a result. It is, therefore, especially apposite in his case to consider how far his model of population behaviour holds true for early modern Europe, and for England in particular.

The essence of Malthus's analytic framework can be grasped by considering Figure 1.1. Malthus held that population would tend to grow exponentially in the absence of the checks imposed by the fixed supply of agricultural land, noting that in North America the population of the British colonies and of the youthful United States had consistently doubled every quarter-century since the early years of settlement there.[5] But at some stage, however favourable the initial circumstances, growth must be arrested as the land becomes fully occupied. Once this stage is reached, any further growth in population necessarily causes the price of food to rise and real incomes to fall.[6] The diagram in Figure 1.1, therefore, shows a positive relationship between population size and food prices and a negative one between food prices and real incomes. At this point the negative feedback system may take one of two routes (or, of course, may follow both either alternately or simultaneously). The outer path (the positive check) shows that falling real incomes may cause mortality to rise, thus restoring once more a balance between population and available resources. Or the same result may be achieved by following the inner path (the preventive check). In this case, the effect of falling real incomes is to discourage marriage (either by causing individuals to marry later or refrain from marriage entirely), which reduces fertility and so again reverses the population trend. Equally, of course, an initial fall in population by lowering food prices and thus causing an improvement in real incomes will also be corrected. Population will thus oscillate round some equilibrium level, or, assuming a slow growth in agricultural production (Malthus's arithmetic increase), round a secular trend line.[7]

Malthus set out this model clearly in the *First Essay* and did not thereafter change his view of its logical composition, but he did substantially modify and amplify his discussion of its application to the history of the countries best known to him. In this chapter, for brevity's sake, I shall concentrate on his discussion of English history, taking advantage of the fact that it has recently become possible to measure much more fully and accurately trends in fertility and mortality in England from the mid-sixteenth century onwards.[8]

The most important change of emphasis made by Malthus between the first and later editions of the *Essay* was a much increased emphasis upon the operation of the preventive as opposed to the positive check in recent England history (or in terms of Figure 1.1, on the inner rather than the outer path around the diagram). Between the publication of the

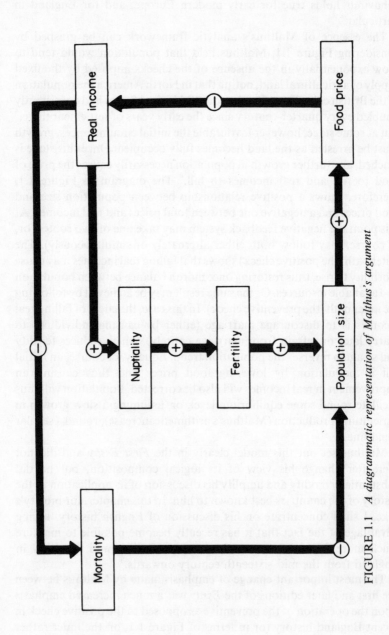

FIGURE 1.1 *A diagrammatic representation of Malthus's argument*

first and second editions, the first English census was taken, and, as part of the same operation'. Rickman, the organiser of the first four English censuses, secured a vast mass of empirical data about totals of baptisms, burials and marriages during the eighteenth century.[9] When Malthus wrote the first edition he was ignorant even of the most elementary facts about the size of the population and its rate of growth. He supposed, for example, that the population of Britain was about 7 million.[10] Three years later the census showed the true total to be 10.9 million, or 56 per cent larger than he had supposed. Once the Census of 1801 had been published he had available to him the bulk of the data which have been used since then, for the parish register returns collected by Rickman have been the empirical foundation of most subsequent work.

Reflection upon the newly available census and parish register data, combined with a much more extensive acquaintance with comparable information from other countries, convinced Malthus that in the English case the preventive check played the predominant role in restraining population growth. In the first edition he laid stress upon the evidence of malnutrition visible among the labouring classes,[11] and displayed great concern about their ability to withstand the temptation of an imprudently early marriage, given the way in which the Poor Laws operated, though he noted that 'a spirit of independence still remains among the peasantry',[12] which helped them to resist such temptation. The nature of the problem he expressed in the following passage:

> Every obstacle in the way of marriage must undoubtedly be considered as a species of unhappiness. But as from the laws of our nature some check to population must exist, it is better that it should be checked from a foresight of the difficulties attending a family, and the fear of dependent poverty, than that it should be encouraged, only to be repressed afterwards by want and sickness.[13]

He was not, however, very optimistic that foresight would prevail.

Later Malthus came to see matters in a different light. The positive check was relegated to a comparatively minor role in his analysis of recent English experience, and more generally that of Europe, compared with other parts of the world. As he put it, '... in modern Europe the positive checks to population growth prevail less, and the preventive checks more than in past times, and in the more uncivilized parts of the world',[14] or again, '... an infrequency of the marriage union from the fear of a family ... may be considered ... as the most powerful of the checks, which in modern Europe, keep down the population to the level of the means of subsistence'.[15] In his discussion of mortality, Malthus laid increasing stress upon its wayward and unpredictable impact and tended to promote overcrowding to an equal place with malnutrition as prime agents in increasing the death rate amongst the poor. A typical passage from the later edition of the *Essay* runs as follows when discussing the effects of famine and death:

> How far these 'terrible correctives to the redundance of mankind' have been occasioned by the too rapid increase of population, is a point which it would be very difficult to determine with any degree of precision. The causes of most of our diseases appear to us to be so mysterious, and probably are really so various, that it would be rashness to lay too much stress on any single one; but it will not perhaps be too much to say, that *among* these causes we ought certainly to rank crowded houses, and insufficient or wholesome food, which are the natural consequences of an increase of population faster than the accommodation of a country with respect to habitations and food will allow.[16]

Reverting to the representation of the logic of Malthus's argument as set out in Figure 1.1, therefore, it may be said that the later Malthus, while continuing to stress the closeness of the links between population growth, changes in food prices, and fluctuations in real income, favoured the inner track rather than the outer, or marriage rather than mortality, as the factor primarily responsible for keeping population and economic resources in balance so far as early modern England was concerned. How far does modern scholarship substantiate this interpretation?

Fortunately, it is now possible to plot changes in population size, nuptiality, fertility and mortality in England from 1541 onwards, and the work of Phelps Brown and Hopkins has made available indices of changes in the price of a basket of consumables and in real wages over the same period, though there is a greater margin of uncertainty about the accuracy of these measures, especially in the case of real wage trends. The strength of each link in the feedback loops shown in Figure 1.1 can thus be tested for early modern English history.

In Figure 1.2 the relationship between rates of population growth and changes in the consumables' price index is shown (the index weights of the food components were as follows: farinaceous food 20, meat and fish 25, butter and cheese 12½, drink 22½; making a total of 80 for food items

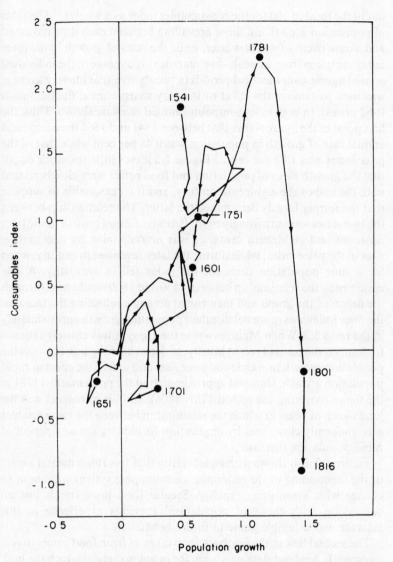

FIGURE 1.2 *Compound annual growth rates of population and an index of the price of consumables (per cent per annum). See text for fuller explanation*

SOURCE Wrigley and Schofield, *Population History of England*, figure 10.2, p. 405

out of the total of 100 for the consumables index as a whole).[17] The rates of population growth are those prevailing between each date indicated and a date twenty-five years later, while the rates of growth in the price index are taken from a twenty-five year moving average of the individual annual figures over identical periods (a twenty-five year moving average was used to remove the effect of the very sharp annual fluctuation in food prices). In both cases compound annual rates are shown. Thus, the first point in the figure shows that between 1541 and 1566 the compound annual rate of growth in population was 0.48 per cent while that of the price index was 1.85 per cent.[18] Figure 1.2 leaves little room for doubt that the growth rates of population and food prices were closely related until the end of the eighteenth century, and it is reasonable to suppose that the former largely determined the latter. The relationship between the two series was surprisingly tight. Periods of rapid growth in the later sixteenth and eighteenth centuries was accompanied by accelerating rises in the price index, while during the later seventeenth century, when for a time population declined, the index fell in sympathy. A line epitomising the relationship between 1550 and 1800 would pass through the origin of the graph and then rise at an angle reflecting the fact that the price index was more volatile than population growth approximately in the ratio 3:2. When Malthus wrote the *Essay* it was entirely rational for him, on the basis of recent history, to detect a strong link between the population growth rate and food price rises and to fear the effect of rapid population growth. He stood approximately at the point marked 1781 in the figure (covering the period 1781–1806), and his retrospect was the long sweep of years in which the relationship between the two variables was uniformly close, and by implication forbidding for any period of rapid population increase.

Figure 1.2 also shows with equal clarity that this fundamental aspect of the functioning of the economic–demographic system was about to change with astonishing rapidity. Secular food price trends lost all connection with those of population. Previous experience in this instance was a fallible guide to future behaviour.

The second link in the feedback loop takes us from food prices to real incomes. It need not detain us long, for in any society in which the bulk of all consumer expenditure is devoted to food, any change in its price is almost certain to be mirrored by an opposite change in real incomes. In Figure 1.3, the same method as in Figure 1.2 is used to set out the relations between population growth and real wage changes. It is so closely similar to Figure 1.2 that it calls for little comment in this context. The trend in the cluster of points representing growth trends before 1800

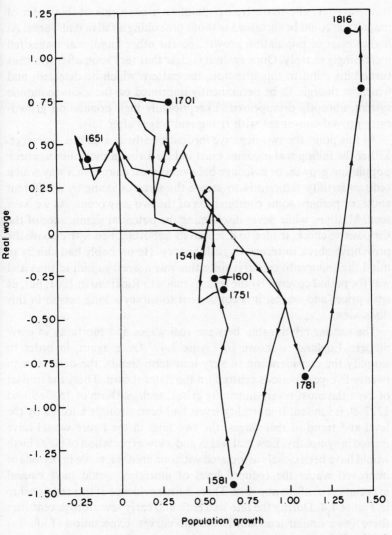

FIGURE 1.3 *Compound annual growth rates of population and an index of real wages (per cent per annum). See text for fuller explanation*

SOURCE Wrigley and Schofield, *Population History of England*, figure 10.4, p. 410

does not, in this case, pass through the origin of the graph. Instead it implies that there was a secular rise in productivity in early modern England at a rate of between one quarter and one half of 1 per cent annually, since real wages rose at about this rate when population was stationary, or, alternatively, a population growth rate of this order of magnitude could be sustained without provoking a fall in real wages. At higher rates of population growth, on the other hand, real wages fell increasingly sharply. Once again it is clear that very soon after Malthus turned his mind to this question, the pattern which he detected, and which he thought to be permanently imprinted on the socio-economic system, abruptly disappeared. Exceptionally high population growth rates proved consonant with rising real wages after 1800.

At this point the two negative feedback paths in Figure 1.1 diverge. Either the falling real incomes must induce a rise in mortality to check population growth, or marriage behaviour must change in a way which reduces fertility sufficiently to secure the same outcome by a different route, or perhaps some combination of the two may occur. As we have seen, Malthus, while never disclaiming the potential significance of the the positive check, tended to discount its importance compared with the preventive check in recent English history. He probably had chiefly in mind the eighteenth century, since this was nearest to him in time and was the period covered by the returns made to Rickman in 1801, but, as with prices and wages, it is convenient to survey a long period in this discussion.

The secular relationship between real wages and mortality in early modern England is shown in Figure 1.4.[19] Once again, in order to simplify the consideration of very long-term trends, the data refer to twenty-five-year periods centred on the dates shown. Thus, the impact of even the most severe mortality crises, such as those of 1557–9 and 1727–9, is limited. If mortality levels had been strongly affected by the level and trend of real wages, the two lines in the figure would have moved in sympathy. Low real wages and a low expectation of life at birth would have been closely associated with one another, while in periods of improved wages the reduced level of mortality would have caused expectation of life to improve. There is little evidence of this relationship in Figure 1.4. During the late sixteenth and early seventeenth centuries there was a similar tendency in the two curves. Expectation of life was falling slightly as real wages plunged to extremely low levels. But apart from this brief period, the lack of evidence for the 'expected' relationship is striking. Mortality worsened steadily for half a century after real wages had begun to recover in the seventeenth century, improved sharply but then again worsened between *c*.1680 and *c*.1730 while real wages rose without interruption, and in the next three-quarters of a century down to Malthus's day improved steadily, though real wages fell sharply towards the end of the eighteenth century. Clearly mortality in

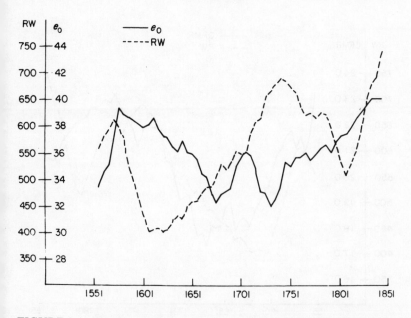

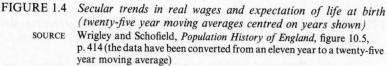

FIGURE 1.4   *Secular trends in real wages and expectation of life at birth (twenty-five year moving averages centred on years shown)*

SOURCE   Wrigley and Schofield, *Population History of England*, figure 10.5, p. 414 (the data have been converted from an eleven year to a twenty-five year moving average)

early modern England did not act as an equilibrating mechanism preserving the balance between population and resources.

We may turn finally, therefore, to nuptiality and fertility as the presumptive agents in achieving the balance. Figure 1.5 repeats once more the real wage graph shown in the last figure, but also shows a measure of nuptiality rather than mortality. The latter takes the form of a twenty-five-year moving average of a modified crude marriage rate, representing the number of first marriages per 1000 persons aged 15 to 34.[20] Fluctuations in the rate reflect the combined impact of changes in marriage age and the proportion who never married. While the 'fit' of the two graphs is not perfect, it strongly suggests that nuptiality responded to changes in the trend of real wages with a lag of about thirty years.[21] The extent of the change in nuptiality was very considerable. It can be shown that age at first marriage for women probably varied by about three and a half years from *c.*23 to *c.*26½ years between its minimum and maximum, and that the proportions who never married (both sexes combined) may have ranged from *c.*5–8 per cent to 16–20

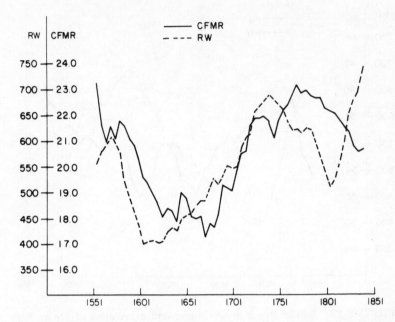

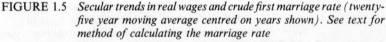

FIGURE 1.5   *Secular trends in real wages and crude first marriage rate (twenty-five year moving average centred on years shown). See text for method of calculating the marriage rate*

SOURCE   Wrigley and Schofield, *Population History of England*, figures 10.9 and 10.11, pp. 425 and 428

per cent.[22] The timing of the changes in these two nuptiality variables were such as to reinforce one another in their effect on fertility.

Back projection allows the calculation of the gross reproduction ratio. In Figure 1.6 its fluctuations are compared with those in the marriage rate already shown in Figure 1.5. It appears that the secular changes in trend of the gross reproduction ratio accord closely with those in the marriage rate, though changes in fertility tend to lag slightly behind those in nuptiality. In a fuller discussion there would be much to be said about the detailed behaviour of the two graphs and their relation to each other, but constraints of space prohibit an extended treatment in this short paper. Nor is such a discussion necessary in order to establish the strength of this final link in the chain of negative feedback which restrained population growth in early modern England through the preventive check. It may, however, be noted that analysis of fertility and mortality produced by back projection demonstrates that changes in fertility exercised a substantially greater influence than changes in

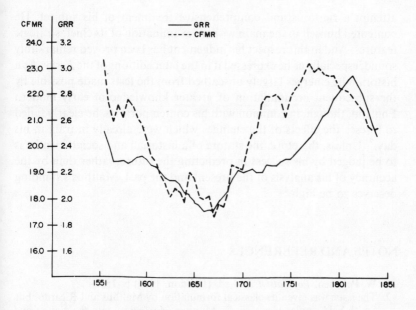

FIGURE 1.6   *Secular trends in the crude first marriage rate and the gross reproduction ratio (twenty-five year moving averages centred on years shown*

SOURCE   Wrigley and Schofield, *Population History of England*, figure 10.11, p. 428

mortality on population growth rates throughout most of the early modern period. It was not simply the case, therefore, that fertility moved in sympathy with economic trends whereas mortality did not: the fertility changes were also decisive in changing population growth rates. The fluctuations in fertility were in turn almost solely a function of changes in the timing and incidence of marriage since age-specific marital fertility rates varied only trivially. Marriage commanded the demographic stage in early modern England.[23]

There is, of course, far more to be said about the operation of the positive and preventive checks in the centuries immediately before the *First Essay* than is contained in the six figures which have been used here as a means of summarising a mass of data. Nothing has been said, for example, of short-term variations in prices, nuptiality, fertility, and mortality. Nor have changes in relationships over time been discussed; nor regional variation. Only a gross and summary picture has been attempted. But perhaps this is broadly appropriate. Malthus did not attempt a rigorous and comprehensive treatment of his subject. He contented himself in the main with an examination of its chief, strategic features. And in this respect his judgement has been proved remarkably sound, especially as he expressed it in the later editions of the *Essay*. As a historian he emerges largely unscathed from the tests made possible by the subsequent accumulation of greater knowledge of early modern England, though, in common with his contemporaries, he clearly failed to foresee the effects of the changes which were already in train in his day.[24] Unless, therefore, the stature of a historian and social scientist is to be judged by his success in predicting the future, rather than by the accuracy of his analysis of the present and the past, Malthus's standing deserves to be high.[25]

NOTES AND REFERENCES

1. W. Petersen, *Population*, 2nd ed. (London, 1969) p. 151.
2. The issue was given its classical formulation by Malthus and Ricardo, but Smith held similar views. T. R. Malthus, *An Inquiry into the Nature and Progress of Rent, and the Principles by which it is Regulated*, (London, 1815). D. Ricardo, *On the Principles of Political Economy and Taxation* (London, 1817) chapter 2 ' On rent'. The relevance of Smith's views on this aspect of economic growth is discussed in E. A. Wrigley, 'The Process of Modernization and the Industrial Revolution in England', *Journal of Interdisciplinary History*, III (1972) 225–59.
3. T.R. Malthus, *An Essay on the Principle of Population*, Royal Economic Society facsimile of the 1798 edition (London, 1926) p. 232. Hereafter, *First Essay* refers to this edition.
4. In this light H. L. Beale's dismissal of Malthus is not only ungenerous but oddly grounded for an historian. 'The historian's estimate of the *Essay on Population*', he wrote, 'is usually far this side of idolatry. He sees it in relation to contemporary fact and to *post-Malthusian development*, and to his pragmatic sight it appears largely irrelevant to both' (my italics). H. L. Beales, 'The Historical Content of the *Essay on Population*', in D. V. Glass (ed.), *Introduction to Malthus* (London, 1953) pp. 21–2.
5. *First Essay*, op. cit., pp. 105–7. The fundamental importance of the interpretation of the very rapid growth of the population of the English colonies in North America in the controversy between Malthus and Godwin has received too little stress. Godwin clearly felt that Malthus's view of the matter to be very damaging to his position, if it were true. In his *Of Population: An Inquiry Concerning the Power to Increase in the Numbers of Mankind, Being an Answer to Mr Malthus's Essay on that Subject* (London, 1820), Godwin attempted to prove that large-scale immigration was the cause of the exceptionally rapid increase in the population of North America. Shortly afterwards Malthus published a crushing rejoinder, as a principal element in his 'Population', supplement to the fourth, fifth and

sixth edition of the *Encyclopaedia Britannica*, VI (Edinburgh, 1824) pp. 307–33. Most unusually he resorted to a sophisticated demographic analysis of the age data of the early US censuses to show that he was right in supposing that a very high intrinsic growth rate was the dominant cause of the rapid population rise. The accuracy of his analysis has recently been endorsed by A. J. Coale, 'The Use of Modern Analytical Demography by T. R. Malthus', *Population Studies*, XXXIII (1979) 329–32.

6. *First Essay*, op. cit., pp. 29–30.
7. This process is vey clearly set out by Malthus in ibid., pp. 29–31.
8. The demographic data used in Figures 1.2 to 1.6 were drawn from the work of the SSRC Cambridge Group for the History of Population and Social Structure. Their derivation is described in E. A. Wrigley and R. S. Schofield, *The Population History of England 1541–1871: A Reconstruction* (London, 1981) chapter 7, and the figures can be found on pages 405, 410, 414, 425 and 428.
9. Rickman secured returns from each parish of the annual totals of baptisms and burials for every tenth year from 1700 to 1770 and for each year 1780 to 1800; and of marriages for each year from 1780 to 1800. Their characteristics are discussed at length in Wrigley and Schofield, ibid., appendix 7.
10. *First Essay*, op. cit., p. 23.
11. See, for example, his remarks about the sons of labourers: *First Essay*, op. cit., p. 73.
12. Ibid., p. 84.
13. Ibid., pp. 89–90.
14. T. R. Malthus, *An Essay ...* 4th ed., vol. I (London, 1807) p. 579.
15. Ibid., p. 580.
16. Ibid., p. 565.
17. E. H. Phelps Brown and S. V. Hopkins, 'Seven Centuries of the Prices of Consumables, Compared with Builders' Wage Rates', *Economica*, XXIII (1956) 296–314. The data taken from Phelps Brown and Hopkins and used in figures 1.2 and 1.3 are discussed and the operations carried out on them are described in Wrigley and Schofield, op. cit., appendix 9.
18. Malthus died in 1834. The last point in the diagram is for 1816 and, therefore, relates to the quarter-century 1816–41; it may be regarded as covering the latest period of which Malthus could have had personal knowledge.
19. In figures 1.4 and 1.6 the graphs are taken to 1841 for the reason stated in note 18.
20. English parish registers very seldom record the marital status of all brides and grooms consistently and from an early date. The evidence enabling the proportion of first marriages within total marriages to be estimated is discussed in Wrigley and Schofield, op. cit., chapter 7.
21. There is a much fuller discussion of the lag and of the imperfections in the data which make its measurement difficult in Wrigley and Schofield, op. cit., chapter 10.
22. *See* table 7.26 and figure 7.15 in ibid. More detailed information about changing English nuptiality patterns in the early modern period may be found in E. A. Wrigley and R. S. Schofield, 'English Population History from Family Reconstitution: Summary Results 1600–1799', *Population Studies*, XXXVII (1983) 157–84.

23. The evidence to substantiate the brief epitome of English population history given in this paragraph may be found in Wrigley and Schofield, op. cit., especially chapters 7 and 10. *See also* R. M. Smith, 'Fertility, Economy and Household Formation in England over Three Centuries', *Population and Development Review*, VII (1981) 595–622; and E. A. Wrigley, 'The Growth of Population in Eighteenth-Century England; a Conundrum Resolved', *Past and Present*, (1983) 121–50.

24. Malthus's historical judgement was not, however, infallible. For example, his assumption that population invariably reacts to an opportunity for increase by a rapid rise in numbers does not square well with English population history in the century and a half following the Black Death.

25. I have explored other aspects of Malthus's work in relation to recent historical scholarship in 'Elegance and Experience: Malthus at the Bar of History', in D. C. Coleman and R. S. Schofield (eds), *The State of Population Theory in 1984* (forthcoming).

2 Malthus: The Origins of the Principle of Population?[1]

B. STAPLETON

The *Essay on the Principle of Population*, first published in 1798, was said by Malthus to have originated as a response to William Godwin's essay on 'Avarice and Profusion' published in his *Enquirer*[2] in 1797. Previously, Godwin had produced his *Enquiry Concerning Political Justice* in 1793 and both his works predicted a future society in which social and economic inequalities would disappear. Such a utopian vision, achieved by a natural order of progress, was also promoted by Marie-Jean-Antoine-Nicolas Caritat, Marquis de Condorcet in his *Esquisse d'un Tableau Historique des Progres de l'Esprit Humain*, published in France in 1794 with an English edition appearing the following year, and it has been stated that the speculations in both these latter publications, along with the essay on 'Avarice and Profusion', provoked Malthus into writing the *First Essay*.[3]

There is little doubt that the *First Essay* was a response to the writings of Godwin and Condorcet since it contains numerous references to the two authors, chapters eight and nine being concerned with Condorcet's writings whilst chapters ten to fifteen are closely connected with Godwin's work. Although these two proponents of the perfectibility of society appear to have been the initiators of Malthus's response, it is most unlikely that, except for the chapters related to their works, they could be held responsible for the content, structure and arguments advanced in the *First Essay*. Those, presumably, must have been influenced by Malthus's own environment, experiences and the people with whom he associated. Hence, a possible explanation of the views expressed in the *First Essay* may reasonably be sought from an examination of Malthus's own background. This presents a problem, since between 1788 and the publication of the *First Essay* in 1798 his whereabouts are unknown; 'of his doings, between the ages of twenty-two and thirty-two, we know almost nothing'.[4] Patricia James, Malthus's biographer, refers to the period as both 'Malthus's fallow decade' and 'the unknown decade'.[5] However, from scattered references it may be possible to determine where Robert Malthus resided for most, if not all, of the decade.

I

In February 1766, the first baptism entry in the Anglican parish register of Wotton, Surrey states

> Malthus – Thomas = Robert, Son of Daniel Malthus of the Rookery Esq[ui]r[e], and Henrietta = Catherine his wife, was privately baptised 14th February (born 13th).[6]

Although the Malthus family residence lay in Dorking, the parish church there lay farther away from The Rookery than Wotton church which lay close across the nearby boundary (see figure 2.1). Daniel Malthus was clearly no ordinary local resident. The title 'Esquire' and the private, as opposed to church, baptism were both indicative of some social standing in the community. As the eldest child and only son of Sydenham Malthus he had inherited the familial estate on his father's death in 1757. Sydenham had been a successful lawyer at Lincoln's Inn, a Director of the South Sea Company, and had acquired land in Hertfordshire and Cambridgeshire. His son, Daniel, went to Oxford, leaving without a degree, then followed his father into Lincoln's Inn, but abandoned the law. Two years after coming into his inheritance Daniel, then a married man with two children, bought Chert Gate Farm west of Dorking in Surrey and converted it into The Rookery. There Robert Malthus was born, the second son and sixth child of the seven which Daniel and Henrietta were to produce.

From 1768, when Daniel sold The Rookery, to 1786 the Malthus family appear to have been highly mobile and thus difficult to trace. In 1773 they were tenants of part of Claverton House, near Bath in Somerset, where Robert also attended school. At the age of 16, in 1782, Daniel sent Robert to be educated by Gilbert Wakefield at a Dissenting Academy located midway between Liverpool and Manchester at Warrington, in Lancashire, and the following year when the school

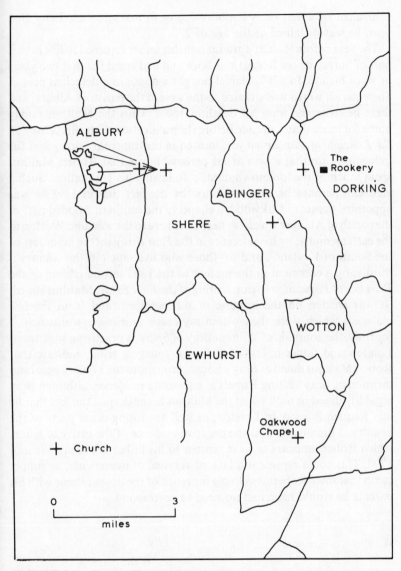

FIGURE 2.1   *Surrey: The Malthus parishes*

closed he moved with Wakefield to continue his education at the latter's home in Bramcote near Nottingham. In 1784, when Daniel was living at Cookham, Berkshire, Robert became a student of Jesus College, Cambridge and graduated early in 1788 as ninth Wrangler, the equivalent of a first class honours degree in mathematics. Later that year, he was ordained at the age of 22.[7]

The year before Robert's graduation, his father returned to live in that part of Surrey where Robert was born and had spent the first two years or so of his life. In 1787, Daniel bought a house in a detached part of Shere parish which was situated to the west in the parish of Albury, and there he remained until his death in 1800.[8] Thus the Malthus family home for more than a decade before the publication of the first *Essay on the Principle of Population* was located in central rural Surrey and the indications are that it was at his parents' house that Robert Malthus spent much of the 'unknown decade' following his graduation. Such a view can perhaps be supported first by the fact that in 1793 he was appointed curate of Oakwood, a chapel in the southern wooded part of the parish of Abinger which lay between Shere to the west and Wotton to the east; secondly, by his reference in the *First Essay* to 'the labourers of the South of England', and to 'those who live much in the country';[9] thirdly, by a comment in the preface to the 1803 second edition of the *Principle of Population* where, writing of the *First Essay*, Malthus stated: 'It was written on the impulse of the occasion, and from the few materials which were then within my reach *in a country situation*';[10] fourthly, the Journals of William Bray of Shere, a practising solicitor in London and father-in-law of Robert's youngest sister, indicate that Robert Malthus dined at Bray's house throughout the 1790s. There is no mention of Bray visiting Robert at a separate residence, although Bray regularly dined or took tea at the Malthus home despite the fact that he was frequently away in London, as well as visiting other parts of the country.[11] Finally, there is the negative evidence of the rarity of letters which Robert appears to have written to his father between 1788 and 1798. This could represent a lack of survival of documents, or simply mean that since Robert was living for much of the time at home with his parents he would have had no need to correspond.

II

Taken together these varied points suggest that the environment from which the *First Essay* emerged was that of a comfortable middle-class family in the heart of rural Surrey where its author could indulge his pastimes of walking, riding, hunting and shooting.[12] It was this background and this locality, which, along with 'the few materials', would seem to have influenced Malthus's thinking when he was producing his famous *Principle of Population*. Accordingly, though he had clearly been busying himself with very little in the years between leaving Cambridge and becoming a curate,[13] he was able to write of the stratum of society into which he was born that 'the middle regions of society seem to be the best suited to intellectual improvement'[14] and furthermore that 'extreme poverty, or too great riches may be alike unfavourable'[15] to the growth of mind. Having asserted the mental superiority of those with whom he associated, country gentry, clergy and professional men, he turned his attention to the social group which was at the centre of his thoughts; 'the principle argument of this essay tends to place in a strong point of view the improbability that the lower classes of people in any country should ever be sufficiently free from want and labour to obtain any high degree of intellectual improvement'.[16]

Thus, the result of raising the wages of labourers from 18 pence (7.5p) to five shillings (25p) a day 'would make every man fancy himself comparatively rich and able to indulge himself in many hours or days of leisure',[17] in much the same way presumably as the wealthier middle class behaved. To support his view he quotes some local evidence: 'The labourers of the South of England are so accustomed to eat fine wheaten bread that they will suffer themselves to be half starved before they will submit to live like the Scotch peasants.'[18] A comment curiously at variance with his observation that 'those who live much in the country' notice that

> the sons of labourers are very apt to be stunted in their growth and are a long while arriving at maturity. Boys that you would guess to be fourteen or fifteen, are, upon enquiry, frequently found to be eighteen or nineteen. And the lads who drive plough, which certainly must be a healthy exercise, are very rarely seen with any appearance of calves to their legs; a circumstance, which can only be attributed to a want either of proper or sufficient nourishment.[19]

It is also at variance with his recognition of the advantages accruing from higher wages paid to workers in America 'where the reward of labour is at present so liberal, the lower classes might retrench very considerably in a year of scarcity without materially distressing themselves'.[20]

However, the major reason for his interest in the lower classes is their crucial role in the operation of the central principle of the *First Essay* – 'Population, when unchecked, increases in a geometrical ratio. Subsistence increases only in an arithmetical ratio.'[21] Having indicated the operation of the preventive check of later marriage in all ranks of society in England,[22] Malthus asserts that the positive check, infant and child deaths through malnutrition and disease, 'is confined chiefly ... to the lowest orders of society',[23] because it is these people who continue to have more children than they can support, and citing Adam Smith in corroboration, Malthus states that

> if potatoes were to become the favourite vegetable food of the common people, and if the same quantity of land was employed in their culture as is now employed in the culture of corn, the country would be able to support a much greater population, and would consequently in a very short time have it.[24]

Population thus invariably increased when the means of subsistence increased, and that increase, if unchecked, would be in a geometrical progression with population doubling in twenty-five years, a figure arrived at because it was the 'ratio of increase which is well known to have taken place throughout all the Northern States of America'.[25] American colonial population is said to have grown from some 400 000 to about 2 500 000 in 1776,[26] mostly as a result of immigration, a factor which also contributed to the 50 per cent growth between the first American census in 1790 which recorded 4 000 000 people and the fourth of 1820, in which 10 million were enumerated, although the major cause of growth in this thirty-year period was natural increase. Since the population expanded from a relatively small size in a land of vast and underutilised geographical area, America was statistically and spatially a somewhat exceptional example for Malthus to employ, but clearly one which would aptly demonstrate his theory.

Thus, as a result of actual experience, this ratio of increase of American population Malthus says 'we will take as our rule; and say, That population, when unchecked, goes on doubling itself every twenty-five years or increases in a geometrical ratio'.[27] The ratio of increase is then applied to Britain; 'the population of the Island is computed to be about seven millions',[28] and at the end of a century would have reached 112 million whereas the means of subsistence would support only 35 million.

Problems, however, would have arisen before the population had reached 28 million since there would have been sufficient increase in food supply to feed only 21 million people.[29] The consequent rise in food prices 'would immediately turn some additional captial into the channel of agriculture',[30] but agricultural output would only be able to respond very slowly to the rising prices of provisions, and increasing poverty would be inevitable. Such problems were inescapable since Providence had ' ordained that population should increase much faster than food'.[31] The Principle of Population is thus elevated to a part of natural law ordained from above and exists because man is naturally 'inert, sluggish, and averse from labour, unless compelled by necessity'[32] to be otherwise.

Consequently any development which interfered with the operation of the Principle, by tending to raise the level of population without increasing food supply, would by definition be harmful. And in England Malthus was certain that such was the result of the operation of the Poor Laws that the condition of the poor was actually worsened in two ways: first, by their tendency 'to increase population without increasing the food for its support';[33] and, secondly, because 'the quantity of provisions consumed in workhouses upon a part of the society, that cannot in general be considered the most valuable part, diminishes the shares that would otherwise belong to more industrious, and more worthy members'.[34] Furthermore, the Poor Laws resulted in a weakening of the spirit of independence among the peasantry, inducing men 'to marry from a prospect of parish provision with little or no chance of maintaining their families in independence'.[35] They 'diminish both the power and the will to save among the common people' who seem 'always to live from hand to mouth' and 'seldom think of the future'.[36] Without the Poor Laws men would be more prudent since thoughts of death or sickness would deter them from going to the alehouse and dissipating their earnings for fear their families would starve. Thus the Poor Laws removed one of the strongest checks to idleness and dissipation and allowed men to marry 'with little or no prospect of being able to maintain a family in independence'.[37]

What was required was the encouragement of agriculture to provide more employment whilst raising the levels of food supply.[38] However, England's recent historical experience was quite different. Instead, Malthus notes, 'the commerce of this country, internal as well as external, has certainly been rapidly advancing during the last century'.[39] But because increasing wealth has been mainly the produce of labour and not land, the funds for maintaining labour have only risen slowly and the increasing national wealth 'has had little or no tendency to better the condition of the labouring poor' and a much greater proportion of them 'is employed in manufactures, and crowded together in close and unwholesome rooms'.[40] And the greater the proportion of population in manufacturing, and fewer consequently in agriculture, meant the poor were worse off. Furthermore, Malthus argues that enclosure and related expansion of pastoral farming plus the growth of large farms had reduced the numbers employed in agriculture in the last century. Consequently, any increase in population must be employed in manufacturing, in which economic fluctuations and changing fashions had resulted in increasing numbers of paupers who had exchanged 'the healthy labours of agriculture, for the unhealthy occupations of manufacturing industry'.[41] This prejudice against manufacturing industry was perhaps the result of his stay in Warrington at the impressionable age of 16, since that town, manufacturing sailcloth, glass, ironwares and linens,[42] must have presented a stark contrast to rural Somerset. However, trade fared no better in Malthus's economic thinking since he stated that foreign commerce 'will be found . . . to contribute but little to the increase of the internal funds for the maintenance of labour'.[43] With such negative views on the economic contribution of manufacturing industry and overseas trade, it is hardly surprising that Malthus was concerned about population growth. It is clear he was aware that economic growth was taking place, but was unable to recognise the advantages of the production of surplus manufactures for export in exchange for imported foodstuffs. He tended to view the economy as a closed one, despite the knowledge that Holland was dependent on food imports.[44] Growth, unfortunately for Malthus, was occurring in industry and trade, not agriculture, and the result was poverty. Hence, the 'great increase of the poor rates, is, indeed, of itself, a strong evidence, that the poor have not a greater command of the necessaries and conveniences of life'.[45] Malthus's primary solution was 'the total abolition of all the present parish-laws'[46] because they interfered with the Principle of Population. Secondly, premiums were to be given for expanding and encouraging agriculture and, thirdly, serious attempts should be made to weaken the institutions which caused agricultural labourers to be paid less than the labourers in trade and manufacture. Finally, he advocated the establishment of county workhouses.[47] Thus the Principle of Population meant that the tradition established in Elizabethan times of the relief of poverty by public assistance was unacceptable, except in the most extreme cases.

III

The references to the labourers of the south of England make it clear that in the formulation of his views, Malthus was influenced by the people he saw around him and the events he encountered. Some of those events, in his capacity as curate at Oakwood, would have brought him into contact with the labourers and their families, since the baptism of their children would have been one of Malthus's duties. Those baptisms are recorded in the registers of Oakwood chapel and in the decade from 1788 to 1798 show an average of sixteen each year, a figure over three times greater than the average annual number of burials for the same period, which numbered only five.[48] It seems impossible to believe that Malthus could have been unconscious of, or was uninfluenced by, such evidence. Yet there is no indication that, despite his first-class honours degree in mathematics, he ever utilised the local parish register information in a numerate manner, notwithstanding the fact that he demonstrated his awareness that at least two preceding writers had made demographic calculations based on parish register baptismal and burial entries. Malthus referred to Richard Price's use of such data in his 'Observations on Reversionary Payments' and to Thomas Short's attempts to compare the proportion of baptisms to burials in the century before 1650 with the proportion from the late seventeenth century to 1750.[49] He criticised Price for using extracts from the registers which were for periods of insufficient extent by which to judge the real growth of population because it was not possible to infer the 'increase for the twenty years before, or . . . for the twenty years after' the five or ten year periods Price has examined.[50] This was sound demographic comment and when applied to the registers of those parishes with which Malthus would have been most familiar, Wotton, Shere and Abinger with Oakwood chapelry, it produces interesting results.

At Wotton (see Figure 2.2(a)), for the whole of the seventeenth and eighteenth centuries, when baptism entries are measured against burials, little noticeable population growth occurred, especially between 1670 and 1740. Between 1780 and 1800 there was actually a surplus of burials. At Abinger, after baptism surpluses in the early seventeenth century to the mid 1630s the next eighty years indicate an almost stable population, before the numbers appear to rise steadily, with the exception of the 1740s when the levels of baptisms and burials are much the same (Figure 2.2(b)). After 1730 Shere registers indicate steady but unspectacular growth of the parish's population (Figure 2.3(a)). However, only in Malthus's own curacy at Oakwood does an unequivocal rise in population occur (Figure 2.3(b)), which is sufficient to ensure that when the baptisms and burials of Wotton, Abinger and Oakwood are aggregated there appears a quite clear and marked rise in the population of the combined parishes after 1740 (Figure 2.4).[51]

28

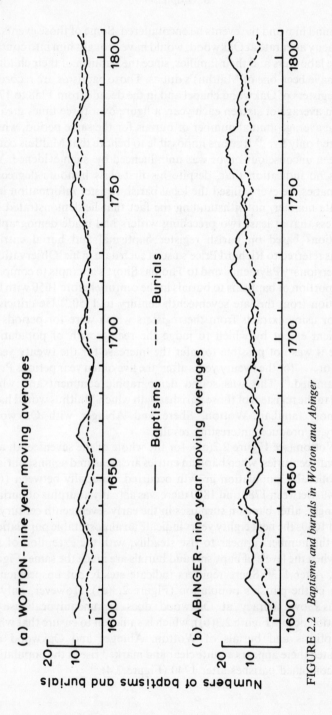

FIGURE 2.2 *Baptisms and burials in Wotton and Abinger*

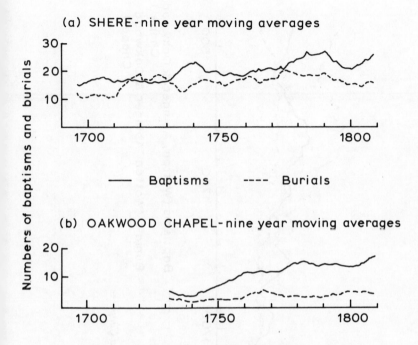

FIGURE 2.3   *Baptisms and burials in Shere and Oakwood Chapel*

This trend of rising population was undoubtedly one of concern not only to Malthus but to others with whom he would have associated in the locality. A letter written in November 1794 to the Bray family at Shere from Mr Duncomb at Newdigate, a parish some 13 kilometres south-east of Shere, gave figures of births and burials from the parish register for every tenth year from 1693 to 1793 inclusive, indicating that the number of births for the eleven specified years totalled 138 and the burials seventy-one. Duncomb wrote that the population of Newdigate was greatly increased but building had not kept pace, only one house having been built in forty years.[52]

With the connections between the Bray and Malthus families being so strong no doubt William Bray, knowing of Robert Malthus's interest in the subject, would have discussed the letter with him at one of their frequent meetings. Duncomb was only providing further evidence of a phenomenon which they already knew was a problem in their own

30

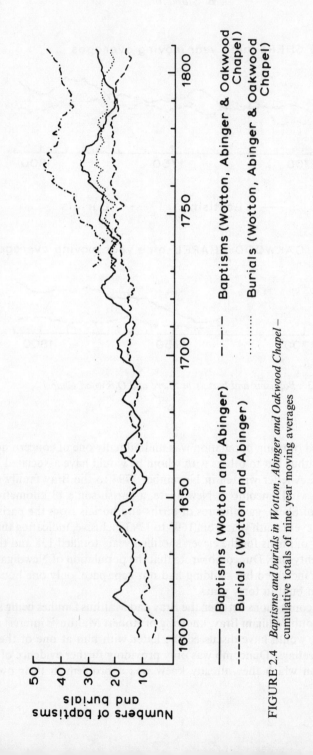

FIGURE 2.4 *Baptisms and burials in Wotton, Abinger and Oakwood Chapel –*
cumulative totals of nine year moving averages

locality, since it was being highlighted by the considerable increases in poor rate expenditure which they were being required to pay. There could be no clearer demonstration of the Principle of Population in operation.

The accounts of the expenditure on poor relief for Wotton, Abinger and Shere parishes all survive for various parts of the eighteenth century. Wotton's beginning in 1708, show an almost 300 per cent (296 per cent) increase from the first five years' (1708–12) total expenditure of £540 6s 2d (£540.31) to the last five years' (1796–1800) total of £2139 0s 6¼d (£2139.03), but the decade which saw the largest increase was the 1790s in which expenditure soared by some 76 per cent.[53] Abinger's overseers of the poor disbursements commence in 1732 and produce an increase of 186 per cent between the 1730s annual average expenditure of £175 12s 8d (£175.63) and that of 1796–1800 which averaged annually £502 2s 2¼d (£502.12), although the increase was more evenly spread over the years, with a more modest rise of almost one third in the 1790s.[54] The payments to the poor at Shere survive for a much shorter period, only beginning in 1776. In the first five years (1776–81) £1681 12s 1d (£1681.61) was expended. The last five years of the century saw that sum rise to £2804 with the increase in the 1790s amounting to 37 per cent. Fortunately, at Shere the survival of the Overseers of the Poor Receipt Book affords a minor insight into the Malthus family, since among the payers is listed for the first time on the ninth of January 1787 'Mr. Malltiss' (the name became Malthus in 1792) who was rated at £34, plus £4 for 'Oughtreds Meadow', and in the parish as a whole he was the seventeenth highest payer. Daniel Malthus's first half-dozen sixth-monthly payments totalled £28 6s 0d (£28.30), and the last six, prior to the publishing of the *First Essay*, £37 3s 0d (£37.15) an increase of just over 30 per cent.[55] Although the percentage increase in annual relief payments in the 1790s was lower in Shere than in Wotton, this smaller increase would seem to reflect the fact that levels of poor relief in Shere were then much higher than in the neighbouring parishes. For instance, the proportion of the population of Shere receiving relief was higher, and the proportion being assessed for payment was lower, than in both Wotton and Abinger. Consequently, the average contribution of each assessed individual in Shere was higher than elsewhere (see Table 2.1). In addition Daniel Malthus's payments amounted to almost twice the average level for the parish as a whole (for example, in February 1800, Daniel's widow Henrietta paid £6 13s 0d (£6.65) on a rate of 3s 6d in the pound when the average payment for all those assessed was £3 8s 10d (£3.44). With such considerable increases in the

TABLE 2.1 Contributors to and recipients of poor relief in 1801 in Abinger, Wotton and Shere in the county of Surrey

	Population in 1801	Poor relief contributors	Proportion* of population contributing to poor relief (contributors × 4.75) % ages	Recipients of poor relief	Proportion* of population in receipt of poor relief (recipients × 4.75) % ages	Total sums paid in 1801 £ s d	Average contribution £ s d
Abinger	632	70	53	35	26	308 6 4	4 8 1 (at the 3/6 rate)
Wotton	441	48	52	35	37.6	148 15 9	3 2 0 (at the 2/6 rate)
Shere	871	78	43	75	40.8	403 7 6	5 3 5 (at the 5/0 rate)

* It has been assumed that both contributors and recipients represent households, hence a multiplier of 4.75 for mean household size has been applied to produce the percentages. See P. Laslett and R. Wall, *Household and Family in Past Time* (Cambridge, 1972) pp. 125–58.

payments for poor relief in the eighteenth century it is perhaps not surprising that Malthus would find it necessary to comment on them in the *First Essay*,[56] since the sums paid were mainly obtained from families like his own. And it was clearly not too difficult to forge a link between the rising poor relief payments and the growing population without attempting any analysis of the structure or causes of poverty.

For nowhere in the *First Essay* is there any attempt to recognise that there existed in Britain a large body of impotent poor, the aged, the sick, the widowed and children on whose fate Malthus failed to utter a single syllable. Reading the *Essay* conveys the impression that the poor were all young able-bodied adults with ever growing families.[57] Even so, any reference to the effect of rising prices upon their incomes is conspicuously absent. What Malthus did was to focus his attention and argument on the able-bodied poor and particularly on their moral condition. And it is this focus that the Royal Commission on the Poor Law of 1832–4 repeated, as did the legislation which followed it. Though Malthus claimed 'to refer frequently to things as they are as the only way of making one's writings practically useful to society',[58] there is little evidence to support his claim in relation to either the administration and practical workings of the Poor Law, or the recipients of relief, despite his repeated linking of the Principle of Population with Poor Law policy.

The conspicuous absence of any reference to the structure of poverty in the *First Essay* is thrown more sharply into relief when compared with Malthus's unpublished pamphlet, *The Crisis, A View of the Present Interesting State of Great Britain, by A Friend of the Constitution*. Once again Malthus expounded on the virtues of the middle classes and country gentlemen[59] and then went on to say:

> But though it is by no means to be wished that any dependent situation should be made so agreeable, as to tempt those who might otherwise support themselves in independence; yet as it is the duty of society to maintain such of its members as are absolutely unable to maintain themselves, it is certainly desirable that the assistance in this case should be given in the way that is most agreeable to the persons who are to receive it. An industrious woman who is left a widow with four or five children that she has hitherto brought up decently, would often gladly accept of a much less sum, than the family would cost in the work-house, and with this assistance added to her own exertions, might in all probability succeed in keeping herself and her children from the contamination of a society that she has surely just reason to dread. And it seems peculiarly hard upon old people, who perhaps

have been useful and respectable members of society, and in their day, 'have done the state some service', that as soon as they are past their work, they should be obliged to quit the village where they have always lived, the cottage to which time has attached them, the circle of their friends, their children and their grand-children, and be forced to spend the evening of their days in noise and unquietness among strangers, and wait their last moments forlorn and separated from all they hold dear.

It is an old saying that home is home, be it ever so homely; and this sentiment certainly operates very strongly upon the poor. Out of the reach of most of those enjoyments that amuse the higher ranks of society, what is there that can attach them to life, but their evening fire-side with their families in a house of their own; joined to the consciousness that the more they exert themselves the better they shall support the objects of their affection. What is it but a sentiment of this kind that tempts many who have lived in the ease and luxury of [domestic] service, to forego these advantages, to marry, and submit to the labour, the difficulties, the humbler condition and hard fare, that inevitably attend the change of situation? And surely no wise legislature would discourage these sentiments, and endeavour to weaken this attachment to home, unless indeed it were intended to destroy all thought and feeling among the common people, to break their spirit, and prepare them to submit patiently to any yoke that might be imposed upon them.[60]

The contrast between the compassionate approach to poverty and the recognition of the problems of the aged, widowed and children in Malthus's unpublished *The Crisis* and the deafening silence on the subject in the *First Essay* is clear and striking. It was a silence which Malthus was to maintain throughout subsequent editions of the *Essay*, in which much of the approach of the *First Essay* was repeated,[61] ameliorated only by a suggestion in favour of the *gradual* abolition of the Poor Laws.[62] Even so, this would apply only to those alive at the time of legislation since neither any legitimate child born one year after, nor any illegitimate child born two years after abolition would be entitled to any parish assistance.[63]

It is difficult to explain these diametrically opposite views on the treatment of poverty or to imagine what may have caused such dramatic changes to occur in a matter of only two years. *The Crisis* appears to be Malthus referring to things as they really were – observations on reality, the scientific reasoning of Population Malthus. By 1798, such an analysis of poverty as *The Crisis* contained did not fit the arguments about the Principle of Population and its causes put forward in the *First Essay*, the guiding tenets of which appear to be the moral judgements and sentiments of Parson Malthus. The dynamic behind the more moral than scientific fundamental presuppositions of the *Essay* may well have been a financial one. In the *First Essay* Malthus comments 'that nearly three million pounds are collected annually for the poor and yet they are still in distress', and states that even if eighteen shillings (90p) in the pound, instead of four shillings (20p), were raised by the wealthier classes for disbursement to the poor, the only result would be higher prices of the essentials of life which the poor required.[64] Events, he later considered, were to prove him right, for in reference to the high prices of 1800 and 1801, Malthus noted that 'the supposition which I have made of a collection from the rich of eighteen shillings in the pound has been nearly realised; and the effect has been much as I might have expected'.[65]

IV

Since, as shown above, local poor relief costs had been rising rapidly in the 1790s it seems probable that Malthus's *First Essay* was at least influenced, if not partially caused by, the growing financial burdens the costs imposed on families like his own and his friends. The local evidence, however, suggests that Malthus was perhaps too strongly influenced by some contemporary events. Nevertheless, had he taken account of his own criticism of Richard Price's use of parish register material and looked at the local registrations over a much longer time span, the arguments he uses in the *First Essay* suggest he would not have recognised any evidence which would have led him to form any other conclusion than the one he enunciated. For when he examined Price's statement that the proportion of births to deaths was higher at 124 to 100 from Queen Elizabeth's time to the middle of the seventeenth century, by comparison with the 111 to 100 from the late seventeenth century to the middle of the eighteenth century, he finds this wholly to be expected as more good land would have been available for cultivation in the earlier stages than later, when the population of England 'had accommodated itself very nearly to the average produce of [the] country'.[66]

Malthus, although he knew of Gregory King's work,[67] was not in any position to quantify the size of the nation's population. Nevertheless, he shows he was aware of the slowing down in the rate of population growth which occurred in England between approximately the mid-seventeenth and mid-eighteenth century, a century in which it is now thought that the national population grew from some 5½ million people to only 6 million.[68] His explanation for this trend was that discouragements to marriage, war, depopulation of large towns, the close habitations and insufficient food of many of the poor had prevented population from increasing beyond the means of subsistence.[69] He discounted the possibility that any agrarian developments 'could remove the pressure of it [population] for a single century'.[70] Yet the evidence of the expansion of agricultural output at a pace faster than population growth during the century 1650–1750 is inescapable. The price of wheat fell steadily. In the 1640s the average price per annum at Eton College, some 32 kilometres from Abinger, was 51s 7d (£2.58) per quarter, whereas by the 1740s it had fallen to 26s (£1.30).[71] Wimpey wrote that 'all history cannot furnish twenty such years of fertility and abundance as from 1730 to 1750 when the average prices were the lowest ever known'.[72] Not surprisingly, the average price of the loaf in London fell over the same period from 6s 6d to 4s 6d producing real savings for the poorer members of the community. Since, from the 1670s to the late 1760s, England became a substantial exporter of surplus grain (there being only four years 1728, 1729, 1757 and 1758 when any significant imports of wheat or flour occurred before 1765)[73] at a time when there were more, not fewer, people to be fed, the evidence clearly points to considerable improvement in agricultural output.

Furthermore, it is apparent that for long periods of up to a century the major principle of the *First Essay*, that population should increase much faster than the means of subsistence, did not apply to England, since despite increasing real incomes for the majority of the population there was no tendency to earlier marriage and the consequent production of surplus population over subsistence which Malthus stated would be the result of improved circumstances.[74] The poor of England had not always behaved as the Principle of Population stated they would, and had Malthus used his mathematical skills to explore the local parish registers with a more open mind he might have arrived at a conclusion rather different from the monocausal explanation into which be made all historical change fit. But then, like all of us, he was a man of his time and being conscious of what he could see happening around him to the population and the associated rising relief payments to the poor, he neglected to use some of the most valuable of those few materials which were then within his reach in a country situation.

NOTES AND REFERENCES

1. This chapter is an amended and expanded version of that which was given at the International Conference on Historical Demography in Paris 27–29 May 1980, and subsequently published in J. Dupaquier (ed.), *Malthus Past and Present* (London, 1983) pp. 45–59.
2. T. R. Malthus, *An Essay on the Principle of Population*, Royal Economic Society facsimile of the 1798 edition (London, 1926) p. 1. Hereafter, *First Essay* refers to this edition.
3. For example Malthus, *An Essay . . .* in A. Flew (ed.), *Malthus* (Harmondsworth, 1970) p. 9.
4. P. James, *Population Malthus* (London, 1979) p. 34.
5. Ibid., pp. 40 and 55.
6. G[uildford] M[uniment] R[oom], PSH/WOT/1/1, Wotton Parish Register 1596–1812.
7. James, op. cit., pp. 13–34 for biographical details.
8. GMR, PSH/WOT/1/1, Wotton Parish Register 1596–1812; the burial of 'Daniel Malthus, Esquire, of Albury in this county, aged 70' is recorded on 14 January 1800, and on 12 April 1800 'Henrietta Catherine, widow of Daniel Malthus Esquire, late of Albury in this county, aged 67' was buried.
9. *First Essay*, op. cit., pp. 132 and 73.
10. T. R. Malthus, *An Essay . . .* 7th ed. (London, 1973) p. 1 (my italics).
11. GMR, 85/1/33–41, Bray Collection, The journals of William Bray 1790–8. In 1794, 1797 and 1798 Bray listed the miles he travelled in England either by carriage or on horseback. They totalled respectively 1759 miles, a prodigious 2665 miles and 1280 miles. In those years Robert Malthus dined 2, 1 and 3 times respectively with Bray. Conversely, Bray visited Mr and Mrs Malthus 5 times in 1797 and twice in 1798. The surviving diaries of William Man Godschall, the father-in-law of another of Malthus's sisters do not commence until after the publication of the *First Essay* and so provide no guide to the unknown decade.
12. *First Essay*, op. cit., p. 225.
13. James, op. cit., pp. 40–1. Mrs James also considers here that Malthus had his 'first experience of a settled home . . . during these ten years in Surrey'.
14. *First Essay*, op. cit., p. 367.
15. Ibid.,
16. Ibid., pp. 217–18.
17. Ibid., p. 79.
18. Ibid., p. 132.
19. Ibid., p. 73.
20. Ibid., p. 131.
21. Ibid., p. 14. Not, it should be noted, self-evident ratios.
22. Ibid., pp. 63–6.
23. Ibid., p. 71.
24. Ibid., pp. 136–7, and Adam Smith, *The Wealth of Nations*, 6th ed., E. Cannan (ed.), (London, 1950) p. 179.
25. *First Essay*, op. cit., pp. 185–6. This statement was later supported by census figures of the white population of America from 1790, 1800 and 1810

in Malthus's *Summary View* . . . published in 1830. *See* D. V. Glass (ed.), *Introduction to Malthus* (London, 1953) p. 128. However, J. Potter in 'The Growth of Population in America 1700–1860', in D. V. Glass and D. E. C. Eversley (eds) *Population in History* (London, 1965) p. 662, indicates that the American population grew at less than Malthus's rate of doubling every twenty-five years.
26. E. B. Greene and V. D. Harrington, *American Population before the Federal Census of 1790* (New York, 1932) pp. 4–7.
27. *First Essay*, op. cit., p. 21.
28. Ibid., p. 23. Malthus's computation, when compared with the 1801 Census, underestimates the population of Britain by over 50 per cent.
29. Ibid., p. 189.
30. Ibid., p. 310.
31. Ibid., p. 361.
32. Ibid., p. 363.
33. Ibid., p. 83.
34. Ibid., p. 84.
35. Ibid., p. 85.
36. Ibid., pp. 86–7.
37. Ibid., p. 89.
38. Ibid., pp. 96–7.
39. Ibid., p. 312.
40. Ibid., pp. 312–13.
41. Ibid., pp. 315–25.
42. J. Aikin, *A Description of the Country from Thirty to Forty Miles Round Manchester* (London, 1795) pp. 300–4.
43. *First Essay*, op. cit., p. 336.
44. Ibid., p. 311.
45. Ibid., pp. 320–1.
46. Ibid., p. 95.
47. Ibid., pp. 95–7.
48. GMR, PSH/OK/1/1, Oakwood Chapel Register.
49. *First Essay*, op. cit., pp. 121–5.
50. Ibid., p. 121.
51. GMR, PSH/WOT/1/1, Wotton Parish Register, PSH/SHER/1/1–2, Shere Parish Registers, and PSH/OK/1/1, Oakwood Chapel Register. In view of the fact that the Oakwood baptism register states that many of the parents lived in either Wotton or Abinger, aggregating the baptism totals would seem sensible. Clearly the Chapel was catering for families in the southern parts of both parishes since it was nearer than the two parish churches. Note also that baptism/ marriage ratios fell in the early eighteenth century by comparison to earlier and later peaks in the combined parishes.
52. GMR, 85/2/8 (642) Bray Collection.
53. Surrey Record Office, LA4/17/5,6,7,8. Wotton Overseers' Disbursements, 1708–1800.
54. Ibid., P1/7/1,2,3,4. Abinger Overseers' Disbursements, 1732–1800.
55. Ibid., P10/1/1–2. Shere Poor Books 1776–1800.
56. *First Essay*, op. cit., pp. 320–1.
57. Ibid., pp. 72–3, for example.

58. G. F. McCleary, *The Malthusian Population Theory* (London, 1953) p. 167, quoting from a letter of 26 January 1817 to David Ricardo.
59. W. Empson, 'Life, Writings and Character of Mr Malthus', *Edinburgh Review*, LXIV (1837) 479.
60. W. Otter, *Memoir of Robert Malthus* (London, 1836) p. xxxvi, cited in James, op. cit., pp. 53–4.
61. Malthus, op. cit., *An Essay* . . . 7th ed., Book III, pp. 38–51.
62. Ibid., pp. 64, 200–9.
63. Ibid., p. 201.
64. *First Essay*, op. cit., pp. 75–9.
65. Malthus, op. cit., *An Essay* . . . 7th ed., Book III, p. 40.
66. *First Essay*, op. cit., p. 125. In the light of this observation, Malthus's solution to the problem of rising poverty by expanding agricultural employment and productivity (as in *First Essay*, p. 96) appears to be somewhat paradoxical, since presumably less good land would have been available at the end of the eighteenth century than in 1750.
67. Ibid., p. 125.
68. E. A. Wrigley and R. S. Schofield, *The Population History of England, 1541–1871* (London, 1981) pp. 207–10 and appendix 3.
69. *First Essay*, op. cit., p. 126.
70. Ibid., p. 16.
71. B. R. Mitchell and P. Deane, *Abstract of British Historical Statistics* (Cambridge, 1962) pp. 486–7.
72. J. Wimpey, *Rural Improvements* (London, 1775) pp. 492–3, cited in G. E. Mingay, 'The Agricultural Depression, 1730–50', *Economic History Review*, 2nd series, VIII (1956) 336.
73. Mitchell and Deane, op. cit., p. 94.
74. *First Essay*, op. cit., p. 77, and *see* E. A. Wrigley, 'Family Limitation in Pre-Industrial England', *Economic History Review*, 2nd series, XIX (1966) 82–109; R. B. Outhwaite, 'Age at Marriage in England from the Late Seventeenth to the Nineteenth Century', *Transactions of the Royal Historical Society*, 5th series, 23 (1973) 55–70; Wrigley and Schofield, op. cit., pp. 255–6, 422–4.

3 The Demographic Impact of the Old Poor Laws: More Reflections on Malthus

J. P. HUZEL

I

In a previous article it was argued provisionally that the Old Poor Law, and in particular the allowance system, did not operate to promote population increase by lessening the preventive check to marriage on the part of the labouring poor. This conclusion stood in direct contradiction to the views of T. R. Malthus and numerous of his contemporaries who viewed pre-1834 poor relief as a crucial catalyst, not only for the rapid expansion of the lower orders, but also for the attendant growth of poverty itself.[1] Subsequent writing on this theme has been negligible. What has emerged, however, tends to support my earlier argument. G. S. L. Tucker, for example, found no significant positive correlation between fertility ratios by county in 1821 and levels of per capita poor expenditures over the period 1817–21.[2]

The purpose of the present chapter is to provide more conclusive evidence in refutation of a Malthusian relationship between Poor Law family income transfers and demographic change. In addition, it is intended to explore a closely related theme; namely the hypothesis, again adopted by Malthus and especially the Poor Law Commissioners of 1834, that parish allowances in addition to facilitating population growth also rooted the labourer to his parish of settlement thus restricting labour mobility.

Malthus's belief that the Old Poor Law caused population growth has

40

been documented.[3] The Old Poor Law, however, according to Malthus, had another important impact on population beyond causing its natural increase. The combined effect of the Settlement Laws and the availability of allowances in the parish of settlement operated to restrict labour mobility, thus impeding the free market mechanism:

> Were I to propose a palliative, and palliatives are all that the nature of the case will admit, it should be, in the first place the total abolition of all present parish laws. This would at any rate give liberty and freedom of action to the peasantry of England, which they can hardly be said to possess at present. They would then be able to settle without interruption, wherever there was a prospect of a greater plenty of work and a higher price for labour. The market of labour would then be free, and those obstacles removed which, as things are now, often for a considerable time prevent the price from rising according to the demand.[4]

The *1834 Poor Law Report*, however, was far more emphatic: 'if, therefore the Allowance System did not find a surplus population it indubitably created it, and fixed it to the spot; for on the day the labourer (single or married) accepted parish allowance, he and his became serfs and rooted to the soil'.[5] Another section of the report concluded that 'the labourer, if he thinks his parish a good one, that is, one in which public or private relief is profusely distributed, is averse to endanger his existing settlement, by leaving it'.[6] And when T. H. Holland, sometimes vestry clerk at Bermondsey, was asked why English labourers had not taken employment he replied that 'the facility of obtaining parochial relief indisposes them to exert themselves or seek about to procure employment, or to take the labour which is given to the Irish'.[7]

Such views concerning labour immobility, like those dealing with the impact of parish allowances on population increase, have coloured even the more recent historiography of rural labour in England's Industrial Revolution. Styles, of course, has severely questioned the degree to which the Laws of Settlement impeded labour mobility.[8] Arthur Redford, in his classic work on migration, places the emphasis squarely on generous poor relief: 'On the whole, however, it seems probable that the action of the Old Poor Law in restricting immigration was not so much due to the effects of the settlement system as to the mistaken and lax administration of poor relief in the southern counties previous to the Poor Law Amendment Act of 1834.'[9] T. S. Ashton, in his now classic *The Industrial Revolution 1760–1830* (1948), stated uncategorically that

Speenhamland 'led to an overpopulation of the agricultural village, similar to that which existed on a larger scale in Ireland, and (what is to the present purpose) reduced the pressure on the labourers to move'.[10] E. J. Hobsbawm, in *Industry and Empire* (1968), claimed that if the agricultural labourer 'had sense, he would raise a large family, for a wife and children meant extra earnings, and, at certain times, an extra allowance from the Poor Law' and that Speenhamland 'immobilized the labourer'.[11]

The remainder of this chapter will examine the demographic impact of the Old Poor Law on both population increase and labour mobility

II

Three tests will be made to examine the Malthusian view that the Old Poor Law led directly to higher birth and marriage rates and in turn to population increase. The first focuses on the short-term demographic impact of the abolition of the allowance system in 22 parishes spanning 15 counties. The second test contrasts 11 parishes operating the allowance system with 18 non-allowance parishes within the County of Kent. The third utilises some 49 parishes, again within the County of Kent, to compare the demographic effects of child allowances according to the order of child at which such payments commenced. It should be noted that the term 'allowance-system' is defined as allowance-in-aid-of-wages paid to the able-bodied on a scale geared to family size. The latter two exercises will test not only for population increase *per se*, but also for migration.

Mark Blaug, in 1964, regretted the fact that instructions were not given to the Commissioners of the *1834 Poor Law Report* to inquire when or why the policy of subsidising wages in the form of family allowances was abandoned.[12] A perusal of the *Report*, however, does reveal that as far as individual parishes were concerned the Commissioners were preoccupied with the termination of such allowances and not with their inception. Almost sixty cases were discovered where the date at which the allowance system was abolished could be ascertained. Particularly interesting in this regard was Edwin Chadwick's section on 'Dispauperised Parishes' which discussed the abolition of the allowance system in fifteen rural parishes in Berkshire, Hertfordshire and Buckinghamshire between 1822 and 1832.[13] Other cases are scattered throughout the *Poor Law Report* and many are found in the *Rural Queries*.

Of the total of sixty cases where the date of the abolition of the allowance system was specified, all cases where the reform occurred midway through the 1820s were noted, for it was in this decade that the HO 71 returns provided vital demographic information.[14] Thirteen such rural parishes emerged and four towns of 3000 inhabitants or more. In addition, all cases for which aggregative demographic totals were in possession of the Cambridge Group for the History of Population and Social Structure were utilised, thus adding four more rural parishes and one urban.[15]

The method of analysis is as follows: birth, marriage, death and infant mortality rates were calculated for each rural parish for two roughly equal time periods: (1) for the years when the allowance system was in effect and (2) for the years immediately following its abolition. The number of years examined on each side of the date of abolition was approximately the same for each case. The crude rates were calculated by relating the mean annual number of births, deaths and marriages to the mean population for each of the two periods. The latter is based on the average of the annual population totals calculated for each parish by comparing the increase between the censuses (1821 and 1831) with the natural increase (the difference between births and deaths) and assuming any net migration to be evenly distributed over the ten years. No standard correction factors were applied uniformly to all parishes to take account of underregistration. The clergymen's comments in the HO 71 returns, however, estimating the number of births, deaths and marriages unregistered were taken into account where possible and added to the vital events registered. Infant mortality was calculated by relating the number of deaths, twelve months or under, to the number of births in the allowance and post-allowance years respectively. The same procedure was repeated for the five towns. Overall mean values for the rates were then calculated separately for the group of rural and town parishes contrasting the allowance with the post-allowance period.

The group of parishes examined is by no means a proper sample for any particular area or county. The cases were selected by taking all parishes mentioned in the *1834 Poor Law Report* which abolished the allowance system between 1824 and 1828 and by including all cases where information was in possession of the Cambridge Group. There is no reason to suspect any bias in the cases chosen. The fact, moreover, that the parishes examined were considered by the Poor Law Commissioners as instances where allowances had been solidly entrenched and where dramatic changes in administration had occurred renders them highly suitable for testing.[16] The year in which the allowance system was abolished was taken as the starting date of the post-allowance period. Tables 1 and 2 more fully illustrate the method and present the results.

TABLE 3.1 Demographic comparison of seventeen rural parishes where allowance system was abolished

(A) Demographic structure during the allowance period

1	2	3	4	5	6	7	8	9	10
Parish and county	Years under* allowances	Mean annual number for period of			Base pop for period	Crude rates per 1000			Infant† mortality rates per 1000 births
		Births	Deaths	Marr.		Births	Deaths	Marr.	
Woburn (Beds)	1811–12	37.2	31.9	10.3	1581	23.53	20.18	6.51	
Winkfield (Berks)	1801–12	44.5	28.3	10.6	1452	30.65	19.49	7.30	
Leckhamstead (Bucks)	1821–26	15.0	7.2	4.0	523	28.68	13.77	7.65	144.4
Downham (Cambs)	1821–23	45.3	23.7	15.7	1382	32.78	17.15	11.36	125.0
Linton (Cambs)	1826–31	59.8	27.5	11.5	1678	35.64	16.39	6.85	
Stanford Rivers (Essex)	1821–24	29.3	14.0	5.5	811	36.13	17.26	6.78	102.6
Thaxted (Essex)	1821–27	42.8	29.14	15.0	2123	20.16	13.70	7.06	80.0
Westerham (Kent)	1821–24	53.5	32.8	6.8	1776	30.12	18.47	3.83	158.9
Farthinghoe (Northants)	1821–24	15.5	4.8	2.8	481	32.22	9.98	5.82	48.4
Bishop's Stoke (Hampshire)	1821–25	27.4	14.0	4.4	1004	27.29	13.94	4.38	80.3
Livermere (Suffolk)	1821–26	10.3	5.5	1.3	273	37.73	20.15	4.76	112.9
Brede (Sussex)	1821–29	36.5	17.2	10.0	974	37.47	17.66	10.27	117.1
Hartfield (Sussex)	1821–27	42.7	9.7	23.7	1484	28.77	15.97	6.54	117.1
Hellingly (Sussex)	1821–25	60.6	22.4	8.2	1357	44.66	16.51	6.04	59.4
Northiam (Sussex)	1821–24	44.8	29.8	7.0	1352	33.14	22.04	5.18	72.6
Withyham (Sussex)	1821–27	38.4	21.9	12.9	1444	26.59	15.17	8.93	96.7
Leamington Hastings (Warw.)	1821–26	12.3	10.2	2.7	449	27.39	22.72	6.01	121.6
Overall Mean						31.35	17.09	6.78	101.53

(B) Demographic structure during the post-allowance period

1	2	3	4	5	6	7	8	9	10
Parish and county	Years under* allowances	Mean annual number for period of			Base pop for period	Crude rates per 1000			Infant† mortality rates per 1000 births
		Births	Deaths	Marr.		Births	Deaths	Marr.	
Woburn (Beds)	1822–32	44.0	31.9	10.5	1742	25.26	18.31	6.03	
Winkfield (Berks)	1813–24	53.2	28.6	8.0	1558	34.14	18.36	5.13	
Leckhamstead (Bucks)	1827–30	13.5	14.3	6.5	525	25.71	27.24	12.38	148.1
Downham (Cambs)	1824–30	49.6	35.1	12.0	1649	30.08	21.29	7.28	129.7
Linton (Cambs)	1832–37	72.1	35.1	12.3	1678	42.97	20.92	7.33	
Stanford Rivers (Essex)	1825–30	27.7	14.5	4.2	863	32.10	16.80	4.87	72.2
Thaxted (Essex)	1828–30	45.3	34.3	20.0	2255	20.08	15.21	8.87	88.2
Westerham (Kent)	1825–30	59.8	33.7	6.2	1896	31.54	17.77	3.27	117.0
Farthinghoe (Northants)	1825–30	15.0	10.5	2.8	475	31.58	22.11	5.89	122.2
Bishop's Stoke (Hampshire)	1826–30	30.2	18.4	7.2	1028	29.38	17.90	7.00	106.0
Livermere (Suffolk)	1827–30	10.8	3.5	2.5	396	27.28	8.84	6.31	116.3
Brede (Sussex)	1830–37	42.8	19.3	11.8	1099	38.94	17.56	10.74	
Hartfield (Sussex)	1828–30	42.7	23.0	9.3	1530	27.91	15.03	6.08	70.3
Hellingly (Sussex)	1826–30	58.0	21.6	8.4	1456	39.84	14.84	5.77	55.2
Northiam (Sussex)	1825–30	64.9	31.7	11.8	1397	46.47	22.69	8.47	54.0
Withyham (Sussex)	1828–30	52.3	22.3	18.3	1551	33.72	14.38	11.80	101.9
Leamington Hastings (Warw.)	1827–30	14.8	9.5	3.0	454	32.60	20.93	6.61	84.7
Overall Mean						32.32	18.25	7.28	97.37

* = Total years assessed in allowance period = 106
  Total years assessed in post-allowance period = 99
† = Infant mortality data are not available for Cambridge Group Information

SOURCES PRO HO 71 *Poor Returns*; and *Rural Queries*, and aggregate totals in possession of the Cambridge Group for The History of Population and Social Structures.

The total number of years in the allowance and post-allowance periods for the rural parishes and the towns is almost equivalent – 106 and 99 years in Tables 3.1 (A) and (B) respectively, 30 and 35 respectively in Tables 3.2 (A) and (B). The overall mean values of birth, death, marriage and infant mortality rates cannot be considered as fully accurate indications of absolute levels. Although, as pointed out earlier, additions were made to specific parishes where clergymen indicated underregistration, in some cases their comments were inconclusive. The vicar of Leckhamstead, for example, estimated two deaths annually unentered but stated as well that he could not offer any exact estimation of the number of untabulated births. In other cases where no estimates were given on the HO 71 forms, resultant crude rates appear suspiciously low – for example, in Table 3.1 (A) the birth rates for Woburn and Thaxted, the death rate for Farthinghoe, and the marriage rates for Westerham, Bishop's Stoke, and Livermere. In Table 3.1 (B) the birth rates for Woburn and Thaxted again appear low along with the death rate for Livermere and the marriage rates for Westerham and Stanford Rivers. Tables 3.2 (A) and (B) similarly exhibit a few seemingly deficient rates particularly for St Werburgh and East Grinstead. No uniform correction factors were applied to these cases under the assumption that any deficiencies in registration were constant in both allowance and post-allowance periods. This would seem likely since none of the clergymen specified changes in the quality of registration. Moreover, the majority of cases cited above for possible underregistration in the allowance period exhibit similar tendencies in the post-allowance period, again suggesting that where deficiencies did occur they were applicable to both time periods. Only in the instances of Leckhamstead, Farthinghoe, and Livermere where the death rates fluctuate considerably from Table 3.1 (A) to (B) do changes in registration quality appear likely.[17] It is similarly assumed for the infant mortality rates, where deficiencies are more likely to occur, that the quality of registration was constant. Thus for comparative purposes in contrasting the relative levels of rates in the periods before and after the abolition of allowances the calculations were soundly based.

Table 3.3 presents in summary form the results for both rural and town areas. With respect to the seventeen rural parishes, the Malthusian hypothesis that the allowance system operated as a significant inducement to marriage and births is not substantiated by the evidence. The mean overall birth rate rose 3.09 per cent in the post-allowance period and the marriage rate revealed a greater rise of 7.37 per cent. Taking parishes on an individual basis, moreover, ten out of seventeen

TABLE 3.2 Demographic comparison of five towns where allowance system was abolished

(A) Demographic structure during the allowance period

Town and county	Years under* allowances	Mean annual number for period of			Base pop for period	Crude rates per 1000			Infant† mortality rates per 1000 births
		Births	Deaths	Marr.		Births	Deaths	Marr.	
St Werburgh (Derbys.)‡	1821–25	136.8	104.6	58.6	5525	24.76	18.93	10.61	175.4
Falmouth (Cornwall)	1821–27	222.9	146.3	60.7	6685	33.34	21.88	9.08	92.3
E. Grinstead (Sussex)	1821–27	97.9	55.3	15.9	3259	30.04	16.97	4.88	93.6
Stratford Upon Avon (Warw.)	1821–23	120.0	58.3	32.7	3276	36.63	17.80	9.98	94.4
Ashford (Kent)	1813–20	80.0	43.0	17.9	2653	30.15	16.21	6.75	
Overall Mean						30.98	18.35	8.26	113.9

(B) Demographic structure in the post-allowance period

Town and county	Years under* allowances	Mean annual number for period of			Base pop for period	Crude rates per 1000			Infant† mortality rates per 1000 births
		Births	Deaths	Marr.		Births	Deaths	Marr.	
St Werburgh (Derbys.)‡	1826–30	152.4	124.8	63.0	6058	25.16	20.60	10.40	161.4
Falmouth (Cornwall)	1828–30	230.0	160.0	78.7	7104	32.38	22.52	11.07	119.9
E. Grinstead (Sussex)	1828–37	112.8	56.6	15.2	3475	32.46	16.29	4.37	62.1
Stratford Upon Avon (Warw.)	1824–30	145.9	89.0	34.9	3476	41.97	25.60	10.04	116.2
Ashford (Kent)	1821–30	81.1	54.2	13.1	2791	29.06	19.42	4.69	113.9
Overall Mean						32.21	20.87	8.11	113.9

* = Total years assessed: under allowances, 30; post-allowances, 35.
† = Infant mortality data are not available for Cambridge Group Information.
‡ = Within the Borough of Derby.
SOURCES Same as for Table 3.1.

increased their marriage and birth rates upon abolition of allowances. If the demographic impact of allowances had been of a Malthusian nature one would have expected birth and marriage rates to fall markedly upon abolition. No such trends emerge.

TABLE 3.3   *Summary of demographic changes in rural and town parishes*

Crude rate	17 rural parishes		% change	5 Towns		% Change
	(A)	(B)		(A)	(B)	
Births per 1000	31.35	32.32	+3.09%	30.98	32.21	+3.97%
Deaths per 1000	17.09	18.25	+6.79%	18.35	20.87	+1.37%
Marr. per 1000	6.78	7.28	+7.37%	8.26	8.11	−1.81%
Infant Mort. per 1000 births	101.53	97.37	−4.10%	113.9	113.9	0%

(A) = Allowance period, (B) = Post-allowance period

The changes in the levels of mean infant mortality rates, again referring to Table 3.3, also cast doubt on the hypothesis suggested by Blaug that the allowance system operated to save infant lives.[18] If this had been the case, one would have expected a marked rise in infant mortality upon cessation of the allowance system. The fall of 4.10 per cent in the post-allowance period certainly does not confirm any such relationship. The fact that the overall death rate rose in the post-allowance period (6.79 per cent) does leave open the possibility that the allowance system had some effect on keeping overall mortality down. It must be pointed out, however, that excluding the parishes of Leckhamstead, Farthinghoe and Livermere where a change in death registration completeness was suspected, the overall mean death rate rises from 17.62 in the allowance period to only 18.00 in the post-allowance period, or only 2.16 per cent. It would appear, then, that the change of administration had little effect on mortality.

The town parishes exhibit roughly similar trends. The marriage rate experiences a slight fall (1.8 per cent) indicative of relative stability. The rise in the birth rate and the completely unchanged level of infant mortality also support the conclusions made with respect to the rural parishes. The overall general death rate likewise reveals minimal change.

The above evidence renders highly dubious the Malthusian argument that the allowance system provided a crucial incentive to marriages and births. It likewise reveals no relationship between allowances and infant mortality of the type suggested by Blaug.

III

Computerisation of parish data for the County of Kent allows for a second test of the Malthusian Poor Law population hypothesis, including the possible impact of the allowance system on migration. Questions No. 24 and No. 25 of the *Rural Queries,* circulated to Kent parishes in 1832, provide information concerning the payment of child allowances and/or allowance-in-aid-of-wages to the able-bodied.[19] The forty-nine replies to these questions allow for a fourfold classification of parishes regarding Poor Law administration: those which paid all-owance-in-aid-of-wages to the able bodied and child allowances on a scale geared to family size (11 parishes); those which paid allowances-in-aid-of-wages but not according to any scale relating to the number of children (2 parishes); those which paid no supplement to wages of the able-bodied, but did pay child allowances by scale (18 parishes); and last, those which paid neither allowances-in-aid-of-wages nor child allowan-ces by scale (18 parishes).[20] For a second test of the Malthusian hypothesis it was decided to select the first and last of the above categories for demographic comparison, that is, parishes paying all-owances-in-aid-of-wages geared to family size and those paying no allowances whatsoever. A contrast between parishes practising the type of allowance system so castigated by Malthus and the Poor Law Commissioners and parishes completely devoid of these methods should provide a sufficient test. If the allowance system was as dominant a factor in demographic change as the Malthusian hypothesis suggests, the allowance parishes should reveal not only higher rates of population increase but also higher birth and particularly marriage rates. They should also exhibit lower rates of out-migration and, if Blaug's suggestion is valid, lower rates of infant mortality.

Table 3.4 compares the allowance and non-allowance groups of parishes across eleven demographic variables mostly applicable to the 1820s. Employing demographic indices for the 1820s assumes, of course, that the classification of parishes based on the year 1832 (when the *Rural Queries* were circulated) is applicable to the previous decade. That this assumption is generally valid is revealed in the replies to question No. 39 of the *Rural Queries* which asked for 'the particulars of any attempt which had been made in your neighbourhood to discontinue the system (after it has once prevailed) of giving Parish Allowances to able-bodied labourers in the employ of individuals (on their own account or on that of their families)?' All replies from the allowance parishes (9 out of 11 answered the question) indicated that no such attempts had been made.[21] Typical of such replies were, 'I know of no attempt' (Bapchild), and 'We have made no attempt in this parish, nor do we know any that have' (Egerton). In addition, three parishes (Lenham, Sundridge and Speldhurst) indicated that the allowance system began in the early 1820s. These replies imply a continuity of the system from the 1820s at least. Of the non-allowance parishes (9 out of 18 replied), seven indicated that the system had never prevailed in their parishes: 'Never had prevailed' (St Michael, Harbledown), 'Has not prevailed in this Parish at all in any matter whatever' (St Peter, Thanet). Two parishes said that it had prevailed once – no dates were specified – but had been entirely discontinued (Gillingham and Thornham). This evidence certainly would suggest that those parishes not practising the allowance system in 1832 were immune from the practice in the 1820s as well.

Table 3.4 reveals the results of the comparison. Most rates are expressed as values per 1000 per annum except percentage population

TABLE 3.4   *Demographic comparison of allowance and non- allowance parishes in rural Kent*

Demographic indices	Allowance parishes (11)		Non-allowance parishes (18)	
	Total all parishes	Mean value	Total all parishes	Mean value
% Population change 1801–11	156.75	14.25	163.34	9.13
% Population change 1811–21	205.59	18.69	297.90	16.55
% Population change 1821–31	90.86	8.26	235.80	13.10
Death rate/1000 1813–20	191.62	17.42	366.66	20.37
Death rate/1000 1821–30	204.16	18.56	324.36	18.02
Birth rate/1000 1821–30	381.59	34.69	648.00	36.00
Marriage rate/1000 1821–30	65.78	5.98	134.86	7.49
Infant mort. rate 1821–30	1573.22	143.02	1619.64	89.98
Migration rate/1000 1821–30 per annum	−90.09	−8.19	−40.50	−2.25
Natural change rate/1000 1821–30 per annum	+177.32	+16.12	+323.64	+17.98

SOURCES *Census* 1801, 1811, 1821, 1831; PRO/HO 71; *Rural Queries* change which is expressed as a straight percentage increase from census to census.[22] All unregistered vital events which were specified in the HO 71 returns were added to the totals registered. The 'TOTAL all parishes' column contains the sums of the various rates for all parishes in the allowance and non-allowance groupings. The mean values are obtained by dividing these sums by the total number of parishes in each grouping (that is by 11 and 18 respectively).

A glance at the comparative mean values in Table 3.4 once again indicates no connection of a Malthusian type between allowances and population. The allowance parishes reveal a lower percentage population increase in the decade 1821–31. Their marriage and birth rates are lower than the non-allowance parishes and hardly supportive of allowances operating as a crucial incentive to more marriages and births. The hypothesis that allowances may have operated by lowering infant mortality is likewise not substantiated, allowance parishes possessing a higher overall rate than their non-allowance counterparts. The overall death rate is roughly similar in both groups, the allowance group revealing a slight increase in the 1820s over its level in the 1810s. Comparing rates of natural change per 1000 per annum in the 1820s, allowance parishes again reveal a lower mean value.

A most important feature of Table 3.4 concerns the comparison of migration rates per 1000 per annum in the two groups of parishes. These offer little evidence of allowances rooting labourers to their parishes. There was, contrary to the assertions of Malhus and numerous Poor Law Commissioners, greater out-migration in parishes where the allowance system prevailed. More persons per 1000 per annum were, in fact, leaving these parishes than were marrying in them. Taking rural parishes in Kent as a whole, moreover, there emerges a similar relationship between poverty levels in general and the degree of out-migration.

Table 3.5 divides 344 rural Kent parishes into five categories strictly in terms of mean per capita poor expenditure levels for the decade 1821–30,[23] and compares the rates of migration in each category over the same decade. It should be noted that parishes in rural Kent as a whole were net losers of population. Within this broad trend a clear pattern emerges revealing greater out-migration the higher the per capita poor expenditure range, parishes in the 35s plus, and 30–34s ranges possessing above average rates of loss. High poverty levels certainly do not appear to have restricted labour migration, but, on the contrary, probably encouraged it. In short, rural labour would more likely migrate from poverty stricken parishes even where allowances

TABLE 3.5   *Migration rates and per capita poverty levels in Kent rural parishes, 1821–30*

Per capita poor expenditure range 1821–30	No. of* parishes	Migration rate/1000 per annum 1821–30	
		Total all parishes	Mean value
35s +	49	− 842.80	− 17.20
30–34s	83	− 860.71	− 10.37
20–29s	77	− 426.58	− 5.54
15–19s	68	− 398.48	− 5.86
0–14s	67	− 115.241	− 1.72
Total	344	− 2641.92	− 7.68

* i.e. parishes for which HO 71 material was available.
SOURCES *Census* 1821 and 1831; PRO HO 71; *Poor Returns*.

were paid than from parishes less subject to such difficulties.[24]

The above evidence with respect to Kent, as in the previous intercounty analysis of allowance parishes, casts severe doubt on the interaction between the allowance system and population posited by Malthus and his contemporaries, and also must qualify Blaug's hypothesis concerning the infant mortality mechanism. Indeed, a further glance at Table 3.4 would suggest that, far from causing greater rates of population increase, the allowance system was perhaps, in fact, a reaction to previous demographic change. Although vital rates are not available for the 1810s and 1820s, intercensal rates of population increase seem to indicate this. Percentage population change in the 1800s and 1810s was higher in allowance than non-allowance parishes. Just as Blaug has argued that the allowance system was more a reaction to low wages than a cause, so it might likewise be suggested that this system was a response rather than a stimulus to population increase.

IV

Malthus and the Poor Law Commissioners in their condemnation of the allowance system, tended in most cases to lump together the payment of child allowances and allowances-in-aid-of-wages. Although the two types of relief often were closely associated, it is nevertheless the case that in early nineteenth-century England (Kent being no exception) child allowances were often paid without recourse to allowances-in-aid-of-wages. It could be argued, from a demographic point of view, that the former method of relief especially where paid upon the birth of the first child would be most likely to produce Malthusian results. As a third test of the Poor Law Population hypothesis, it was therefore decided to focus on the payment of child allowances whether combined with allowances-in-aid-of-wages or not.

Utilising, once again, the forty-nine replies to questions No. 24 and No. 25 of the *Rural Queries* it was possible to divide these parishes into five categories in regard to the payment of child allowances. The five categories were: (i) parishes paying allowances on the birth of the first child (6 parishes); (ii) parishes paying allowances commencing with the third child (6 parishes); (iii) parishes paying allowances only on the birth of the fourth child (17 parishes); (iv) parishes paying allowances to 'large' families but not by any set scale (12 parishes); and (v) parishes paying no child allowances whatsoever (8 parishes).[25] Within this fivefold classification one would expect the most dramatic Malthusian effects to reveal themselves in parishes which paid child allowances beginning with the first child.

Table 3.6 compares these groups of parishes across the same ten demographic variables utilised in the previous test (see Table 3.4). For tabular convenience, only mean values for the demographic variables are provided for each group.

A glance at the demographic indices for 'first child' parishes reveals little evidence of Malthusian mechanisms operating with respect to child allowances. The birth rate of these parishes is below that revealed for 'no allowance', 'no scale', and 'fourth child' parishes. The level of the marriage rate in 'first child' parishes is likewise lower than all other groups except 'third child' parishes. If the Malthusian hypothesis was valid one would have expected almost the opposite.

Blaug's suggestion that allowances may have operated via mortality is likewise not supported. Although 'third child' and 'fourth child' parishes reveal low infant mortality rates, the level in 'first child' parishes is the highest of any group. It would appear, as well, that no marked trend emerges with repect to 'first child' parishes regarding the overall death rate for the 1820s. Levels in this decade, moreover, are higher for all scale parishes compared to the previous decade.

In terms of rates of natural change and overall population increase 'first child' parishes rank low compared to other groups. Child allowances even where paid to the first child, then, did not produce

TABLE 3.6   *Demographic comparison of child allowances in rural Kent*

Demographic indices	Classification re child allowances (no. of parishes)				
	First child (6)	Third child (6)	Fourth child (17)	No scale (12)	No allowance (8)
% Population change 1801–11	11.30	17.42	15.98	15.75	13.64
% Population change 1811–21	24.95	26.36	19.05	16.17	12.22
% Population change 1821–31	10.38	2.32	11.58	17.99	13.48
Death rate/1000 1813–20	18.48	19.32	18.00	22.12	20.11
Death rate/1000 1821–30	21.45	22.33	20.45	19.93	22.37
Birth rate/1000 1821–30	31.05	30.34	33.65	31.19	32.20
Marriage rate/1000 1821–30	6.21	5.81	8.85	11.55	9.18
Infant mort. rate /1000, 1821–30	130.83	105.56	104.21	123.21	125.95
Migration rate/1000 1821–30	−2.64	−17.43	−5.01	+4.20	+4.99
Natural change rate /1000, 1821–30	+9.60	+8.01	+13.20	+11.26	+9.83

SOURCES   *Census* 1801, 1811, 1831; PRO/HO 71; *Rural Queries.*

greater overall population increase in the 1820s as would have been expected under Mathusian assumptions.

A comparative glance at migration rates again casts doubt on the view of Malthus and contemporary propagandists against the Old Poor Law that allowances severely inhibited labour mobility. Although fewer people were leaving 'first child' as opposed to 'third' or 'fourth child' parishes, nevertheless all scale parishes reveal net losses through migration in the 1820s. Parishes either paying allowances by no scale or not utilising any form of allowances reveal net migration gains in the same decade.

A further perusal of Table 3.6 suggests that child allowances, far from activating mechanisms resulting in rapid population growth, were possibly a result of such growth. Rates of population increase in those parishes resorting to child allowances by scale in the 1820s and early

1830s were, on the whole, higher in the 1810s than in parishes never resorting to scales or allowances. Rates of increase were particularly high between 1811 and 1821 in parishes later providing allowances commencing at the 'first' or 'third child'. The pattern here is quite similar to that evinced in the earlier comparison of allowance and non-allowance parishes.

V

These findings are of considerable import. First, they lead one to conclude that the allowance system under the Old Poor Law must be ruled out as a causal factor in population increase during the Industrial Revolution, whether through the mechanism of encouraging marriage, or through reducing infant mortality. The evidence suggests that the Malthusian proposition should be turned on its head. It is much more plausible to contend that the allowance system, far from acting as a crucial catalyst to population increase, was a response to it. The rapid growth in numbers in the first two decades of the nineteenth century, combined with a depressed agriculture in the post-Napoleonic war period, produced severe surplus labour problems. For many magistrates and overseers the only realistic solution within the context of a society governed (albeit with diminishing force) by moral notions of the right of the poor to subsistence, was to supplement wages or provide relief in accordance with family size.

Secondly, one may assert that far from being content to rely on the dole and procreate in response to its largesse, the rural underemployed moved in search of work. To be sure, the aggregative migration rates do not tell us exactly who moved. For couples already burdened with young children this was no doubt a hazardous risk and the likelihood of staying put – whether allowances prevailed or not – would be strong. Even if one concedes that it was mainly single and young males who left, this is a far cry from the Malthusian assertion that such persons, lusting after the dole, married early, and remained in their parishes. Such lines of reasoning would suggest that far more heed be paid to J. D. Marshall's warning that 'the stereotype of a highly mobile midlands and northwest, and a stagnating south, must now be questioned'.[26]

Thirdly, the examination of the Malthusian Poor Law Population hypothesis constitutes a historical case study within the wider demographic literature concerning the impact of government policy on fertility. Considerable attention has been devoted to the impact of twentieth-century family allowance schemes on the birth rates in countries such as France, Belgium and Canada.[27] Much current demographic research, of course, is being directed towards the effects of family planning programmes on family size in developing nations. Although the allowance system under the Old Poor Law was a much more *ad hoc* affair than the centrally planned programmes of the twentieth century, its negligible demographic impact serves as a basic reminder that fertility is a complex phenomenon deeply rooted in the social, economic and cultural structures of societies and therefore not easily influenced by administrative measures.[28]

NOTES AND REFERENCES

1. *See* J. P. Huzel, 'Malthus, the Poor Law and Population in Early Nineteenth-Century England', *Economic History Review*, 2nd series, XXII (1969) 430–52.
2. G. S. L. Tucker, 'The Old Poor Law Revisited', *Explorations in Economic History*, XII (1975) 239. Tucker also ran partial correlations under his 'split model' where he separated his counties into arable East and pasture West. Again no significant results emerged.
3. Huzel, loc. cit., 430–3.
4. T. R. Malthus, *An Essay on the Principle of Population* (London, 1798) pp. 95–6. In later editions he states: 'The whole business of settlements even in its present amended state, is contradictory to all ideas of freedom. And the obstructions continually occasioned in the market of labour by these laws have a constant tendency to add to the difficulties of those who are struggling to support themselves without assistance.' This point was first made, of course, by Adam Smith.
5. 'Poor Law Reports', B[ritish] P[arliamentary] P[apers], XXXVII (1834) 58–9.
6. S. G. and E. O. A. Checkland (eds), *The Poor Law Report of 1834* (Harmondsworth, 1974) p. 246.
7. Ibid., p. 248.
8. *See* P. Styles, 'The Evolution of the Law of Settlement', *University of Birmingham Historical Journal*, IX (1963–4) 33–63.
9. A. Redford, *Labour Migration in England 1800–50*, 2nd ed. (Manchester, 1964) p. 80.
10. T. S. Ashton, *The Industrial Revolution 1760–1830* (London, 1948) p. 111.
11. E. J. Hobsbawm, *Industry and Empire: An Economic History of Britain Since 1750* (London, 1968) pp. 83–4. See also E. J. Hobsbawm and G. Rudé, *Captain Swing* (London, 1969) p. 50: 'Henceforth it would be madness for a labourer, sure of at least his crust at home, to venture anywhere else.' For an extended discussion on the historiography of the relationship between the Old Poor Law and population increase see Huzel, loc. cit., 437–40.

12. M. Blaug, 'The Poor Law Report Reexamined', *Journal of Economic History*, XXIV (1964) 231.
13. *See* 'Poor Law Report', loc. cit., XXIX, part 2, 22–85.
14. For a discussion of the Home Office 71 returns in the Public Records see Huzel, loc. cit., 447. These returns provided vital statistics for the 1831 Census. They contain for each parish in England and Wales yearly totals of baptisms, burials and marriages over the period 1821–30. The burials for each year are further broken down by age at death. In addition they include comments on defective registration.
15. The parishes are as follows:

Parish and County	R or U*	Year**	Source
Leckhamstead (Bucks)	R	1827	'Rural Queries', *BPP*, XXXIII (1834) Q. 39.
Downham (Cambs)	R	1824	'Poor Law Report', loc. cit., XXVIII, 594.
Stanford Rivers (Essex)	R	1825	Ibid., 225.
Thaxted (Essex)	R	1828	Ibid., 227.
Westerham (Kent)	R	1825	Ibid., 208.
Farthinghoe (Northants)	R	1825	Ibid., 408–11.
Bishop's Stoke (Hampshire)	R	1826	'Rural Queries', loc. cit., Q. 39.
Livermere (Suffolk)	R	1827	Ibid.
Hartfield (Sussex)	R	1828	Ibid.
Hellingly (Sussex)	R	1826	Ibid.
Northiam (Sussex)	R	1825	Ibid.
Withyham (Sussex)	R	1828	Ibid.
Leamington Hastings (Warws)	R	1827	Ibid.
St Werburgh (Derbys)	U	1826	'Poor Law Report', loc. cit., XXIX, 17.
Falmouth (Cornwall)	U	1828	Ibid., 427.
E. Grinstead (Sussex)	U	1828	Ibid., 312.
Stratford-Upon-Avon (Warws)	U	1824	Ibid., 17.
Woburn (Beds)***	R	1813	'Rural Queries', loc. cit., XXVIII (1822) 153.
Winkfield (Berks.)***	R	1813	Ibid., XXXIII (1834) Q. 39.
Linton (Cambs)***	R	1832	Ibid.
Brede (Sussex)***	R	1830	Ibid.
Ashford (Kent)***	U	1821	'Poor Law Report', loc. cit., XXVIII, 212.

*   R for rural and U for urban
**   Year of Abolition of Allowances
*** Parishes for which the data come from the Cambridge Group.

16. The administrative change at Stanford Rivers in 1825, for example, was described as a 'bold effort at reform' where weekly pay was 'at once struck off'. Total poor expenditure dropped from £1191 in the year 1821 to £560 in the year 1825. Farthinghoe likewise reported a dramatic fall in poor expenditure upon its reform in 1825 when relief was stopped to 'all but extreme cases'. Falmouth, reformed in 1828, refused regular outdoor to the poor and 'able-bodied men applying for relief' were 'offered the house with their families'. Such comments were typical of the parishes under examination. For source references to the above statements see note 15 above.

17. It should be noted, however, that these are three of the smallest parishes under consideration and that, on this account, greater fluctuations might be expected.

18. M. Blaug, 'The Myth of the Old Poor Law and the Making of the New', *Journal of Economic History*, XXIII (1963) 174.

19. *See* 'Poor Law Report', loc. cit., XXX–XXXIV, the 'Answers to Rural Queries'.

20. The Kent parishes falling into these categories were:

    (A) *Parishes paying both allowances-in-aid-of-wages and child allowance by scale.* (11) . . . Lenham, Wrotham, Bapchild, Edenbridge, Brenchley, Egerton, Goudhurst, Marden, Speldhurst, Sundridge, Westwell.

    (B) *Parishes paying allowances-in-aid-of-wages but not according to any scale relating to the number of children.* (2) . . . Preston-next-Faversham, West Wickham.

    (C) *Parishes not paying allowances-in-aid-of-wages but paying child allowances by scale.* (18) . . . Hawkhurst, Higham, Nonington, Eastry, Ash-next-Sandwich, Ashurst, Bexley, Bidborough, Chalk, Chiddingstone, Farningham, High Halden, Horsmonden, Leigh, Pembury, Rolvenden, Wilmington, Boughton Monchelsea.

    (D) *Parishes not paying allowances-in-aid-of-wages nor child allowances by scale.* (18) . . . Chilham, Chislehurst, St Lawrence-in-Thanet, Chislet, Cobham, Barham, Chevening, St Michael Harbledown, Gillingham, Lamberhurst, Harrietsham, Hartlip, Milstead, Northfleet, Murston, St Peter-in-Thanet, Rodmersham, Thornham.

21. The parishes replying were Lenham, Wrotham, Bapchild, Edenbridge, Brenchley, Egerton, Goudhurst, Marden, Speldhurst, Sundridge, Westwell. For the specific replies see 'Rural Queries', loc. cit., XXXIII, Q. 39, under the specific parishes.

22. Birth, marriage, death, migration and natural change rates are calculated on base population for each parish arrived at by taking the mean of the population in 1821 and in 1831. The natural change rate per 1000 per annum represents the total births for the period 1821–31 minus the total number of deaths. This was further divided by ten to arrive at a per annum figure and then expressed per 1000 of the base population. The migration rate is similarly calculated, only initially the natural change was subtracted from the population difference between the 1821 and 1831 Census.

23. Per capita poor expenditure for each parish was calculated for the period 1821–31 by taking the total of poor expenditure for each year from 1821 to 1830, dividing by ten to obtain an annual average, and relating this to the base population for the decade. The latter was obtained by summing the

population in 1821 and 1831 and dividing by two.

24. For the further argument that labour demand, particularly in the area of London, was crucial to labour mobility *see* J. P. Huzel, *Aspects of the Old Poor Law, Population, and Agrarian Protest in Early Nineteenth-Century England with Particular Reference to the County of Kent* (Unpublished Ph.D. thesis, University of Kent, 1975) pp. 192–4, 250–2.
25. For Kent parishes which fall into these categories *see* ibid., p. 433.
26. *See* J. D. Marshall, *The Old Poor Law, 1795–1834* (London, 1968) pp. 42–3.
27. For reference to these studies *see* Huzel, loc. cit., 451, n.2.
28. I would like to thank the Canada Council for funding the research for this paper. Thanks are also extended to Professor Alan Armstrong for helpful criticism of an earlier draft and to the Cambridge Group for the History of Population and Social Structure for access to data in their possession. For a critique of the original article on which this paper is based *see* D. Levine, 'Parson Malthus, Professor Huzel, and the Pelican Inn Protocol: A Comment', *Historical Methods*, XVII (1984), and my reply 'Parson Malthus and the Pelican Inn Protocol: A Reply to Professor Levine', idem., 21–7.

4 Malthus in Scandinavia 1799

LARS MAGNUSSON

In his *Essays in Biography*, J. M. Keynes praised the second edition of *An Essay on Population* in the following terms:

> [P]olitical philosophy gives way to political economy, general principles are overlaid by the inductive verification of a pioneer in sociological history, and the brilliance and high spirits of a young man writing in the last year of the Directory disappear.[1]

Malthus admitted that the first edition had been written 'on the impulse of the occasion and from the few materials which were within my reach in a country situation'.[2] In preparation for the second edition, Malthus read extensively, gathered statistical materials and travelled. The most interesting outcome of these studies was the motion of moral restraint, which gave the theory of population a totally new approach. The theory seemed originally to have been one of the most dismal in a dismal science, and the author admitted this indirectly in the preface to the second edition; 'I have endeavoured to soften some of the harshest conclusions of the first Essay.'[3]

It is often maintained that the evidence provided in the second edition in support of the law of population was very weak. We shall note later that this judgement appears appropriate for the Norwegian studies, but not, on the whole, for the Swedish case. This essay proposes to discuss the relevance of the empirical material Malthus gathered on Scandinavia for his second edition, especially in relation to his interpretation of this evidence for his grand theory of population. Our discussion is placed in the context of the current debate among Swedish scholars concerning Malthus's interpretation of Scandinavian population during the eighteenth and nineteenth centuries. However, lack of space compels us to treat only the main trend of this discussion.

The Scandinavian studies were based on previously published statistical materials. The Swedish materials in particular were highly reliable. This is attributable to the establishment of the Swedish *Tabellverket* in 1749 whose main task was to collect population statistics from every parish in the Kingdom of Sweden. In addition, Malthus and three academic friends visited the Scandinavian countries and Russia in 1799. They were accompanied by the famous British explorer Edward Daniel Clarke. They travelled through Denmark and reached Hälsingborg on the south-west coast of Sweden. They then proceeded to Gothenburg via the provinces of Halland and Bohuslän. From there Clarke took the main road to Stockholm, while Malthus and his friends travelled north to Norway. In Norway they stopped at Christiania (Oslo) and visited the southern part of the country. They then crossed the border into Sweden and proceeded to Stockholm, and from there they followed the Swedish north-eastern coastline through Norrland to Finland and Russia.[4]

Malthus depicted Norway in extremely favourable terms:

> In the summer of the year 1799, the Norwegians appeared to wear a face of plenty and content . . . and I particularly remarked that the sons of housemen and the farmers boys were fatter, larger and had better calves to their legs, than boys of the same age and in similar situations in England.[5]

He provided mortality figures that were comparatively very low – according to Malthus the crude death rate was only 20.8 (per 1000). He attributed this to preventive checks operating in the form of late marriages. Late marriage functioned as a form of moral restraint and was caused by institutional, ecological and economic factors. He indicated that a number of institutional factors were particularly important in this context, for example, special inheritance laws and the military system. A more important factor was the shortage of arable land in Norway. Of course, this was primarily due to natural factors, yet this condition was aggravated by a specific social and economic structure that favoured pasture. In this economy, there was a fear that expanding farming acreage would deplete the forests. This form of pastoral economy together with a specific institutional framework militated against early marriages, and consequently resulted in low marital fertility and low mortality.[6] Population increase never reached the point where positive checks would become necessary. Malthus was also highly impressed by the official Norwegian position concerning the population problem: 'Norway is, I believe, almost the only country in Europe, where a traveller will hear any apprehensions expressed of a redundant population, and where the danger to the happiness of the lower classes of people from this cause is in some degree understood.'[7]

Malthus's description of Sweden, on the other hand, was hardly favourable at all. His travelling companion, Clarke, described the Swedish situation in terms which Malthus most likely assented to:

> When we entered Sweden from Denmark, we were struck with the superior liveliness of the Swedes; but in entering it now from Norway we received a very different impression. To add to the general wretchedness of the country, a greater dearth had prevailed, during the former winter, than the oldest persons ever remembered . . . The people had saved themselves from starving, by eating the bark bread, and a grass we afterwards found to be sorrel . . . In everything, the appearance of the people was strangely contrasted with that of the Norwegians. The latter wear red caps. The Swedes, in their broad-brimmed hats, without any buttons upon their black coats, looked like so many quakers in mourning.[8]

Although more nuanced, Malthus's account of Sweden is essentially the same as Clarke's. In the context of his theory of population, he described the Swedish situation in the following terms:

> [I]ts population has a strong tendency to increase; and that it is not always ready to follow with the greatest alertness any average increase in the means of subsistence, but that it makes a start forward at every temporary and occasional increase of food, by which means it is continually going beyond the average increase, and is repressed by periodical returns of severe want, and the diseases arising from it.[9]

In contrast to Norway, the Swedish situation was characterised by active working positive checks to population growth. According to Malthus, Sweden had extremely high mortality figures even with its low level of urbanisation. Swedish statistics also revealed that population growth during the latter half of the eighteenth century was strongly correlated to harvest fluctuations, which appeared only further to strengthen his conclusions.[10] In this context, the economic policy of the Swedish government annoyed Malthus: 'Yet notwithstanding this constant and striking tendency to overflowing numbers, strange to say! the government and the political economists of Sweden are continually calling out for population, population.[11]

Malthus's interpretation of Swedish population movements for the eighteenth and early nineteenth centuries remains a controversial issue among Swedish scholars in the fields of history, demography and economics. The Malthusian viewpoint was accepted in principle by Eli Heckscher, who particularly emphasised what he saw as a strong, positive correlation between population growth and means of subsistence for the eighteenth century. In an article in 1943, he discussed the relevance of the Malthusian model for Sweden, and his empirical findings appear to verify the presence of a strong, positive correlation between harvest fluctuations and mortality for this century. He concluded that this 'without doubt verifies Malthus's construction, both the theory and its application for the Swedish development'.[12] More recently, T. McKcown has argued in favour of a Malthusian interpretation of Swedish population movements for the eighteenth and early nineteenth centuries.[13]

Although Heckscher agreed essentially with Malthus, he made some interesting remarks. First, he critised the extremely low figures Malthus presented for Norway. According to Heckscher, the real crude death rate for the later eighteenth century was approximately 25.0 instead of Malthus's 20.8 (per 1000).[14] Secondly, he argued that Malthus overemphasised the differences between Norway and Sweden. Heckscher maintained that the similarities between the two countries were striking. Low mortality and marital fertility were not peculiar to Norway but rather a distinctive feature of all Scandinavian countries (except Finland) as opposed to continental Europe:

> Everything sems to point at that Denmark, Norway and Sweden during the 18th century had a lower – and presumably a much lower – nativity than mainland Europe during the same time. The crude death rate on the other hand, 26 to 28 per 1000, seems to correspond to Germany as late as in the 1870s and South Europe about 1900.[15]

Heckscher attributed this to the low level of urbanisation in Scandinavia, which did not exclude the possibility of a strongly operative Malthusian law of population. On the contrary, the strong correlation between harvest fluctuations and mortality demonstrated that this was the case.[16]

Moreover, Heckscher hints at a paradox in the Malthusian interpretation. Ironically, the early nineteenth century is a period of demographic transition. At the time of Malthus's visit to Sweden, strong underlying forces were necessitating demographic changes, at least in the longrun. After 1810 the death rate fell rapidly, while the birth rate remained unchanged. This led to a population boom, expecially for the 1820s. Malthus noted this in the sixth edition of the *Essay* and sought to explain the declining mortality in a special postcript to the chapter on Sweden:

> [T]he healthiness of the country . . . has continued to advance since 1805. This increase is attributed to the progress of agriculture and industry, and the practice of vaccination. The gradual diminution of mortality since the middle of the last century is very striking.[17]

Since Heckscher, the Malthusian interpretation of Swedish population development has been disputed. Criticism has been directed at the interpretation of fluctuations in the death rate before 1820 and at the causes for the population boom after 1820. Gustaf Utterström has been especially critical of Heckscher's position (and thereby Malthus's) theory) that harvest fluctuations were the main factor underlying mortality for the pre-1820 period. Instead, Utterström emphasises other main factors:

> Lack of food was seldom the sole cause of increases in mortality and far from always the principle cause. Epidemics, whether connected or not with war and famine, also played a large part. Climate, the standard of housing and hygiene were all of importance.[18]

He also notes that a positive correlation between harvest fluctuations and changes in the death rate does not mean that the first variable is the cause of the second. Instead, Utterström finds that both variables are strongly correlated with a third: climate.[19]

In a recent essay, G. Fridlizius has made similar objections to the Malthusian interpretation. Likewise, he questions the existence of a causal relationship between harvests and changes in the death rate for eighteenth-century Sweden. Moreover, he has attempted to estimate the possibility of such a relationship. He has correlated corn prices against the crude death rate with a one year lag. The working assumption here is that in a strict Malthusian interpretation, there should be a positive correlation between the two variables with a one year lag. (Corn prices are, of course negatively correlated with harvest fluctuations.) However Fridlizius arrives at a significant positive correlation between corn prices and the crude death rate *for the same year*. He explains this finding in the following terms:

The factors which influence the outcome of the harvest but not the harvest itself also determine changes in mortality. Weather conditions contributing to poor harvests also caused endemic diseases such as tuberculosis and influenza to be prevalent and thereby raised overall mortality.[20]

Fridlizius also relates the marriage rate to corn prices but does not find any significant correlation. Finally, he compares fertility with the real wages of workers for the entire period of the mid-eighteenth to the mid-nineteenth century in an attempt to prove that a Malthusian context was absent from the long-term development process.[21] Periods of falling real wages do not appear to have had any effect on overall fertility and 'indicate the operation of preventive checks, in the form of a lower marriage frequency, higher age at marriage or lower marital fertility'.[22]

The criticisms of Utterström and Fridlizius must be situated in the context of a general critique of the application of the Malthusian model to Europe in the transition from an agrarian to an industrial society. J. D. Chambers has stressed the autonomy of mortality in relation to economic variables in pre-industrial Europe as well as the significance of factors other than economic development as the 'cause' of the decline in mortality in the eighteenth and early nineteenth centuries.[23] Indeed, Gustaf Utterström is one of the founders of this theory which nowadays seems to be, as W. A. Armstrong stated, 'increasingly accepted'.[24]

Fridlizius has also criticised Malthus's explanation from the sixth edition. He argues that the post-1820 population boom in Sweden was not causally connected with expanding agriculture nor the embryonic industrialisation of that period. On the contrary, growing population itself constitutes an important prerequisite for agricultural development and proto-industrialisation in the early nineteenth century. And it is an important long-term factor contributing to the Swedish industrial breakthrough from the 1850s onwards. Fridlizius also notes that because of its effects on society's age structure, a fast rising population leads to a rising demand for consumption goods. The role of the demand factor in the explanation of the industrial revolution had, of course, already been stressed by Elizabeth Gilboy in the 1930s.[25] Of the 1850s we learn that, 'The changes in population structure during that decade must have resulted in a large increase in household formation, with an increased demand for housing and various consumer goods,'[26]

This general attack on the Malthusian position made possible a Keynesian interpretation of population development in the transition from an agrarian to an industrial society. As a consequence of improvements in hygiene, a growing immunity of the human host, and so on, population growth is approached as an independent variable and an important causal factor in economic development. The collection of essays in W. R. Lee, *European Demography and Economic Growth* (1979) provides a good example of this Keynesian approach. Lee's interpretation of the German development is typical of the entire book:

> Indeed the evidence provided . . . : emphasise the exogenous nature of population growth, and its strict independence of either increased agricultural output, or nascent industrialisation . . . Furthermore exogenous population growth may well have generated waves of population – sensitive and other types of capital formation, the differential productivity of which would in turn have influenced the rate of expansion of aggregate supply and thus of economic growth in general.[27]

This collection of essays aims in general at providing positive evidence for a suggestion once made by J. R. Hicks: 'One cannot repress the thought that perhaps the whole Industrial Revolution of the last two hundred years has been nothing else but a vast secular boom, largely induced by the unparalleled rise in population.'[28]

Thus far we have seen that the Malthusian interpretation of Swedish (and Norwegian) demographic behaviour has been criticised from different perspectives. However, in recent years the Malthusian position has been defended in part by Swedish scholars. This counter-movement is, of course, not Malthusian in its true sense. It is not probable that any of these scholars would accept the Malthusian law of population, at least not in its strict formulation. Instead, they have taken one of the most fruitful propositions in the Second Essay as their point of departure, a proposition which Malthus never fully explored.

As noted, Malthus explains how preventive checks function in different ecological and socio-economic structures in the extended second edition of the *Essay*. This approach is largely responsible for the substantially less gloomy outlook of this edition. The chapters on Norway and Switzerland are especially significant, in which Malthus seeks to explain why preventive checks in the form of moral restraint are so effective in these countries. He attempts to locate the causes of low nativity, mortality and marriage rates in the ecology and socio-economic framework of a pastoral economy.

Malthus investigated the pastoral economy with its limited natural resources. Specific traditions and customs were developed which functioned to preserve it, and also its distinctive social organisation. A high age of marriage resulted in a relatively low marital fertility and served as an important factor in preserving society and alleviating the pressure on land. Thus in this social and economic structure, social being determined social consciousness (as Marx would have expressed it) even in the sphere of demographic behaviour.

But Malthus never developed this line of thought. Had he done so, it would have subverted the original formulation of his theory of population. Why should this form of behaviour be limited to Norway and Switzerland? Or to a pastoral economy? It is not plausable that other forms of resource allocations systems have corresponding social structures, traditions and demographic behaviour which function to serve the purposes of preservation? If we accept these propositions, then there is no reason why population must expand faster than the means of subsistence; for there is always a set of preventive checks that makes this situation, if not impossible, at least not inevitable.

This approach has been in the forefront of recent Swedish discussion. It was, of course, heavily influenced by the ongoing international debate concerning family formation and population growth in pre-industrial Europe. What many scholars found was that before industrialisation – or 'proto-industrialisation' – there seemed to exist a 'homeo-static equilibrium' between natural resources and population. 'Among peasant populations the necessary connections of household formation to resources which were scarce and which could be aquired only by inheritance formed the decisive structural determinant,' wrote, for example, Hans Medick in a highly influential paper in 1976.[29] This equilibrium was later on upset – we are told – by 'proto-industrialisation' and the development of rural industry which led to a rise in the demand for labour and thus made possible a secular growth of landless population stratas in the countryside. The debate on 'proto-industrialisation' and its demographic consequences paved the way for numerous local studies on family formation in different social, economic and ecological environments. And they all seemed to point out that family formation patterns in Europe before industrialisation were highly influenced by such economic, social and ecological factors.[30]

Various Swedish scholars have applied this approach in their treatment of pre-industrial Sweden. Beginning with an idea that is also prevalent in Malthus's writings, it is ironic that the description these scholars provide of Sweden in the eighteenth and early nineteenth centuries is in stark contrast to Malthus's account. One of the most important contributors in this field has been David Gaunt, who has sought to relate such demographic variables as family size, marital fertility, age at first marriage, and so on, with what he terms specific ecosystems: 'different demographic patterns are brought forth through differences in the local human ecological situation; the economic, social and ecological framework for individual action'.[31]

By studying different geographical regions in Sweden, Gaunt has been able to locate different demographic patterns caused by socio-economic and ecological factors. Small households, late marriages, low marital fertility and high marriage frequency are predominant in the corn-growing manorial areas. A different pattern emerges in the sparsely populated, forested districts of Bergslagen, where the social structure is characterised by a dominant peasant-owner class. Larger households, larger marital fertility and a lower frequency of marriage resulted from the greater work opportunities found in proto-industries, home crafts, mining and so on, together with a more evenly distributed annual work pattern. Gaunt concludes that 'there are at least two demographic structures in seventeenth and eighteenth century Sweden. They exist simultaneously'.[32]

In a similar study treating the Dala parish in Västergötland county in western Sweden in the late eighteenth and early nineteenth centuries, C. Winberg finds that variation in marital fertility, age of marriage, and so on, depended upon one's social position in peasant society. His main results imply that landless peasants had a lower fertility rate and a higher age at first marriage than landowning peasants.[33] I. Eriksson and J. Rogers arrive at similar results in a study on *statare*, a strata of landless agricultural workers. This strata expanded rapidly in the early nineteenth century, replacing peasants and cottagers as the main working force on many estates.[34]

The implication of these and other studies is to challenge the notion of population growth as an autonomous, driving force in the Swedish experience of the transition to industrial society. Instead, these studies indicate that different social strata in peasant society adapted themselves to the existing ecosystems of social relations and resources. Demographic factors fulfilled an important function in preserving the social system. Pre-industrial populations adopted certain moral restraints, to use Malthus's term, and perhaps also vice in order to survive both physically and socially. Population expanded only if the social system changed and/or the agricultural sector developed.

To summarise, according to Malthus, the Swedish situation was characterised by extreme poverty and active working positive checks to population growth. Norwegian conditions were characterised as totally different, due to specific institutional and socio-economic factors that promoted moral restraint. This chapter has discussed this interpretation in the light of recent research and debate in Sweden. Malthus's interpretation of Sweden and Norway has been the subject of debate and criticism from various perspectives. Eli Heckscher, working from a Malthusian position, challenged Malthus's sharp distinction between Norway and Sweden. He argued that both Norway and Sweden were characterised by low mortality and fertility. He also made some criticisms of Malthus's empirical materials. A second critique has had broader implications and has challenged the Malthusian model in its entirety. The contributions of G. Utterström and G. Fridlizius have been especially important in this context, but their approach is not exclusively Swedish. These scholars maintain that population growth in the transition from an agrarian to an industrial society is not to be understood as a simple effect of economic expansion and embryonic industrialisation, as Malthus's interpretation implies. On the contrary, population growth is interpreted as constituting an important causative factor in this transition. We have also noted a third line of thought that has been developing. Its approach is similar to that found in Malthus's discussion of the pastoral economy in the second edition of the *Essay*. Here Malthus sought the causes for low nativity, mortality and marriage rates in the ecology and socio-economic structure of the pastoral economy. Specific demographic behaviour was noted as an important factor in preserving the social structure. Various scholars have applied this theoretical approach to the Swedish situation. They have found that different demographic structures existed contemporaneously in pre-industrial Sweden, and that the socio-economic and ecological structures are important determining factors. Once again, the role of a rapidly developing agricultural sector is emphasised in the explanation of population growth in the transition from an agricultural to an industrial society.

NOTES AND REFERENCES

1. J. M. Keynes, *Essays in Biography* (London, 1951) p. 99.
2. T. R. Malthus, *An Essay on the Principle of Population*, 4th ed. (London, 1807) vol. 1, p. v.
3. Ibid., p. ix. *See also* K. Smith, *The Malthusian Controversy* (London, 1951).
4. E. F. Heckscher, 'Malthus och den nordiska befolkningsutvecklingen under 1700–talet', *Ekonomisk Tidskrift*, 45 (1943) 191 ff., and G. Utterström, *Jordbrukets Arbetare* (Stockholm, 1957) vol. 1, p. 81 f.
5. Malthus, op.cit., p. 316.

6. Ibid., pp. 308–20.
7. Ibid., p. 324.
8. E. D. Clarke, *Travels in Various Countries of Europe, Asia and Africa*, part 3, vol. 2 (London, 1823) pp. 89–90.
9. Malthus, op.cit., p. 334.
10. Heckscher, loc.cit., 207.
11. Malthus, op.cit., p. 335.
12. Heckscher, loc.cit., 202.
13. T. Mckeown, R. G. Brown and A. G. Record, 'An Interpretation of the Modern Rise of Population in Europe', *Population Studies*, 3 (1972) 345–82.
14. Heckscher, loc.cit., 193.
15. Ibid., 205–6.
16. Ibid., 206 f.
17. Malthus, *An Essay*, 6th ed. (London, 1825) vol. 1, p. 298.
18. G. Utterström, 'Some Population Problems in Pre-Industrial Sweden', *Scandinavian Economic History Review*, II (1954) 103–65.
19. Utterström, op.cit., vol. 1, p. 207.
20. G. Fridlizius, in W. R. Lee (ed.) *European Demography and Economic Growth* (London, 1979) p. 345.
21. Ibid., p. 346.
22. Ibid., p. 346.
23. *See* for example, J. D. Chambers, *Population, Economy and Society in Pre-Industrial England* (Oxford, 1972).
24. *See* ibid., p. vii, the preface by W. A. Armstrong.
25. E. Gilboy, 'Demand as a Factor in the Industrial Revolution', in R. M. Hartwell (ed.), *The Causes of the Industrial Revolution in England* (London, 1967).
26. Lee, op.cit., p. 364.
27. Ibid., pp. 158–9.
28. J. R. Hicks, *Value and Capital* (Oxford, 1974) p, 302
29. H. Medick, 'The Proto-Industrial family Economy: The Structural Function of Household and Family During the Transition from Peasant Society to Industrial Capitalism', *Social History*, 3 (1976) 303.
30. *See*, for example, P. Kriedte, H. Medick and J. Schlumbom, *Industrialisierung vor der Industrialisierung* (Gottingen, 1977), and F. Mendels, 'Proto-Industrialization: The First Phase of the Industrialization Process', *Journal of Economic History*, XXXII (1972) 241–61.
31. D. Gaunt, 'Pre-Industrial Economy and Population Structure', *Scandinavian Journal of History*, 2 (1977) 184. *See also* his 'Natural resources – Population – Local Society: The Case of Pre-Industrial Sweden', *Peasant Studies*, VI (1977) 137–41.
32. Gaunt, ibid., 'Pre-Industrial Economy', 209 f.
33. C. Winberg, *Folkökning och Proletarisering*, (Göteborg, Meddelanden från Historiska Institutionen vid Göteborgs Universitet, 1975).
34. I. Eriksson and J. Rogers, *Rural Labour and Population Change* (Uppsala, 1978).

5 Malthusianism in South-West France in the Nineteenth and Twentieth Centuries

FRANÇOIS PRADEL DE LAMAZE

It is very unlikely that the name, and, even more so, the work of Malthus was known (or would be today) to the ordinary people of south-west France in the nineteenth century. Fellow clerics, however, perhaps confusing this poor man for the anti-papist devil, consigned him to hell. Thus a certain priest, Massabie, officiating at Douelle, in the department of Lot, thundered from the pulpit: 'the ideas and narrow calculations of the Malthusian school have erupted. Today an only son gives a house to an only daughter'.[1] But one would have certainly surprised the peasant of Gers or Lot if one had told him that his demographic behaviour would later be studied and quoted as an archetypal example of Malthusianism in France.

Moreover, as always where Malthus is concerned we must be cautious. In this book, which begs to interpret the man's work, we risk oversimplification, confusing, for example, what Malthus said with the interpretation current in the France of today, which reduces his demographic message to little more than one of voluntary limitation of fertility. There is much more to say than this, but the reader must spare us that in this short chapter.

Although statistical data are unreliable in France before the nineteenth century, it can be said that before Malthus the south-west of France was distinguished from the rest of the country by a low rate of fertility, and the nineteenth and twentieth centuries serve only to confirm this characteristic. Certainly other regions of the country

71

(Normandie and Bourgogne, for example) experienced identical phenomena, and undoubtedly for similar reasons, but the specific case of the south-west and its immense size (Aquitaine, Midi-Pyrénées and Limousin comprising about one quarter of the territory of France), justifies the special interest of study (see Figure 5.1).

Indeed one has the tendency today to think that the homogeneity of a

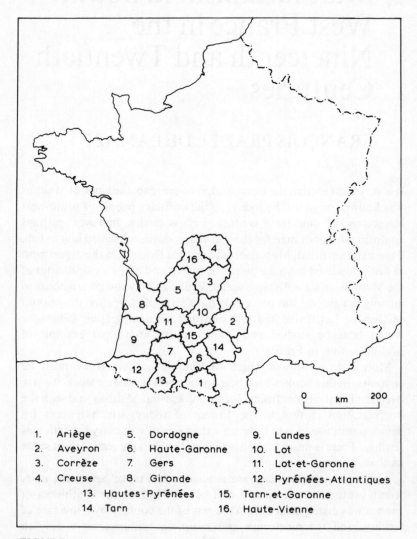

1.	Ariège	5.	Dordogne	9.	Landes
2.	Aveyron	6.	Haute-Garonne	10.	Lot
3.	Corrèze	7.	Gers	11.	Lot-et-Garonne
4.	Creuse	8.	Gironde	12.	Pyrénées-Atlantiques
	13. Hautes-Pyrénées		15.	Tarn-et-Garonne	
	14. Tarn		16.	Haute-Vienne	

FIGURE 5.1   *Departments of south-west France*

'Malthusian' pattern of demographic behaviour in this area is of long standing. On the contrary, at the beginning of the nineteenth century, there was a great contrast in those patterns: very low fertility in the centre of the region (the departments of Gers, Lot-et-Garonne and Tarn-et-Garonne), in contrast to very high fertility in the surrounding departments (Aveyron and Corrèze in particular). Disregarding the departments of Gironde and Haute-Garonne which, with the two large towns of Bordeaux and Toulouse, had a demographic pattern which was closer to the national one, one can observe a clear diffusion or contagion of 'Malthusian' behaviour from the plains to the mountains.

In effect, geographical conditions were determining factors in the nineteenth century: the plain of the Garonne allowed for the existence of an agriculture, which, while not rich, was at least above mere subsistence level: while in the mountains, on the contrary, in the Pyrénées or the Massif Central, agricultural cultivation could hardly stretch to ensure basic survival. For this reason and provided that demographic pressure was reasonably controlled, it was possible for a family on the plains to hold its own, or even grow richer, from simple agricultural resources. In contrast, in the mountains, and whatever the size of the family, the need for external means of supplementing income was all but permanent. From this base there developed two very different patterns of behaviour from the nineteenth century: *a priori*, it was possible, and often desirable for the small farmer, who was often an owner occupier, in Gers or Lot-et-Garonne to adjust the size of his family to that of his land; but for the family settled in Corrèze, Creuse or Aveyron, the constant concern was to ensure a complementary and external means of income, either through local paid activities (through major works like the creation of roads and railways, and sometimes also domestic work for local manufacturers) or, more often, through seasonal migration of great and small distances (such as to the building trade in Paris, Bordeaux or Toulouse). Whether seasonal or casual, migration soon became permanent, through the increasingly heavy demand for labour from growing industry most often situated north of the Loire.

The development of the population (as depicted in Tables 5.1 and 5.2 and the appendixes)[2] is, in this respect, instructive. In Gers the population declined in a continuous fashion, falling from 312 000 inhabitants in 1831 to 274 000 in 1886; in contrast in Corrèze regular growth was the normal pattern, the population increasing from 294 000 to 326 000 over the same period. In the first case, the fall in population was due essentially to a deficit of births in relation to deaths, a deficit which seemed all the more pronounced as the population aged: from

1846 to 1851 Gers lost 4300 inhabitants through natural means and a further 3100 through emigration; from 1856 to 1861 it lost an additional 4500 through an excess of deaths over births. In the second type of department, in contrast, natural increases often largely compensated for a migratory deficit: for the same period 1846–51, the excess of births in Corrèze was 5400 while the migratory deficit was 2100. These figures must be treated cautiously, taking into account the incompleteness of the data, but nevertheless they do demonstrate the contrast well.

In the middle of the nineteenth century therefore one can distinguish two types of department with widely differing demographic behaviour:

TABLE 5.1 *Total population 1801–1975 (in thousands)*

Grouping of departments	1801	1831	Maximum population (year of maximum)	1911	1921	1975
Gers, Lot-et-Garonne, Tarn-et-Garonne	785	901		673	594	651
Lot, Tarn, Hautes-Pyrénées, Landes, Pyrénées-Atlantiques, Dordogne	1695	2046	2178 (1851)	1895	1723	1911
Ariège, Aveyron, Corrèze, Creuse, Haute-Vienne	1221	1458	1680 (1891)	1528	1358	1158

TABLE 5.2 *Evolution of the population 1846–51 and 1931–6 (in thousands)*

Grouping of departments	Population in 1846	1846–1851 natural balance	migratory balance	Population in 1931	1931–1936 natural balance	migratory balance
Gers, Lot-et-Garonne, Tarn-et-Garonne	903	− 10.2	− 7.1	605	− 10.4	+ 15.2
Lot, Tarn, Hautes-Pyrénées, Landes, Pyrénées-Atlantiques, Dordogne	2166	+ 34.6	− 35.4	1723	− 10.0	− 12.4
Ariège, Aveyron, Corrèze, Creuse, Haute-Vienne	1578	+ 36.8	− 25.6	1293	− 9.4	− 15.5

on the one hand was the group comprising Gers, Lot-et-Garonne and Tarn-et-Garonne whose population decreased by natural means generally producing a deficit of deaths over births, a trend of natural decrease which was emphasised by a rate of emigration of little importance; and on the other hand, there was the group comprising Corrèze, Creuse, Haute-Vienne, Aveyron, Ariège, Lot and Tarn, where population increased due to a high birth rate, in spite of important migratory movements dominated by emigration. The other departments (Dordogne, Pyrénées-Atlantiques and Landes) had much less regular behaviour, either because of urbanisation, which was important, or because of the presence of both types of demographic pattern, particularly in Dordogne.

The different patterns of behaviour produced sharp contrasts (as in Table 5.3 and the Appendixes). From the point of view of age structure, Gers, Lot-et-Garonne and Tarn-et-Garonne stand out with an already ageing population in 1861, but in which at all ages there was a balance between men and women. At the same time in the surrounding departments the population was young, but showed important disparities in the distribution between the sexes: generally, a shortage of men was noticeable in the 20–40 year age group, ages when men in particular were most affected by migratory movements of both a temporary and permanent nature. From the point of view of the birth rate (for which see Table 5.4 and Appendixes) complementary demographic phenomena are noticeable: in Gers there were 213 children aged between 5 and 9 years for every 100 women aged between 25 and 29, and there were 271 in Creuse.[3]

These demonstrable contrasts get smaller by the end of the nineteenth century in some departments, though not until the First World War in

TABLE 5.3   *Ratio between old and young people in 1861, 1901 and 1975**

Grouping of departments	1861	1901	1975
Gers, Lot-et-Garonne, Tarn-et-Garonne	0.411	0.609	0.910
Lot, Tarn, Hautes-Pyrénées, Landes, Pyrénées-Atlantiques, Dordogne	0.236	0.376	0.891
Ariège, Aveyron, Corrèze, Creuse, Haute-Vienne	0.183	0.308	1.106

*Ratio of the number of people aged 65 years or more for every child under 15 years of age.

TABLE 5.4   *Fertility in 1861, 1901 and 1975**

Grouping of departments	1861	1901	1975
Gers, Lot-et-Garonne, Tarn-et-Garonne	197.4	174.4	210.2
Lot, Tarn, Hautes-Pyrénées, Landes, Pyrénées-Atlantiques, Dordogne	230.9	226.1	213.2
Ariège, Aveyron, Corrèze, Creuse, Haute-Vienne	244.2	252.9	206.2

*I have chosen as the measure of fertility the ratio of the number of children between 5 and 9 years to every 100 women between 25–29 years. This measure, summary though it is, has the advantage of eliminating the effects of migrations, which are very significant for the younger women.

others. Using the same measure of fertility (that is surviving children aged 5 to 9 years per 100 women aged 25 to 29), the variation which was considerable in 1861 (at its lowest 184 children per 100 women in Tarn-et-Garonne, and at its greatest 271 in Creuse) became very slight a century later: at its lowest 181 in Haute-Vienne, and at its greatest 232 in Creuse in 1975.

Ignoring the departments of Gironde and Haute-Garonne, this homogenisation in the patterns of demographic behaviour concerning births was produced by the close proximity of places and the subsequent diffusion of similar behaviour as if by contagion. Initially, in 1861, the three most 'Malthusian' departments were located next to one another: only Tarn-et-Garonne and Lot-et-Garonne had fewer than 200 children per 100 women (still using the same measure of fertility) and Gers scarcely more. The same was true in 1901 with the three adjoining departments of Lot, Tarn and Haute-Pyrénées now also barely above 200, while the most distant departments of Corrèze, Creuse and Aveyron maintained high fertility (see Figure 5.2).

Following the First World War, by contrast, fertility increased slightly in the middle of the region, while it decreased considerably in the surrounding departments. Since then there has been a great homogeneity of demographic behaviour patterns in the whole of the south-west. Today (in 1975 that is), with the exception of Haute-Vienne, all the departments under review have a fertility rate, using the same measure as before, which varies narrowly from 205 in Lot-et-Garonne to 232 in Creuse.

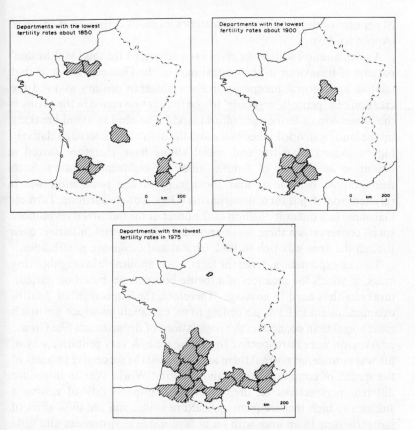

FIGURE 5.2 *Departments with the lowest fertility rates in 1850, 1900 and 1975*

When rates of fertility are compared during the twentieth century, broadly speaking, at the lowest levels, migration has continued to play a role by accentuating the drop in population in two ways. First, it assumed more importance by becoming permanent (seasonal migration virtually disappeared) and particularly by including women who were much less mobile in the nineteenth century than today, and secondly, migration made an important contribution to the lowering of the birth rate because emigration affected women in the most fertile age group. The net effect was to accentuate the lower birth rate. In addition, between the two World Wars in all the departments of the south-west there were more deaths than births, and today, after some respite from this trend in the 1950s, that has become the norm once more.

The result of all this is, as the evidence shows, a considerable ageing of the population, such that certain of the departments today have nearly

20 per cent of the people, and sometimes more, over the age of 65 years (Appendix 5.3).

An explanation which has often been advanced for this 'Malthusian' pattern of behaviour in the central part of the Garonne valley is that relative agricultural prosperity in the eighteenth century allowed the creation of a 'petite bourgeoisie' whose foundation rested in the main on the possession of fertile agricultural lands. The need to avoid breaking up the land by divided inheritance and the desire to conserve a relatively high standard of living and social status have therefore forced a limitation on the size of families since the eighteenth century. Such demographic behaviour, and the ageing of the population which resulted from it, put these departments (Gers, Lot-et-Garonne, Tarn-et-Garonne) in a difficult position at the onset of the industrial revolution: social conservatism there was opposed to all industrial initiative, even though the area was rich in both capital and economic possibilities.

Such an explanation, given the facts, is not applicable in neighbouring areas, in which the creation of a 'petite bourgeoisie' based on agricultural wealth is hard to envisage. Therefore, the 'contagion' of 'Malthusianism' ought to have, according to us, explanations which are much more social than economic: the populations of departments like Creuse or Aveyron were introspective for a long time. A very primitive way of life was considered normal there and it needed the successive impacts of the spread of communications and the First World War to introduce different perspectives on life. The virtual impossibility of raising a sufficiently high income from agriculture alone, and the difficulties of industrialising in an area with an unfavourable environment and little capital wealth, therefore forced families, desirous of a very different standard of living, either into a family exodus or a very clear reduction in family size.

APPENDIX 5.1   *Evolution of the population from 1801–1975 (in thousands)*

| Department | 1801 | 1831 | Maximum population at date shown | | 1911 | 1921 | 1975 |
			middle of 19th cent	end of 19th cent			
Ariège	196	254	267 (1851)		199	173	139
Aveyron	318	359		416 (1886)	369	333	278
Corrèze	244	295		328 (1891)	309	274	241

APPENDIX 5.1 *Evolution of the population from 1801–1975 (in thousands)*
(cont.)

| Department | 1801 | 1831 | Maximum population at date shown | | 1911 | 1921 | 1975 |
			middle of 19th cent	end of 19th cent			
Creuse	218	265		284 (1891)	266	228	147
Dordogne	409	483	506 (1851)		437	397	373
Gers	258	312			222	194	175
Landes	224	282	310 (1856)		289	264	287
Lot	261	284	296 (1851)		206	177	150
Lot-et-Garonne	299	347			268	240	292
Pyrénées-Atlantiques	355	428	452 (1841)		433	403	535
Hautes-Pyrénées	175	233	251 (1851)		206	186	228
Tarn	271	336	363 (1851)		324	296	338
Tarn-et-Garonne	228	242			183	160	184
Haute-Vienne	245	285			385	350	353

APPENDIX 5.2 *Evolution of the population 1846–51 and 1931–6 (in thousands)*

| Department | Population 1846 | 1846–1851 | | Population 1931 | 1931–1936 | |
		natural balance	migratory balance		natural balance	migratory balance
Ariège	270	+ 5.5	− 8.6	161	− 3.6	− 2.5
Aveyron	389	+ 12.3	− 7.3	324	+ 0.3	− 9.4
Corrèze	318	+ 5.4	− 2.1	264	− 1.4	—
Creuse	286	+ 8.4	− 7.0	208	− 3.8	− 2.2
Dordogne	504	+ 7.8	− 5.6	384	− 1.7	+ 5.0
Gers	314	− 4.3	− 3.1	193	− 3.7	+ 3.0
Landes	298	+ 7.2	− 3.2	257	− 1.6	− 4.2
Lot	294	+ 4.9	− 3.2	167	− 5.1	+ 1.0
Lot-et-Garonne	346	− 4.2	− 0.7	248	− 4.0	+ 9.2
Pyrénées-Atlantiques	458	+ 3.7	− 14.5	422	+ 2.3	− 11.6
Hautes-Pyrénées	251	+ 4.4	− 4.7	190	− 2.2	+ 0.8
Tarn	361	+ 6.6	− 4.2	303	− 1.7	− 3.4
Tarn-et-Garonne	243	− 1.7	− 3.3	164	− 2.7	+ 3.0
Haute-Vienne	315	+ 5.2	− 0.6	336	− 0.9	− 1.4

80

APPENDIX 5.3 *Comparative distribution of population by age (in percentages)*

Department	1861			1975		
	less than 20 years	20–64 years	65 years or more	less than 20 years	20–64 years	65 years or more
Ariège	38.8	55.0	6.2	25.7	51.9	22.4
Aveyron	38.3	55.0	6.7	27.5	52.8	19.7
Corrèze	41.3	53.3	5.4	26.1	53.4	20.5
Creuse	40.1	54.6	5.3	24.5	50.3	25.2
Dordogne	36.3	59.4	4.3	26.7	53.2	20.1
Gers	30.4	61.0	8.6	27.3	53.1	19.6
Landes	39.9	55.2	4.9	28.9	52.9	18.2
Lot	34.1	58.3	7.6	26.9	52.9	20.2
Lot-et-Garonne	29.3	61.7	9.0	28.3	53.8	17.9
Pyrénées-Atlantiques	36.8	56.2	7.0	29.5	53.7	16.8
Hautes-Pyrénées	36.1	56.8	7.1	28.4	54.7	16.9
Tarn	35.4	58.1	6.5	28.2	53.6	18.2
Tarn-et-Garonne	29.0	62.0	9.0	28.5	53.2	18.3
Haute-Vienne	41.0	54.9	4.1	25.7	54.8	19.5

APPENDIX 5.4 *Fertility in 1861, 1901 and 1975**

Department	1861	1901	1975
Ariège	248.3	224.5	222.4
Aveyron	245.7	264.5	223.1
Corrèze	228.3	271.7	207.2
Creuse	271.0	243.4	231.6
Dordogne	230.1	225.7	208.0
Gers	212.7	177.0	212.0
Landes	263.7	244.0	219.6
Lot	219.6	201.5	215.1
Lot-et-Garonne	194.1	172.2	205.0
Pyrénées-Atlantiques	219.3	252.8	214.4
Hautes Pyrénées	231.3	200.4	210.7
Tarn	227.9	208.4	212.1
Tarn-et-Garonne	183.9	174.5	217.2
Haute-Vienne	232.3	249.3	181.4

* I have chosen as the measure of fertility the ratio of the number of children aged between 5 and 9 years to every 100 women between 25 and 29 years. This measure can be free, at least in part, from migratory problems. Women of this age, indeed, are and were for the most part non-migratory.

NOTES AND REFERENCES

1. Cited in A. Armengaud, *Les Français et Malthus* (Paris: Presses Universitaires de France, 1975) p. 19, and which was taken from the *Bulletin de la Société des Etudes du Lot*, VI (1880).
2. The tables and appendixes have been constructed by the author from the various census returns of the *Statistique Générale de la France*.
3. This measure of fertility is certainly rather crude but it can be independant of the main statistical difficulty of including migratory effects. Initially, or when it is a matter of comparing different levels of fertility, this measure can be considered synonymous to the 'sum of reduced births'.

Part II
Land: The Primacy of Agriculture

6 The Course of Rents in the Age of Malthus

G. E. MINGAY

I

In Malthus's day rents formed a major element of the national income. The researches of Phyllis Deane and W. A. Cole indicate that at the beginning of the nineteenth century land accounted for more than half of British national capital, and rents produced a fifth of the national income. Farm capital also loomed large in the total capital stock, accounting in 1832 for as much as a fifth of the country's capital other than land.[1]

The greater part of farm capital, however, belonged to tenants rather than landowners. The majority of landowners undertook little or no commercial farming: in Malthus's time their great investment was in the land: non-farming private and institutional landowners owned the great bulk of it, about four-fifths to nine-tenths of the whole. The remainder, only something between 10 and 20 per cent of the farmland, was owned by the farmers. Rent was the landowner's return for his investment in the land and for the more or less permanent amenities of the land which he provided: the farm buildings, hedges, walls and fences, drains and embankments, access roads, and the wider transport improvements secured by investment in turnpikes and canals. It was not an excessive return: net of outgoings farm rents represented only about 3 or 4 per cent of the capital value of the land.[2] A higher return, indeed, could be obtained from mortgages, government stock and Bank and East India stocks, urban land or canal shares. But none of these provided the bonus of political power, local influence and social prestige which was the unique advantage of land.

The farmers, the great majority of them tenants as we have noted, saw land as producing three rents, or in effect a gross return which was divided among three claiments. One rent, or one-third of the total return, went to repay the farmer's outlays – his expenditure on stock and implements, on wages, tithe and parish rates, and his living expenses; another rent, or second *tranche* of the gross return, represented the farmers's profit, generally believed to represent an average of about 10 per cent on his farm capital; and the remaining rent was the one paid to the landlord. Contemporaries saw the return from the land as having social as well as economic functions. Sir Joseph Banks, the celebrated botanist and a Lincolnshire landowner, believed that after deducting tithe and taxes the land's produce should be divided into four: three parts should go to the tenant, one for his household expenses, another for his farming outlays, and the third 'for improvement of his premises . . . and for providing Portions for his daughters and Capital sufficient to enable his Sons to take farms'; the remaining fourth part should be reserved for the landlord 'for his maintenance and the support and placing out of his family'.[3]

The landlord, too, had a social function: he was not there merely to consume the tenant's surplus. He performed various unpaid functions on behalf of the tenant and, indeed, the whole village community, filling local administrative offices, serving as Justice of the Peace, and thereby responsible for a wide range of duties from maintaining law and order to the regulation of weights and measures, and representing the county or a market town in Parliament. He might seek to advance farm technology and improve farming standards by running an experimental farm, by enclosing and draining common fields and wastes, and he might involve himself in transport developments in order to improve access to distant markets. He was sometimes called upon to protect the farmers against the depredations of vagrants, robbers and pirates, and from all those who might wish to impose new taxes on farm products or otherwise harm the prosperity of agriculture. And he undertook a variety of local but useful responsibilities, supporting charities and schools, writing letters on behalf of tenants and witnessing their wills, even holding their surplus funds (paying the standard rate of interest on them) and taking instructions on their ultimate disposal – just like a private savings bank and trustee. Sir Joseph Banks, evidently a conservative in social matters, thought that the level of rents to be charged should be adjusted with some care so as not to put too severe a burden on the tenant on the one hand, while attempting to ensure on the other that the tenants did not become excessively wealthy. Farmers, he believed, should be able to save enough 'to make their sons Farmers and their Daughters Farmers

Wives, and be happy and cheerful'; but they should not 'grow rich enough to make their sons into Consumers of the Producers of the Earth as Lawyers, Parsons, Doctors, etc., etc.,' which 'classes should be taken from the younger branches of Gentlemen's Families'.[4]

II

There were, of course, wide variations in rents between different estates and between different types of land. Each unit of land is in some sense unique, and many factors might influence the rent charged for it. The actual calculations of the movement of rent over time is not simply a matter of inspecting the figures at the beginning and end of a convenient run of rentals. Rents were affected by absence of new investment and neglect of maintenance, which was not infrequently the case on badly managed estates, particularly those in the hands of absentee owners.[5] The reverse conditions of an active policy of investment and improvement, on the other hand, was reflected in a gradually rising rental. A large-scale enclosure of common fields and commons made for farms that were easier to manage, and might revolutionise the capabilities of the soil and hence enhance attractiveness to farmers, resulting perhaps in a twofold, threefold, even fourfold increase in rents. For the estimation of long-term rent movements it is necessary to eliminate the effect of enclosure since although one may be dealing with land geographically in almost the same place (though there was much redistribution, selling and exchanging of holding at the time of enclosure), it was certainly not the same land in its attractiveness to farmers and hence in its rent-producing capacity.

A futher complication in the calculation of rent movements is that the money amounts which appear in estate rentals are listed only against a string of tenants' names: often the farm itself is not named, neither is the acreage stated. Changes in both the amounts, and in the names, might result from acquisitions or sales of land. Many proprietors were active in the land market. As already remarked, enclosure itself was an occasion for buying, selling and exchanging. But at any time a landowner might buy land in a village in order to round off or otherwise improve his existing farms, or to move towards a sufficient command of the property there to bring about an enclosure, or merely to extend his local influence. In other villages he might sell his land if the estate there were unprofitable or the prospects of mounting an enclosure remote. Estates were in fact shifting agglomerations of properties, neither fixed in total area nor in composition. To take the total rental of an estate at one date and compare it with the rental at a substantially later date is thus a doubtful procedure – often one is not comparing the same land or the same area. And even in the exceptional case when there was no change in the actual land content of an estate there could be significant changes in the composition of the farms. Farms, as operating units, were rarely sacrosanct. In addition to the farmhouse and buildings they generally consisted of a number of fields (or in open villages, field-lands) and closes which could be added to, or subtracted from, as seemed appropriate to the landlord or his agent. Successful tenants were often rewarded by an augmentation of their farms with land taken from the holdings of less successful men. Small tenants might disappear from the rental altogether as their holdings were consolidated to make larger units. Throughout the eighteenth and early nineteenth centuries, indeed, the average size of farms tended to grow, and this occurred without the intervention of large-scale enclosure: it was a fact of life in both villages that retained their common fields and those that had long lost them. The precise calculation of rents, therefore, has to take account not only of the shifting composition of the estate but also of the changing composition of the farm units of which the estate was constituted.

A further factor affecting rent movements was the peculiar process by which rents were changed. On some estates the total rental rose very gradually as individual farms were improved piecemeal and their rents reassessed. On others, especially those on land already enclosed and improved, rents might remain completely unchanged for very long periods of years. When a change occurred it was often the result of the succession of an heir or a complete change in ownership. Then a professional valuer might be called in and a detailed survey made of the farms, field by field, close by close, with an assessment of the personal capacity of each tenant. The old rent and the new valuation were set side by side, and the decision left to the landlord, who in fact often compromised, setting a new rent somewhere between the two figures. In setting the new rent various non-economic factors entered into consideration. Landlords generally did not like to appear grasping: they preferred popularity, as Arthur Young remarked, and an extra low bow and scrape from the tenantry, to an additional five shillings per acre per annum. This was a bad thing for agriculture, Young believed, for he thought that high rents forced farmers into farming more efficiently.[6] In setting new rents, or when making abatements in bad times, many landlords took their cue from the leading proprietor of the district. Their stewards made enquiries to see what the big owner was proposing to do, and they followed suit. So in areas where large estates dominated, their owners tended to establish the ruling level of rents.

One difficulty here was that the great estates tended to be low-rented. There was a convention, accepted by most great proprietors and their stewards, that they should be seen to live up to their role as great proprietors, as leaders and protectors of the rural community; and this meant magnanimity in the matter of rents, if perhaps in little else. Thus in 1830, wrote James Loch, agent to the Sutherland estate: 'Lord Stafford's rents . . . have always been fixed at rather under the general average of the district . . . I mean that the tenants should feel that they hold their lands on rather easier terms than their neighbours. It is fit and proper that those who hold of a great man should do so.'[7] Some proprietors could well afford to follow a policy of deliberately underrenting their agricultural properties because they could draw on other large sources of revenue. Indeed, some deliberately subsidised their farm tenants out of their income from minerals, iron works, canals, docks or urban land. It was his income from shipping, and from coal and ironstone, that enabled John Christian Curwen to become the leading agricultural improver in Cumberland, developing new practices of feeding horses and cattle, setting new standards in dairying, and planting on a vast scale – a million trees on the slopes of Windermere – thus well earning his grandiloquent title of 'Field Marshal in the armies of Agriculture'.[8] Later examples included the Marquess of Bute, who used his coal revenues to keep down the rents of his Glamorgan farm tenants, and the Duke of Sutherland, who diverted his huge Bridgewater Canal income into schemes to help resettle the displaced crofters of his Sutherland estates.

Locally, farm rents could also be influenced by political considerations and by the landowner's passion for sport. There was an understanding that in return for a 'good bargain' the tenant promised at least one of his two county votes to the landlord's candidate at election time. And on the estates of enthusiastic foxhunters and game preservers tenants might enjoy a low rent as compensation for the depredations to which the farms were subject, and for the requirements sometimes imposed on them of bringing up young hounds for the hunt. Hunting in fact was made possible only by the acquiescence of the farmers, who, however, were often keen sportsmen themselves. Some farmers had their own hunts, and others joined those of their landlord, proud to be as well attired and as well mounted as he and his important friends. Lastly, the rent of a particular farm might be affected by the landlord's partiality for certain tenants. When a rental was reviewed it was not unusual for the owner to write against a tenant's name as did Lord Monson in 1810: 'This man is an old servant of the family, so no increase here'; or against another, the rent was to be abated 'in Consideration of Age and Infirmities'; yet another, because he was 'a very industrious man with a large Family'; and again, 'this being an old Tenant Lord Monson did not wish him to be advanced in his Rent, it therefore stands at the Old Rent'.[9]

With so many non-economic, social, personal and capricious factors entering into the matter, it is not surprising that rents on some estates were out of line with the general trend – moving up later, or faster, or less rapidly or perhaps not at all. Indeed, it is surprising, rather, that a general trend can ever be distinguished. That it can is a tribute to the overriding influence of prices.

III

The agricultural surplus represented by rent was not a fixed amount, nor was it directly related to the value of land or the costs of cultivation. It was determined basically by the level of agricultural prices, and for particular kinds and uses of land by the prices of particular farm products, those of grain, cattle, sheep, cheese, and specialised crops like hops, hemp, madder, woad and market-garden produce. Research carried out over the past twenty years or so has established fairly well the broad course of rents in the Malthusian age and the years leading up to it. In the first half of the eighteenth century, and particularly in the decades of the 1730s and 1740s, the generally low and stable levels of farm prices made it difficult for rents to be increased, or even in some areas to be sustained at existing levels. Pressure on rents was such, indeed, that some landlords could avoid abatements only by offering various subsidies to complaining tenants, subsidies which included making repairs to farm buildings, and finding money for seed and parish taxes, even doctors' bills and funeral expenses, all outgoings which were normally regarded as the tenant's responsibility. After mid-century the farming environment gradually improved. Between 1750 and 1790 prices rose fairly steadily, and by the latter date the prices of wheat, barley and oats were about 50 to 75 per cent higher than they had been forty years earlier, while beef and mutton had risen by about 25 per cent. After a lengthy time-lag rents, too, moved upwards. The general rise in rents in areas investigated by the writer was about 40–50 per cent over the period 1750–90, with most of the rise coming after 1770.[10]

There was a sharp break in this gradual upward progress during the war period between 1793 and 1815. Prices rose to unprecedented heights: wheat from an average of some 48 to 58 shillings a quarter in the early 1790s to reach over 100 shillings in 1800, 1801, 1812 and 1813; in only ten of the years between 1793 and 1815 did wheat fall below 75 shillings, in only six below 65 shillings. Barley too rose sharply, as did oats – barley in 1801 reached 90s 7d, twice the pre-war price for wheat – while meat prices also rose, beef in particular – the price of beef actually outpacing that of wheat in several years of the period.[11] The price upsurge was not due to the wartime difficulties of importing: imports of wheat were in fact far larger than before the wars, averaging over 500 000 quarters a year as against under 200 000 quarters in the 1780s; in the worst years imports were particularly heavy: well over a million quarters in both 1800 and 1801, and nearly 1½ million quarters in 1810. But to set against this upsurge of imports was an expansion of the market by about a fifth as by the end of the wars over 2 million mouths had been added to the numbers to be fed. Under the stimulus of high prices the cultivated acreage expanded rapidly – perhaps by as much as a sixth – as some 3 million acres were enclosed by private acts of parliament alone. But the yield of the expanded farmland was heavily diminished by the long runs of extraordinarily bad seasons, which restricted sowing, damaged growing crops, reduced the harvests, and created fodder shortages and heavy losses of beasts for the producers of livestock.[12]

Rents responded to the dramatic change in conditions. According to the Board of Agriculture the rise between 1790 and 1813 in the rent of a hundred acres of arable land was from £88 6s 0d to £161 13s 0d, an increase of 84 per cent. Thomas Tooke believed that rents went up threefold, though this is not borne out by modern investigations of the records of large estates where, it seems, the more general figure is near to that of the Board of Agriculture, about 90 per cent.[13] McCulloch, basing his figures on the property tax, estimated that the average rent of England and Wales had risen in 1800–15 by 52 per cent; from 1810–11 to 1814–15 it rose from 15s 9½d to 18s 4½d, a rise of 16 per cent in only four years of the period.[14]

After 1813 prices fell as the seasons improved and the large area of recently enclosed wastes and commons made its effect felt on production. Wheat was not to touch 100 shillings again for the rest of the century, and came near to doing so only in the bad years of 1817 and 1818. The average price between 1814 and 1830 was about 67 shillings, markedly lower than the average of 1794–1813 which was 83 shillings. The post-war price level, however, was still substantially higher – by nearly 50 per cent – than the average price of 46 shillings which ruled between 1777 and 1793. In these circumstances it is not surprising that rents did not fall very greatly after the wars. The farmers' often difficult process of adjustment to permanently lower price levels, a process at its most painful in 1815–16 and in 1821–3 when prices fell sharply, was met by temporary rent abatements averaging about 20 or 25 per cent. In the early 1820s some landlords, though not all, were obliged to make permanent reductions, in effect converting the abatements into a new lower level of rents. One reason for the limited nature of the fall in rents was that a considerable part of the increase achieved during the war years was the result of heavy expenditures on farm improvements, especially enclosure, so that tenants had the advantage of farming in improved conditions; moreover, the wartime increase in rents had not resulted in any increase in its real, as distinct from its money, burden; indeed, according to the figures of the Board of Agriculture the share of rent in the total costs of cultivation had fallen slightly. A further factor was that over most of the post-war period dairying and fattening areas were less affected by the fall in prices as urban markets expanded and living standards rose. The balance of profitability was shifting in favour of pasture, producing that differential between rents in the pastoral north and west and the arable south and east which Caird was to notice at mid-century.[15]

IV

It was against this background of a sudden revolution in rent levels, followed by a merely partial readjustment in the post-war era, together with the introduction of the controversial and highly protective Corn Law of 1815, that the contemporary discussion of rents by Malthus and his fellow economists must be seen. By 1815 the rapid expansion of towns and industry was well under way, and the growth of a newly enlarged body of non-agricultural food consumers was shifting the balance of English society. Landlords still presided over what was by far the largest sector of the economy – employing a third of the working population in 1811 – but it was no longer self-evident that what was good for agriculture was good for the country at large. And with the new Corn Law the landlords succeeded 'to the position of hatred and opprobrium which the corn dealers and millers had occupied for so many centuries in the eyes of the common people'.[16] The rich farmer, whose sons were now 'dashing bucks flourishing their broadswords' and whose daughters were to be seen 'rattling in their spruce gigs to the milliners and perfumers', was frequently lampooned in the press; even more bitterly reviled was the wicked landlord, luxuriating on a rent-roll 'swollen by the high price which the poor workers were forced to pay for their loaves of bread, and therefore indirectly by the high wages which their employers were forced to pay to prevent them from dying, as some put it, rather than to enable them to live'.[17] The landlords' cry, wrote Byron, was

> down with everything, and up with rent!
> Their good, ill, health, wealth, joy, or
> discontent, Being, end, aim, religion – rent,
> rent, rent!

Thus began the gradually expanding rift between the landed interest and the nation, the rift which came to crisis point in the 1840s with the pressure of radical propaganda, industrial depression and labour unrest, Irish famine and political division, to bring about within a generation the total repeal of the Corn Laws.

Malthus, as is well known, joined in the debate on the side of the landlords. Protection, Malthus argued in a pamphlet of 1815, was necessary not merely to keep farming profitable but also to keep the nation prosperous. Not only was agriculture the largest source of employment, but the consumption of landlords, farmers and labourers made up a vital proportion of the total demand for goods and services.[18] And in his *Principles of Political Economy* Malthus, assuming a marked under-consumptionist stance, argued that the overproduction of goods inherent in a free monetary economy could be met by the consumption of the 'unproductive' classes, among whom he placed landlords, domestic servants, and those whose incomes were derived from the interest paid on funds loaned to the government, the fund-holders (or 'fund-lords' and 'tax-eaters' as Cobbett savagely called them).[19]

Rents, one might also point out, not only supported in large part the landowning class, but were a source of capital for both agricultural improvement and non-agricultural investment. In Malthus's lifetime a large part of the expansion of mining for coal, iron ore, copper, lead and other minerals, the growth of ironworks, limekilns, brick-works, quarries and timber supplies, and the construction of river improvements, canals and harbours were aspects of estate development by landowners. And that large proportion of rents which went merely to build and maintain country houses, to sustain parks, servants, country sports and the whole aristocratic way of life, performed a useful function in maintaining at the same time an unpaid corps of Members of

Parliament, country magistrates and county administrators. The consumption aspect too was not negligible. If there were in 1815 some 15 000 great landowners, gentry and country gentlemen, it must be assumed that they and their families and servants must have totalled something of the order of a quarter of a million people; and to them must be added the large numbers of professional men, London shopkeepers and workers in luxury trades, country tradesmen, village craftsmen and their employees who relied entirely or in large part on the landowners for their living. It would not be fanciful to see rents as supporting altogether at least a million of the current English population of some 11 million. The figures themselves are hazy, but this is not of itself crucial. Rent was an important element in the national income, in the working of the economy, and not least in the maintenance of the nation's social fabric.

NOTES AND REFERENCES

1. P. Deane and W. A. Cole, *British Economic Growth 1688–1959* (Cambridge, 1962) pp. 301, 304, 306.
2. R. J. Thompson, in 'An Enquiry into the Rent of Agricultural Land in England and Wales during the Nineteenth Century' *Journal of the Royal Statistical Society*, LXX (1907), reprinted in W. E. Minchinton (ed.), *Essays in Agrarian History*, II (Newton Abbot, 1968) p. 79, estimated that landlords' investment in drainage, fencing, roads and buildings averaged £12 per acre, and with repairs and upkeep accounted for all but 22.5 per cent of the rent. This figure may have been higher, however, in the early nineteenth century.
3. Quoted in G. E. Mingay, *The Gentry* (London, 1976) p. 85.
4. Ibid.
5. P. Roebuck, *Constable of Everingham Estate Correspondence 1726–43* (Yorkshire Archaeological Society, Leeds, 1976) pp. 9–10, 15–16.
6. G. E. Mingay, *Arthur Young and His Times* (London, 1975) pp. 47–8.
7. E. Richards, *The Leviathan of Wealth* (London, 1973) p. 29.
8. Mingay, op. cit., *Gentry*, pp. 100–1.
9. G. E. Mingay, *English Landed Society in the Eighteenth Century* (London, 1963) pp. 271–2.
10. J. D. Chambers and G. E. Mingay, *The Agricultural Revolution 1750–1880* (London, 1966) pp. 111–12.
11. G. Hueckel, 'Relative Prices and Supply Response in English Agriculture During the Napoleonic Wars', *Economic History Review*, 2nd series, XXIX (1976) 405.
12. Chambers and Mingay, op. cit., pp. 112–15.
13. See T. Tooke, *History of Prices*, vol. 1 (London, 1838) p. 326; F. M. L. Thompson, *English Landed Society in the Nineteenth Century* (London, 1963) pp. 217–20; H. G. Hunt, 'Agricultural Rent in South-East England 1788–1825', *Agricultural History Review*, VII (1959) 100.

14. R. J. Thompson, loc. cit., 60; L. P. Adams, *Agricultural Depression and Farm Relief in England 1813–1852* (London, 1932) p. 33.
15. He found the average rent of fifteen grazing counties to be 31*s* 5*d* per acre, while that of eighteen corn growing counties was only 23*s* 8*d*, a difference of one-third. J. Caird, *English Agriculture 1850–51* (London, 1852) p. 480.
16. D. G. Barnes, *A History of the English Corn Laws* (London, 1930) pp. 148, 151.
17. P. James, *Population Malthus* (London, 1979) p. 276.
18. Barnes, op. cit., pp. 130–1.
19. James, op. cit., pp. 302–3.

7 Conspicuous Consumption by the Landed Classes, 1790–1830

DAVID CANNADINE

The English Aristocracy in the age of Malthus has received relatively little historical attention in recent years. For the political historian, the repression before and after Waterloo and the passing of the Great Reform Act are the most significant events: if the landowners appear at all, it is only as a defiant and then defensive class. For the social historian, the rise of the middle classes receives a further encore, and the making of the working classes gets its premiere: but the aristocracy is largely forgotten. And for the economic historian, the 'wave of gadgets' which swept across industrial England in these years again serves to relegate agriculture and the landed interest to a relatively obscure backwater. How odd all this is. For during this very period, it was the landed classes – however much they may have been challenged – who were still incomparably the most powerful and wealthy social group – a position which they were to retain well into the second half of the nineteenth century.[1] Certainly, Thomas Malthus would have found this picture of his times – so Whiggish and teleological that the landowners were consigned to a premature grave – eccentric, baffling and bewildering. For him then, if not for historians now, the landed classes were at the centre of the stage, as they were also at the centre of his writings. What, therefore, does a study of his work tell us about the aristocracy of the time? And how far is our understanding of his writings in turn enhanced by a fuller appreciation of the aristocratic world within which he lived, thought and wrote?

I

From contemporaries and historians alike, the English aristocracy in the age of Malthus has received a particularly bad press. Here, for example, is the Hon. G. W. E. Russell, basing his opinions on the recollection of his forbears: 'The aristocracy was honeycombed by profligacy . . . Not merely religion, but decency was habitually disregarded . . . All the ancilliary vices flourished with a rank luxuriance. Hard drinking was the indispensable accompaniment of a fine gentleman, and great estates were constantly changing hands at the gaming table.'[2]

More recently, Professor Hobsbawm has painted a very similar picture:

> The first fifty years of industrialism had been so golden an era for the landed and titled Briton . . . Their packs of hounds criss-crossed the shires. Their pheasants . . . awaited the battue. Their Palladian and neo-Classical country houses multiplied, more than at any time before or since, except the Elizabethan . . . The age of steam and the counting house posed no great problems of spiritual adjustment.[3]

Equally censorious is Professor Perkin, who suggests that it was in this very same period that the landed, governing classes 'abdicated their responsibility' to the lower orders, by dismantling the compassionate legislation of paternalism, and by their self-interested enactment of the Corn Laws, which benefited the landowners at the expense of the rest of the community. In the words of one contemporary observer:

> Everywhere, in every walk of life, it is too evident that the upper orders of society have been tending, more and more, to a separation of themselves from those whom nature, providence and law have placed beneath them . . . The rich and the high have been indolently and slothfully allowing the barriers that separate them from their inferiors to increase and accumulate.[4]

Assuredly, there is much evidence which may be marshalled in support of this picture. To begin with, it was certainly the case that the landed classes enjoyed unprecedented material prosperity during the years of the wars with France. From the 1780s, the price of wheat rose spectacularly and inexorably: 45 shillings a quarter in 1789, 84 shillings a quarter by 1800, and an average of 102 shillings between 1810 and 1814 – prices never attained before, and never reached again thereafter. As a result, the rentals enjoyed by landowners rose on average by approximately 90 per cent, albeit with wide variations between different estates from 50 to 175 per cent.[5] But whatever the local differences, this comment by a West Country observer no doubt had general validity:

> The whole of the landed interest are in a state of unexampled and growing prosperity . . . It is notorious that the whole mass of landed proprietors and tenants in this part of the country are comparatively in a much better condition than they were at the commencement of the Revolutionary War with France . . . The same observations will apply still more strongly to the North of England.[6]

Not surprisingly, at a time when agriculture was so extended, it actually increased its contribution to GNP in these years, from 32 per cent in 1801 to 36 per cent ten years later. Financially, at least, the English landed classes had never had it so good.[7]

How was the money spent? One way, as Professor Hobsbawm spotted, was on country house building. For, if the quantitative survey by Professor and Mrs Stone of country house building in Hertfordshire has general validity, then it is clear that the years between 1790 and 1820 saw the construction of country mansions at a peak which had not been reached before, and which was not to be attained again.[8] Likewise, Professor Flinn has looked at the incidence of country house building as revealed in the *Buildings of England* volumes covering Durham, Hertfordshire, Middlesex, Northumberland, Nottinghamshire and Suffolk. There, again, he finds that there was a major peak between the 1790s and the 1830s.[9] More impressionistically, this was the period which saw the extension of Chatsworth and Belvoir to their present size; when Endsleigh and Ashridge were built; and when the Prince Regent sought to prove that he was the grandest aristocrat of them all, with his extravagance at Brighton, Carlton House and Windsor.

Moreover, these sumptuous palaces were adorned with works of art and exotic overseas treasures which betokened an aristocracy as discerning as it was extravagant. Lord Egremont, who died in 1837, had patronised Turner and allowed him to stay at Petworth: on his death a 'group of artists walked before the hearse, with Turner at their head'. The 2nd Earl Spencer (who was so profligate that many acres of the family estates had to be sold so as to meet his debts) and Thomas Grenville collected books with a single-minded obsession which bordered on the insane: Sir Walter Scott once called them 'the most celebrated bibliomaniacs going'. The 5th Duke of Marlborough was popularly known as the Claude of landscape gardening, and was also a keen collector of botanical plants.[10] But even he was outdone in the ubiquity of his extravagance by the 6th Duke of Devonshire, who rebuilt or extended Chatsworth, Devonshire House, Bolton Abbey and Lismore Castle, was a collector, botanist and patron of Paxton, and ran up debts of over half a million pounds in the process.[11] Never in its history did the English landed classes combine patronage, pleasure and profligacy in such equal proportions.

But it was the extravagance of their private lives that was most marked. The gambling mania of the last quarter of the eighteenth century – to which Russell rightly alluded – is well known. Charles James Fox kept a faro bank close by the House of Commons in St James's Street. At Devonshire House, the 5th Duke, his Duchess and his mistress lived together with their offsprings – legitimate and illegitimate – in a bizarre *menage à trots*. However staid may have been the King's court, profligacy and promiscuity went hand in hand in that of his heir. As never before, and in a manner not to be repeated until the Edwardian era, the theatre and the aristocracy were intimately connected, as Leigh Hunt explains:

> Nobility, gentry, citizens, princes – all were frequenters of theatres, and even more or less acquainted personally with the performers. Nobility inter-married with them; gentry and citizens too, wrote for them; princes conversed and lived with them . . . Lords Derby, Craven and Thurlow . . . sought wives on the stage.[12]

Nor was such extravagant self-indulgence confined to the high life of the great metropolis. The countryside too provided ample evidence of lavish expenditure in addition to house building and art patronage. In particular – again as noticed by Professor Hobsbawm – the period saw the perfection of fox hunting as a national, landed pastime. From 1753 until 1800, Hugo Meynell was Master of the Quorn, and was largely responsible for substituting the fox for hare or deer as quarry, and for the breeding of hounds and horses fast enough for effective pursuit. By the 1790s, the shires had become the centre of fox hunting, with packs such as the Quorn and the Duke of Rutland's Belvoir Hounds preeminent. The Prince of Wales patronised hunting; books such as Beckford's *Thoughts on Hunting* were published; and in 1792 the *Sporting Magazine* appeared for the first time.[13] As a display of corporate, landed, establishment solidarity, fox hunting was of prime significance. As early as 1828, 'Nimrod', the sporting journalist, could refer to it with complete sincerity as one of the 'lion-supporters' of the crown. At the same time, the expenditure lavished on the maintenance and breeding of horses and dogs, to say nothing of their accommodation, reached extraordinary proportions. 'It is not right to see hounds lodged better than human beings', lamented one observer on seeing the magnificent kennels and stables at Badminton.[14]

If financial well-being made such activity possible, it also enjoyed the added luxury of legislative legitimation. For during this period, 'parliament's acts, as much as its composition, reflected the dominance of the landlords'. The Corn Laws, for instance, were deliberately enacted so as to keep the price of wheat (and, consequently, agricultural rents) artificially high. Burke's Corn Law of 1773 took 48 shillings as the top price at which home farmers could expect protection; the 1804 Corn Law pushed the figure up to 66 shillings; and the legislation of 1815 raised it to 80 shillings. In a similar manner, the Game Laws were progressively stiffened, reaching their most severe between 1816 and 1827 – a direct response to the expansion in the organised shooting and hunting of game. Until 1827, landowners were permitted to use spring guns to trap and injure poachers, and from 1816 to 1828 any person found at night, armed with a net for poaching, in any forest, chase or park, was to be tried at Quarter Sessions and, if convicted, sentenced to transportation for seven years. Unarmed poachers were liable to imprisonment, with hard labour if caught with another person, and with whipping for second offences. Between 1827 and 1830, no less than one-seventh of all criminal convictions were secured under the Game Laws: the fetish of game preservation by a game-besotted parliament reached its apogee.[15]

II

Thus was it possible for the landed classes to enjoy themselves during the age of Malthus: buoyed up with rents of unprecedented fatness, and protected by legislation of unique selfishness. Such – at least in part – was the proximate landed context within which Malthus, surveying the world from the green acres of Cambridge or Haileybury, evolved his economic philosophy. What did he make of it all? Both in his day and since, many commentators have seen in his work nothing but a defence of the landed lifestyle just outlined. Robert Southey, for example, described the *Essay on Population* as 'the political bible of the rich, the selfish and the sensual'. Nassau Senior claimed that Malthus's work 'owed its currency to the relief that it afforded to the indolence and selfishness of the superior classes'. And Marx, even more savagely, described 'Parson Malthus' in two memorable passages as a 'shameless sycophant of the ruling classes' and a 'professional sycophant of the landed aristocracy, whose rents, sinecures, extravagance, heartlessness, etc, he justifies from the economic point of view'.[16]

In general, historians have largely endorsed this appraisal of Malthus, although usually in more temperate language. Hollander and Gregory were among the earliest to analyse Malthus's thought, and they concluded that he believed that 'the country's well-being depended upon the maintenance of its traditional social structure, of which a prospering landed interest was the keystone'. Meek, following Marx, claimed Malthus's conclusions were 'generally either in the interests of the ruling classes as a whole against the workers, or in the interests of the mere reactionary section of the ruling classes as against the more progressive section'.[17] In the same way, Bernard Semmel has argued that Malthus's economic opinions were 'grounded upon a favourable view of the landed interest', and Professor Glass has described the polemic of 1798 as a 'country-house essay'.[18] More recently, Professor Pollard has reaffirmed the proposition that Malthus wrote from the standpoint of the landowner, and Professor Perkin has described him as 'the premier apologist of the landed classes', and 'the main champion of the leisured, unproductive landed classes among the classical economists'.[19]

How exactly did Malthus win this reputation? How far is it fair to see his work as an apologia for an aristocracy 'honeycombed by profligacy'? Assuredly, his work stands as a sustained and committed defence of the existing social order, and as a deliberate, spirited attack on the ideas of utopian equality generated in the aftermath of the French Revolution. Man, he insists, is not perfectable. Poverty, like riches, is largely ineradicable. Hence it follows that 'the structure of society in its great features, will probably always remain unchanged. We have every reason to believe that it will always consist of a class of proprietors and a class of landowners'.[20] And, to Malthus, this condition was as praiseworthy as it was inevitable. For the continued existence of landed estates provided the greatest incentive to the middling and lower orders of society to work hard. 'If no men could hope to rise or fear to fall in society', he argued, 'if industry did not bring with it its reward, and idleness its punishment, the middle parts would not certainly be what they are.' Or, as he put it elsewhere: 'Every day, landed estates are purchased with the fruits of industry and talents. They afford the great prize, the *otium cum dignitate*, to every species of laudable exertion.' The only reason, he further explained, why the businessman or labourer would toil for eight hours a day in the counting house was 'the desire of advancing his rank, and contending with the landlords in the enjoyment of leisure, as well as of foreign and domestic luxuries'.[21]

Indeed, Malthus's committment to the landed order was more than just economic. For him, at least, an aristocratic policy was the chief guarantee of personal freedom: 'the first formation, and subsequent preservation and improvement of our present constitution, and of the liberties and privileges which have so long distinguished Englishmen, are mainly due to a landed aristocracy'. So he defended primogeniture, on the grounds that it buttressed the system of landed estates which were themselves the indispensable precondition of an aristocratic (and therefore free) constitution.[22] For the same reasons, he looked upon the development of industry and the eclipse of agriculture, with misgivings. 'In the history of the world', he noted in the second edition of the *Essay on Population*, 'the nations whose wealth has been derived principally from manufacturers and commerce have been perfectly ephemeral beings compared with those the basis of whose wealth has been agriculture.' A decade later, continued industrial development obliged him to modify his views. But he still maintained that 'an excessive proportion of manufacturing population does not seem favourable to national quiet and happiness', and argued that, in any well-balanced society, it was 'desirable that its agriculture should keep pace with its manufacturers, even at the expense of retarding in some degree the growth of manufacturers'. To the end of his life, he remained a devotee of the rural order – a man who had criticised Adam Smith for his 'exceptionable' language in attacking the landed interest, and who, in the *Essay on Population*, wrote unashamedly with metaphors drawn from the hunting field.[23]

More specifically, Malthus's veneration for the landed order embraced support for the Corn Laws in a manner which placed him in the opposite camp to most of his fellow political economists. Even his first essay on the subject, in 1814, while written ostensibly with 'the strictest impartiality', made clear his preference for the protectionist case. And in a second pamphlet in the following year, he stated his views unequivocally:

> I . . . am decidedly of opinion that a system of restriction so calculated as to keep us, in average years, nearly independent of foreign supplies of corn, will more effectually conduce to the wealth and prosperity of the country, and by far the largest mass of the inhabitants, than the opening of our ports for the free admission of grain.[24]

The argument developed here – which was to be repeated almost verbatim in *Principles of Political Economy* – suggested that the community of interest between the landlord, enjoying high rentals, and the majority of the population, paying in consequence higher prices for bread, was total: 'there is no class in society whose interests are so nearly and intimately connected with the prosperity of the state'; 'the interest of the landlords is strictly and necessarily connected with that of the state'.[25]

But how was this so? How did Malthus justify – in the national interest – large, landed rentals, whether the product of naturally or artificially high prices? And how did he defend that extravant spending on the part of the aristocracy which such inflated revenues made possible? The core of Malthus's argument was the need in any society for a body of 'unproductive consumers' – an affluent, leisured and largely landed class who, by their excessive spending, 'give a stimulus to production by developing the wants which the manufacturers are to satisfy'.[26] For Malthus, neither the middle classes (who were obsessed with saving and producing, rather than consuming) nor the labourers (who were sunk in ineradicable poverty) could provide adequate, effective demand for such products. Only the landed classes, with their power to spend augmented by their enlarged revenues from high rents, however maintained, could do so. Rental, as he explained as early as 1814, 'is not a mere benefit to a particular individual or set of individuals, but affords the most steady home demand for the manufacturers of this country'. So when, after 1814, there was a fall in agricultural prices, as in rentals, he was filled with alarm: 'this great failure in the power of purchasing, among those who either rented or possessed land, naturally occasioned a general stagnation in all other trades'. More than ever, therefore, it was 'absolutely necessary that a country with great powers of production should possess a body of unproductive consumers'.[27]

In short, Malthus wanted the landowners to *spend*. They should undertake 'substantial repairs of all the cottages on their estates'. They should be prepared, especially in the post-Waterloo depression, 'to build, to improve and beautify their grounds, and to employ workmen and menial servants' as 'the means most within our power and most directly calculated to remedy the evils arising from that disturbance in the balance of produce and consumption, which has been occasioned by the sudden conversion of soldiers, sailors, and various other classes which the war employed, into productive labourers'. And in *A Summary View of the Principle of Population*, his final word on the subject, published in 1830, he reasserted his opinion that it was economically vital for the landowners to be lavish with their purses: 'the want of an adequate taste for the consumption of manufactured commodities among the possessors of surplus produce . . . would infallibly occasion a premature slackness in the demand for labour and produce, a permanent fall in profits, and a premature check to civilisation'.[28]

Of course, this is only a limited section of Malthus's thinking on the economy and society of his day. And to do it full justice, it needs to be set in the complementary context of his laws of population and production, his theories of wealth and value, and his analysis of poverty and the Poor Law. Constraints of space necessarily prevent such a wide-ranging analysis here. But the coherent structure of his thought, and the centrality of the landowners in that system, should by now be apparent. Since population grows geometrically, while production only increases arithmetically, the poor must necessarily be sunk in permanent, largely ineradicable poverty: there can be no adequate home demand on that front. Likewise, with a middle class obsessed with saving and with producing more than it consumed, the home market which they constituted would be small and shallow. Accordingly, there was only the aristocratic, landed élite, with its purchasing power swollen with high prices and high rents, which could supply 'the demand which made the landlord the lynchpin of society, the initiator of the economic cycle, the unproductive consumer without whom the productive classes could not continue to produce more than they consumed'. As Malthus himself put it: 'there must . . . be a considerable class of other consumers, or the mercantile classes could not continue extending their concerns, and realizing their profits. In this class, the landlords no doubt stand pre-eminent'.[29] Thus did he justify both the Corn Laws and aristocratic spending, by identifying prosperous landlords as the key element in home demand, and therefore as the central driving force to economic progress. On the basis of such an analysis, it automatically followed that what was good for the landlords was good for the country as a whole.

III

Such was Malthus's understanding of the contemporary aristocracy. How has it been analysed? How should it be evaluated? How far does it illuminate, and is it illuminated by, the picture of aristocratic life given earlier in this chapter? As with his own writings, any discussion of the analysis by contemporary critics or subsequent commentators of his own writings on the aristocracy must leave out important supporting analysis by them which concerns Malthus's opinions on population and poverty, rent and wealth, value and labour. With that important caveat in mind, several questions demand attention. What did Malthus's contemporaries make of his concept of 'unproductive consumption'? Was he in fact defending the spending habits of an aristocracy 'honeycombed by profligacy'? Was his attempt to make aristocratic spending the key to home demand convincing and successful? How completely did he understand the economic functions of the landed élite, not only as consumers, but also as producers? More generally, were there any other significant trends in aristocratic society at the time which have only become apparent in retrospect, and of which he himself could not have been aware? How far, in short, is Malthus a reliable guide to the aristocratic society of his time?

For Marx, the chief objection to Malthus was that when he said that what was good for the landowners was by definition good for the nation as a whole, what he really meant was that the nation as a whole ought to behave in such a way as to satisfy the landowners' self-interested preferences. 'Malthus', Marx noted, 'reduces the workers to beasts of burden for the sake of production, and even condemns them to live in celibacy and to die of hunger . . . He does his best to sacrifice the demands of production to the exclusive interests of the existing ruling classes'. Likewise, Marx argued, 'Malthus wants bourgeois production insofar as it is not revolutionary, insofar as it is not an historical force, but merely creates a broader and more convenient material basis for the "old" society'. In the same way, Professor Perkin has argued that, however much Malthus was in favour of an aristocratic polity, it is impossible to depict him as the champion of the revived aristocratic, paternal ideal of the 1820s, because his analysis of working-class prospects was too pessimistic.[30] If to this one adds the belief that his work found favour with 'the rich, the selfish and the sensual', then the picture of Malthus as an apologist for the style of life outlined in the first part of this paper seems entirely valid.

But is it? That Malthus advocated aristocratic spending is not open to debate; that he urged aristocratic self-indulgence is much more questionable. In his own life, at least, he was a man of 'moderate' desires, whose tastes were 'simple and unassuming'. Indeed, although he unashamedly enjoyed the pleasures of the chase, he explicitly warned on one occasion that too much hunting, and too much game preservation by 'the owners of the soil' might be 'most unfavourable to the increase of production'.[31] Indeed, his explicit urgings to landowners – already quoted – that they should spend more money so as to provide work for the poor, might well be interpreted as the quintessence, rather than the antithesis, of the revived ideal of aristocratic paternalism. Although it cannot be denied that Malthus urged the aristocracy to spend, there is a case for saying that he wanted them to spend responsibly, rather than self-indulgently. Viewed in this light, Malthus's work should not so much be seen as an apologia for that style of aristocratic life described in the first section of this paper, but rather as a reflection of a more paternal concept of landownership which, historians are increasingly coming to realise, co-existed with the more oft-described picture of profligacy and self-indulgence. Indeed, recent research increasingly suggests that the portrait of the aristocracy outlined earlier is at best one-sided, and at worst unrepresentative. We really do not know how many landowners in the age of Malthus were 'honeycombed by profligacy'. What we do know increasingly is the number who gave rent rebates to their tenants in the bad years after Waterloo, who spent on roads, parks and improvements so as to provide work, and who patronised and subscribed to the great evangelical societies. Some of the aristocracy, as individuals or as legislators, may have 'abandoned their responsibility', but there is ample evidence on other fronts for a heightened, rather than reduced, sense of aristocratic obligation.[32] And, since Malthus did not encourage the aristocracy to be profligate, and occasionally urged them to be benevolent, it is not entirely unreasonable to see in some aspects of his work the tentative articulation of that ideal.

The attempt by contemporaries and later commentators to depict Malthus as a propagandist for patrician profligacy is not, therefore, entirely convincing. A more telling line of criticism was that Malthus had greatly overestimated the amount of effective demand which the aristocratic, 'unproductive consumers' could generate for the economy as a whole. Certainly, Ricardo had very little time for this argument. 'I cannot express in language so strong as I feel it my astonishment at the various propositions advanced', he noted having read Malthus on this subject. 'A body of unproductive consumers', he added, 'are just as necessary and useful to future production as a fire, which should consume in the manufacturer's warehouse the goods which these unproductive labourers would otherwise consume.'[33] More explicitly, Tory paternalists like David Robinson stressed a broader based concept of effective demand than that put forward by Malthus. For him and for others, it was the spending power of the middle and working classes – augmented, rather than undermined, by poor relief – which was the prime motor of economic development.

The poor laws form the great proportion of wages; abolish them, and with your redundant population, wages will speedily fall by half. What will follow? The body of your British labouring orders will be compelled to abandon the consumption of taxed articles, to feed on potatoes and butchers' offal, and to wear rags. In their fall, they must pull down with them not only the small tradesmen, but to a greater extent the larger ones.[34]

To any such argument, Malthus was unequivocally opposed, and constantly reiterated his case that it was only the effective demand exerted by the upper classes which could make any economic impact: 'In the ordinary state of society, the master producers and capitalists, though they have the power, have not the will to consume to the necessary extent. And with regard to the workmen, it must be assumed that, if they possessed the will, they have not the power.'[35] Nevertheless, historical research has been more eager to support the Tory paternalist interpretation of home demand in the industrial revolution than the theory of 'unproductive consumption' put forward by Malthus. For while Gilboy, Eversley and McKendrick all pay oblique or explicit homage to Malthus, their applications of his home demand theory to a broader spectrum of society – either middle or working class – are not so much an extension of his argument, but a positive negation of it, repeating the very case in favour of a broad-based, non-aristocratic demand pattern which he himself had explicitly opposed.[36] Of course, these arguments too are largely hypothetical: latter-day historians have no more precise or aggregate information on the purchasing power of the lower classes than Malthus did in his time for that of their betters. Moreover, some recent research has suggested that the whole home demand argument needs fundamentally rethinking.[37] All that can be confidently asserted at this stage is that, *if* home demand was indeed an important contributory cause to economic progress, 'unproductive consumption' by the élite seems to be of relatively limited significance compared with the more general rise in purchasing power.

Yet, paradoxically, while Malthus may have overestimated the importance of the landowners as consumers, he may have given them insufficient attention as capitalist, industrial producers. Assuredly, he was well aware that, in his lifetime, economic and social changes were taking place around him of more than ordinary significance. Taking the period of the Napoleonic Wars, for example, he noted how

If . . . we turn our view to the quantity of domestic industry set in motion, we believe that in no former period of the same extent has there ever been any approach to the same increase of draining and enclosures, roads and bridges, canals and harbours, paving and other local improvements, machinery, shipping and exciseable commodities.[38]

Such was indeed the case. But what Malthus – in his hostility to too much rapid industrial expansion – did not grasp was the extent to which much of this industrial development took place as a result of aristocratic, rather than middle-class, entrepreneurship. His twofold economic division, between the entrepreneurs who produced more than they consumed, and the landlords who (fortunately, in his view) consumed more than they produced, did not take account of the fact that many of the mines, docks, harbours, canals and urban estates were themselves, during this period, being developed as the result of aristocratic initiative.[39]

But there was an even more significant aspect of contemporary landed society which Malthus missed completely. Very recently, catchphrases like 'unproductive consumption' and 'abdicated responsibility' have been joined by the expression 'aristocratic resurgence'. This refers to the increased power and influence which, even in a time of challenge, crisis and instability, the landed classes were exerting on English government in the years from the 1790s to the late 1820s. Only the baldest summary can be given here of this interpretation. But in support of it might be mentioned: the role of landowners as patrons of entrepreneurs, and as lobbyists on behalf of industry and the new towns at Westminster; the enlarged and preponderant landed presence among officers of the army and navy; the overwhelming aristocratic dominance of universities and higher education; the increased and unprecedented number of aristocratic bishops and clerical magistrates; and the extended, landed civil service and system of honours.[40] None of this, of course, is as spectacular as Fox and his faro bank. But it may, quantitatively, be more significant. At the time, however, it was only radicals who noticed: certainly, there is no evidence that Malthus was aware of it.

IV

Self-evidently, a chapter of this meagre length can no more do full justice to the sublety of Malthus's thought as it applied to the landed classes than it can hope fully to explore the multifaceted nature of their circumstances at the time. Nevertheless, it is to be hoped that this brief attempt to set Malthus's thought more fully within its aristocratic context may have been doubly illuminating. For clearly, as this glance at his writings shows, Malthus was not a crude and slavish defender of an aristocracy 'honeycombed by profligacy'. Nor, as this brief survey of the landowners themselves implies, were all of them 'honeycombed with profligacy' either. In some ways, Malthus may have been too committed, and in others too ignorant, fully to appreciate the diverse circumstances of the landed classes in his time. In certain ways, he overestimated their importance; in other ways, he understated it, or took it for granted. But even if his vision was blinkered by his prejudices and his time, looking over his shoulder at the English landed classes is an illuminating and rewarding exercise. For this historian, at least, consuming the works of 'Parson Malthus' has been far from unproductive.

NOTES AND REFERENCES

1. W. D. Rubinstein, 'Wealth, Élites and the Class Structure of Modern Britain', *Past and Present*, XXVI No. 76 (1977) 99–126.
2. G. W. E. Russell, *Collections and Recollections*, 5th ed. (London, 1898) p. 53.
3. E. J. Hobsbawm, *Industry and Empire* (Harmondsworth, 1969) pp. 80–1.
4. H. J. Perkin, *The Origins of Modern British Society, 1780–1880* (London, 1969) pp. 183–95.
5. F. M. L. Thompson, *English Landed Society in the Nineteenth Century* (London, 1963) p. 220.
6. A. D. Harvey, *Britain in the Early Nineteenth Century* (London, 1978) p. 337.
7. P. Deane and W. A. Cole, *British Economic Growth, 1688–1959*, 2nd ed. (Cambridge, 1967) pp. 160–1.
8. L. and J. C. F. Stone, 'Country Houses and their Owners in Hertfordshire 1540–1879', in W. O. Aydelotte *et al.* (eds), *The Dimensions of Quantitative Research in History* (London, 1972) pp. 113, 116.
9. M. W. Flinn, *The Origins of the Industrial Revolution* (London, 1966) p. 48.
10. D. Spring, 'Aristocracy, Social Structure and Religion in Early Victorian England', *Victorian Studies*, VI (1963) 271.
11. D. Cannadine, 'The Landowner as Millionaire: The Finances of the Dukes of Devonshire, *c.*1800–*c.*1926', *Agricultural History Review*, XXV (1977) 79–82.
12. *The Autobiography of Leigh Hunt* (London, 1878 ed.) pp. 134–5.
13. D. Itzkowitz, *Peculiar Privilege: A Social History of English Foxhunting, 1753–1885* (Brighton, 1977) chapters 1–3.
14. R. Carr, *English Fox Hunting: A History* (London, 1976) p. 138.
15. D. Beales, *From Castlereagh to Gladstone, 1815–1885* (London, 1969) pp. 22, 25, 47.
16. H. A. Boner, *Hungry Generation: The Nineteenth Century Case Against Malthusianism* (New York, 1955) p. 40; Perkin, op. cit., p. 241; R. L. Meek (ed.), *Marx and Engels on Malthus* (London, 1953) pp. 117, 123.
17. J. H. Hollander and T. E. Gregory (eds), *Notes on Malthus' Principles of Political Economy by David Ricardo* (Baltimore, 1928) p. xxiii; Meek, ibid., p. 23.

18. B. Semmel (ed.), *Occasional Papers of Thomas Robert Malthus* (New York, 1963) p. 23; D. V. Glass (ed.), *Introduction to Malthus* (London, 1953) p. vii.
19. S. Pollard, 'Labour in Great Britain', in P. Mathias and M. M. Postan (eds), *The Cambridge Economic History of Europe*, vol. VII (Cambridge, 1978) p. 97; Perkin, op. cit., pp. 220, 239.
20. J. S. Nickerson, *Homage to Malthus* (London, 1975) p. 100; T. R. Malthus, *An Essay on the Principle of Population*, reprint of the 1st ed. of 1798, in A. Flew (ed.), *Malthus* (Harmondsworth, 1970) pp. 132–45, 172–3, 207.
21. Ibid., *Malthus*, p. 207; T. R. Malthus, *Principles of Political Economy* (London, 1820) pp. 238, 470–1.
22. Ibid., *Principles*, pp. 433–7.
23. J. Bonar, *Malthus and His Work*, 2nd ed. (London, 1924) pp. 246–50; *The Pamphlets of Thomas Robert Malthus* (London, 1970) pp. 117–19; Malthus, op. cit., *An Essay*, p. 152.
24. Ibid., *The Pamphlets*, pp. 97, 151.
25. Ibid., p. 162; Malthus, op. cit., *Principles*, pp. 215–17.
26. Bonar, op. cit., p. 300.
27. *The Pamphlets*, op. cit., pp. 163, 190–1: Malthus, op. cit., *Principles*, pp. 179, 463.
28. Ibid., *Principles*, p. 512; T. R. Malthus, *A Summary View of the Principles of Population*, in Flew, op. cit., pp. 246–7.
29. Perkin, op. cit., p. 239; Ibid., *Principles*, p. 466.
30. Meek, op. cit., pp. 122–3, 157; Perkin, op. cit., pp. 240–1.
31. Semmel, op. cit., pp. 266–7; Malthus, op. cit., *A Summary View*, pp. 246–7.
32. Spring, loc. cit., p. 265; Thompson, op. cit., pp. 231–7; D. Roberts, *Paternalism in Early Victorian England* (London, 1979) pp. 19–21; F. K. Brown, *Fathers of the Victorians* (Cambridge, 1961) pp. 354–7.
33. P. Sraffa (ed.), *The Works and Correspondence of David Ricardo*, vol. II 'Notes on Malthus' Principles of Political Economy', (Cambridge, 1951) pp. 421–5.
34. Perkin, op. cit., pp. 246–7.
35. Malthus, op. cit., *Principles*, p. 471.
36. E. W. Gilboy, 'Demand as a Factor in the Industrial Revolution', in R. M. Hartwell (ed.), *The Causes of the Industrial Revolution in England* (London, 1967), pp. 129–35; D. E. C. Eversley, 'The Home Market and Economic Growth in England', in E. L. Jones and G. E. Mingay (eds), *Land, Labour and Population in the Industrial Revolution: Essays Presented to J. D. Chambers* (London, 1967) pp. 212–13; N. McKendrick, 'Home Demand and Economic Growth: A New View of the Role of Women and Children in the Industrial Revolution', in N. McKendrick (ed.), *Historical Perspectives: Studies in English Thought and Society in Honour of J. H. Plumb* (London, 1974) p. 191.
37. J. Mokyr, 'Demand vs. Supply in the Industrial Revolution', *Journal of Economic History*, XXXVII (1977) 981–1008; J. Mokyr and N. E. Savin, 'Stagflation in Historical Perspective: The Napoleonic Wars Revisited', in P. Uselding (ed.), *Research in Economic History*, 1 (1976) 198–259.
38. Anon. (that is, Malthus), 'Thoughts and Details on the High and Low Prices of the Last Thirty Years. By Thomas Tooke', *Quarterly Review*, XXIX (1823) 228.

39. G. E. Mingay, *English Landed Society in the Eighteenth Century* (London, 1963) chapter 8; D. Spring, 'English Landowners and Nineteenth-Century Industrialism', in J. T. Ward and R. G. Wilson (eds), *Land and Industry: The Landed Estate and the Industrial Revolution* (Newton Abbot, 1971) pp. 16–62.

40. M. W. McCahill, 'Peers, Patronage and the Industrial Revolution, 1760–1800', *Journal of British Studies*, XVI (1976) 84–107; P. Lucas, 'A Collective Biography of Students and Barristers at Lincoln's Inn, 1680–1804: A Study in the "Aristocratic Resurgence" of the Eighteenth Century', *Journal of Modern History*, XLVI (1974) 227–61; N. Ravitch, 'The Social Origins of French and English Bishops in the Eighteenth Century', *Historical Journal*, VIII (1965) 309–25; Sir I. de la Bere, *The Queen's Orders of Chivalry* (London, revised ed. 1964) pp. 67, 103, 109, 116, 139, 174–5.

8 Corn Crises in Britain in the Age of Malthus[1]

MICHAEL TURNER

The decade during which Malthus began his published writing, the 1790s, was one of great turbulence in the British economy. Not only was the industrial and commercial expansion of the late eighteenth century at, or close to, full throttle, but population expanded at hitherto unparalleled rates. Increasingly the primacy of agriculture was undermined by this industrialisation and also by urbanisation, and this, of course, put more rather than less pressure on what was still the leading economic sector of the economy (leading in terms of total employment, fixed capital and contribution to national income). While still basically self-sufficient in food supplies, within tolerably small margins, the country nevertheless clung grimly to that position while an increasing proportion of her population was non-food producing. Inevitably this margin of self-sufficiency was attacked, and viciously so during the 1790s, when the coincidence of poor harvests, the war with France and other factors pushed food prices up and out of the reach of many people. It is during this decade and with respect to this crisis that we see Malthus, both as observer and theoretician of troubled times. A minor industry has emerged in Britain which has investigated the national and regional incidence of corn dearth and distress during the French Revolutionary and Napoleonic wars, and principally in the 1790s.[2] This chapter will measure the frequency and extent of the crises, discuss some of the causes, and finally will investigate what Malthus had to say about them and how his views were sometimes at odds with many of his contemporaries.

I

At their most expressive the successive crises took the form of food dearth verging at times of the year in the direction of what one modern

112

authority has called psycho-social famine.[3] This dearth precipitated widespread rural and urban disturbances which expressed themselves in rioting, threatening behaviour and damage to both persons and property.[4] In addition it was fermented by much political agitation; 'Revolutionary' spirit overflowing from France, Jacobinism, underground pamphleteering and seditious newspaper activity, and by the end of the period in question in such activity as Luddism. Indeed, it is sometimes very difficult to disentangle food riots from political and industrial agitation, and in many cases perhaps they should be treated as synonymous acts, that is, discontent over the scarcity of food expressed through political action and industrial disturbances, like wage riots, as well as more obvious food riots.

The government was fully aware of the crisis which faced the country. Some might say they were more aware of the political, almost revolutionary atmosphere of the times, rather than the fact of hungry people.[5] Nevertheless, the 1790s was a fevered decade during which the government continually sought information about the vulnerability of British food resources. A number of inquiries were instigated, culminating in the first crop census, the 1801 crop returns, and many Select Committees were set up, for example on enclosure and the improvement of otherwise unproductive wastes, and particularly on the dearth of provisions and the resulting high prices of food.[6] Almost every year from 1793 to 1801 there was serious concern over food self-sufficiency. This is not to say that Britain had been self-sufficient every year before 1793, not at all, but the extremes of inadequate food supplies in the face of a rising population were manifestly exposed during these years and exacerbated by the conflict with France.

Figure 8.1 depicts the wheat trade balance from 1731 to 1819. It shows the net surplus or deficit of the wheat and wheat flour trade.[7] The crisis of 1766–7 marked one of the first serious inroads into self-sufficiency, a continuation of a narrowing trend of exports over imports culminating in almost permanent net deficit from *c*.1770. For example, before 1760 there were only three years of net deficit, in 1728, 1729 and 1757, in the last of which it was just over 130 000 quarters. In 1767, Britain imported half a million quarters but exported only 5000. By 1790 imports had regularly reached 100 000 quarters and from 1790 to 1820 they were always over 100 000 quarters, apart from two isolated years, and in each of 1800, 1801, 1810, 1817 and 1818 imports exceeded 1 million quarters. Conversely, between 1790 and 1820 exports on only seven occasions exceeded 100 000 quarters. At its worst in 1800, 1801, 1810 and 1818 the *net* deficit exceeded 1 million quarters. These were years truly in the grip of self-sufficiency crises. The worst wartime year was 1810 during which

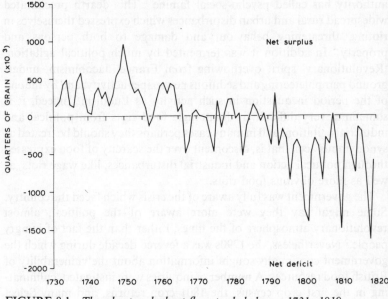

FIGURE 8.1   *The wheat and wheat flour trade balance, 1731–1819*

importation is said to have represented about nine weeks' consumption.[8] This was the worst year and therefore puts into perspective the lower levels of net importation experienced during the remaining war years, or does it? It should not disguise the fact that a permanent situation of net deficit existed, but also, in the light of the standard of living debate, it must be said that 1810 imports representing nine weeks' consumption may have been calculated at pre-1795 consumption levels. If we are correct to believe that wartime consumption and general standards of living were inferior to those in pre-war days, then wartime net imports may have represented a larger share of *real* consumption. We shoud not assume that imports were adequate to meet needs. On the contrary, in spite of this level of importation Britain was still short of basic grain.

To people at large the manifestation of the corn crisis was not felt through the net trading position but rather through their stomachs. This can be highlighted through the movement of food prices, but mainly corn prices, which perhaps was the most sensitive indicator of the dearth and distress because of its relationship with the price of bread. Figure 8.2a shows the course of money–wheat prices for the period 1731–1819. Not all authorities agree on 1800 as the peak of inflation, some give 1811 as an alternative, but the general peaks and troughs are not subject to much doubt.[9] The main wartime crises show up well centred on 1795, 1800 and 1811, with the 'Bread and Blood' crisis of 1816 also prominent. As far as the records indicate J. Stevenson has depicted the crisis in a different way, by quantifying the concomitant food riots which ensued. In 1795–6 there were 74 such disturbances in England, in 1800–1 there were 51, in 1810–13 there were 29 and in 1816–18 there were 22. There is clearly not a good correlation here between the relative sizes of the four price peaks and the four disturbance peaks. There are problems, however, in presenting the crises in this way because the national archives are not a full record of the disturbances.[10] Nevertheless, perhaps Stevenson's figures can be accepted in a relative sense to capture the relative gravity of the different crises. Even this might be difficult to accept for the later part of the period. For example, to what extent was Luddism in 1810–13 or were wage riots throughout the period a form of disguised food riot in the sense that rioters perceived the dearth in different ways through time? In 1800 there was work and money but high prices, but in 1811–12 there was no work and no money, but also high prices. In both cases there were riots. W. F. Galpin has referred to the 'bridgeless gap between the labourer's purse and a loaf of bread', however that gap was created.[11] On the one hand, there may have been genuine shortages at the markets, and on the other, there may have been shortages of the pocket to buy what was available. It may have taken several crises and persistent inflation for people to change their course of action from purely food riots to other expressions of shortage, for example, protests against low wage rates or depressed real wages, or against potential or actual unemployment. In any case, this approach ignores the fact that there was a general prices inflation in train. Notwithstanding the problems of constructing, let alone using a general price index for this period, Figure 8.2b is the money price of wheat deflated against a price index of goods other than cereals.[12] It seems to show that in *real* terms the 1795 price peak was almost comparable to the one in 1800, and that both were greater than the later ones in 1811 and 1816.[13] Furthermore, 1795 represented the first outstanding food prices inflation since the mid-sixties. It set the pace for the general food price level of the war period and perhaps was felt more keenly by people at large as a shock measure. This suddenness or shock may account for the prominence of 1795 in Stevenson's measurement of disturbances; the shock waves diminishing with successive crises, to be replaced perhaps by other disturbances such as wage riots.[14] In addition, the occurrence of riots in 1795–6 came not at the peak of prices but rather in those months when the rate of change of prices upwards was greatest. This accentuates this idea of a shock measure. Similarly, in 1800–1, 'short-term movements in prices were the most important factor in precipitating disturbances'.[15]

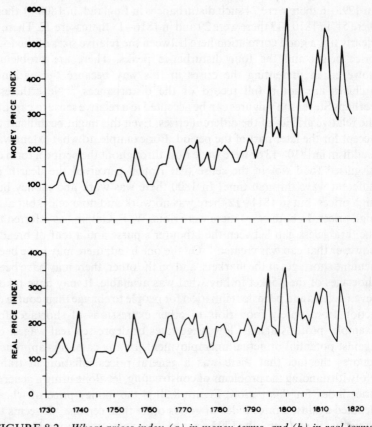

FIGURE 8.2   *Wheat prices index (a) in money terms, and (b) in real terms*

II

If the corn crises had their expression in net trading deficits, inflation peaks and food riots, what factors came together to cause this situation? This is a contentious issue among historians, and, as we will show, it was also a matter of some dispute between Malthus and his contemporaries. The main factors to choose from are the long-run demographic revolution and its associated pressure on aggregate demand, war induced government expenditure inflation, the increase in paper money in circulation – especially after the suspension of cash payments in 1797 – increased freight charges and the Napoleonic continental blockade. Galpin sees a psychological factor at play as well.

> Impressed by the idea of his own self-sufficiency, the Englishman became visibly excited whenever that self-sufficiency was threatened. On every hand he saw visions of impending famine. The press graphically conjured up before his worried brain visions of rice and turnip bread . . . Although his King and Parliament belittled the scarcity, everyone told him of its presence and soon he believed it to be true.[16]

Galpin suggested that as long as foreign supplies were forthcoming the crisis was held in check, but as soon as this foreign supply was threatened attitudes changed. He cites the period of North European Armed Neutrality and the United States Embargo as such threats. 'It was therefore, just the dependence placed upon this supply, though small in itself, just the fear that it might be interfered with, that caused the market to rise so abnormally high.' He therefore put the greatest burden of explanation on the state of foreign supplies, and he is not alone in this belief.[17] However, the contrary weight of evidence which points to poor harvests as the explanation is very strong.

The important point about the war period was not the aggregate number of bad harvests compared with an equivalent period before or after the war, but the extremity and chronology of those bad harvests. Furthermore, they were interspersed by very few bumper harvest years.

> The bad and indifferent years occurred in runs, so that in the absence of a reserve of supplies from the previous year conditions of great dearth ensued. The years from 1794 to 1800 were all remarkable for poor seasons . . . Then after an interval of better seasons, there followed another disastrous series of five very bad years from 1808 to 1812.[18]

Thus even though fourteen of the twenty-eight harvests from 1765 to 1792 were below average, it was the closely confined recurrence of unproductive seasons from 1793 to 1814 which caused the magnitude in the trend of rising prices. In those twenty-two years fourteen wheat harvests were deficient. Odd years of abundance alleviated intermittent failures but not recurrent failures. For example, even though the harvest of 1813–14 was relatively poor the harvest of the previous year was so good that, 'the last of this crop was not consumed before the harvest of 1815'. But set against this example was the gross deficiency of the 1799–1800 harvest in Warwickshire where,

> The consumption of the New Crop began as soon as possible after the Harvest was in, and much of it was threshed out for immediate use, the Stock of Old Corn being, comparatively speaking, none (the Case in most of the Midland Counties); in general there used to be enough to carry on the County for three Months.[19]

The first two crises in 1795 and 1800–1 caused despondency and almost panic alarm in government circles. Looking back, however, it is easy to exaggerate the real severity of the crises, even attended as they were by food riots and disturbances and the Malthusian spectre of famine.[20] Admittedly the worst year of the war for burials appears to have been 1795, with high years also in 1800 and 1810, but the correlation between crises and mortality is statistically weak.[21] From the most recent large-scale work on population history by E. A. Wrigley and R. S. Schofield we discover that for the long period 1541–1871 the relationship between prices and deaths is weak, but it is a positive one, and it mainly suggests a mortality effect in the two years following the year of high prices. But in our period, the age of Malthus – in more general terms the longer period, mid-eighteenth century to 1834 – the mortality/price relationship is very weak and indeed a negative one.[22] Of the forty-five years in the long period 1541–1871 when there was a crude death rate which was more than 10 per cent above the normal trend based on twenty-five year moving averages, only one, 1802–3 was remotely close to the corn dearth years of the French wars. Disregarding the moving averages, this year was the 79th worst year for crude death rate over the whole period of more than 300 years.[23]

The government was most anxious about the state of food supplies between 1795 and 1801. The year 1793 was a good average harvest year, but 1794 was below average as was 1795. The state of the harvest was different for the different grain crops. Though the wheat crop failed in 1795, in terms of a good average year and also compared with 1794, both barley and oats in many places were exceptional crops. However, the failure of wheat in 1795, in spite of good barley and oats, was further worsened because a heavier acreage was sown with wheat that year at the expense of barley and oats. There was not much alarm in terms of impending dearth in the late autumn and early winter of 1794 because although the recent harvest had been below average there was still some surplus from the year before. One of the first reported incidents to reach the Secretary of State for Home Affairs was the seizure of bread and general disquiet at the price of provisions at Kinninghall near Thetford in Norfolk. Further reports reached the Home Office in the winter of 1795, some of them complaining that in spite of the shortages and high prices some of the home supply found its way to France, of all places, from the south coast ports of Shoreham and Newhaven via Jersey and Guernsey.[24] Reports from country districts of corn riots continued into the spring of 1795. The problem appeared to be at its worst in the West Country. Scarcity, high prices and concomitant unrest continued into the summer of 1795 and there was eager anticipation of the new harvest. The failure of this subsequent harvest provoked the government into instituting a number of inquiries, the first of which was in late October 1795.[25] One of the most important national conclusions to emerge from this inquiry was that the produce of the 1795 harvest would not last until the future 1796 harvest, a warning that further scarcity, high prices and unrest would certainly follow. This was indeed the case in late 1795 and early 1796.

In fact the 1796 harvest turned out to be a good one, better than average, and as a result a period of 'relative' plenty existed. This lasted until the summer of 1799, at which time there were renewed fears about harvest failure, scarcity and high prices. Indeed, 1799 was another year of failed harvest. The first fears are contained in the correspondence from December 1799 and continue well into 1800. Agitation in the countryside clearly became more violent or potentially more violent than it had been four or five years earlier, with the destruction of property and threats to farmers, corn merchants and dealers if they did not lower the price of grain. Violent demonstrations continued throughout the whole of the spring, summer and autumn of 1800. An inquiry instigated in late October 1800 to assess the potential of that year's harvest revealed that its produce was insufficient to last until 1801, and fears of further scarcity and high prices were manifest in more disturbances, food riots and the like. The harvest of 1800 was not so much a disaster but rather below average, but more important it was the second successive below average crop. This discounted the chance of storing any grain for the following year, in fact as soon as it was gathered in it was threshed out and consumed. The prospects for 1801 were therefore bleak and net imports reached an all time record high. But the very worst fears were eventually relieved: 1801 was a bumper harvest year, the best in some districts in living memory, and the condition of dearth was dissipated, at least for the time being.[26]

The inflation of prices for agricultural produce during the war years is said to have motivated both an extension of cultivated land by bringing into cultivation otherwise waste and unproductive lands, and also an improvement of existing farming land. In both cases this was achieved, amongst other ways, by enclosure, by bringing the wastes and commons into cultivation, and by eliminating the wasteful features of open-field cultivation.[27] The evidence strongly suggests a relationship between price movements and enclosure, though it is still very much an area of debate and theory.[28] This is not a far remove from Malthus's concept of rent in which land is not only limited in supply but also its quality is uneven. Price rises will induce cultivation of the less fertile acres and/or intensify the cultivation of existing ploughlands. The governments of the day were very concerned and wished to see the less fertile lands brought into productive service as a means of alleviating the dearth and distress.[29] As Sir John Sinclair put it in 1803, 'let us not be satisfied with the liberation of Egypt, or the subjugation of Malta, but let us subdue Finchley Common; let us conquer Hounslow Heath; let us compel Epping Forest to submit to the yoke of improvement'.[30]

There were further scarcities after 1801 but the record of enclosure and reclamation was also very impressive during the war years. So we may speculate on the degree of dearth and distress had it not been for a spatially extensive and temporally intensive enclosure movement.[31] The single most important year in the entire history of parliamentary enclosure in England with the passing of 122 Acts occurred in 1811. The next eight most important years all occurred during the war. The half decade of 1810–14 was the single most important with 547 Acts, a very large proportion of which was for the enclosure and improvement of commons and wastes. The next three most important half decades were 1800–4, 1805–9 and 1795–9 with 450, 430 and 344 Acts respectively. In total, the war years accounted for about 3 million acres of enclosure of which perhaps 1 million was common and waste. About 9 per cent of the land area of England was enclosed in those years.

III

The emphasis of this chapter has been on the two corn crises of 1795 and 1800. In real money terms, and in respect of public shock and surprise at the vulnerability of self-sufficiency, perhaps these first two crises require special consideration. What was the public reaction to high prices in causal terms as distinct from the already evidenced disturbances? This speculation allows me to turn the spotlight in this final section specifically on to related aspects of the so-called 'moral economy' and on to the general theme of this book, the opinions and observations of Malthus himself.[32] He had ample time to observe the dearth and distress of the 1790s and we can take as our text not his most famous works on population but rather his pamphlet of 1800, *An Investigation of the Cause of the Present High Price of Provisions*. He stated that, 'during the last year there was a scarcity, to a certain extent, of all sorts of grain; but it must be at the same time acknowledged, that price was higher than the degree of that scarcity would at first sight appear to warrant'.[33] On a recent visit to Sweden he observed a worse scarcity, but only a doubling of prices compared with a trebling of prices in Britain. He pointed to the universal cry of the common people that, 'there must be roguery somewhere; and the general indignation has fallen upon monopolizers, forestallers, and regraters',[34] to which we could add engrossers. But Malthus did not agree with this 'medieval' indictment of the middleman, or what we might call the negative image of the moral economy. These middlemen were indispensable in conveying the produce from the grower to the consumer; they were not iniquitous in exercising their powers but rather responded to a demand situation artificially created by more generous parish allowances in the face of a fixed supply, a situation of too much money chasing too few goods which therefore resulted in an automatic price rise *over and above that caused by deficient harvests alone*. Malthus does admit that middlemen, no doubt working partly from motives of self-interest, held back their limited supplies and let it dribble on to the market thus contributing to the feeling of scarcity, but at the same time they avoided a true famine.[35]

Humane though it appeared, the process of supplementing poor relief incrementally as prices rose resulted in a larger number of purchasers at a given price than there was a supply to satisfy that demand, hence prices continued to rise, one might say almost in a leap-frogging motion with poor relief. Malthus illustrated this process with a hypothetical situation. Suppose there was a commodity – bread, for example – for which there were fifty purchasers. Suppose further that because of an insufficiency of supply – harvest failure perhaps – there was only enough bread to supply forty people at normal consumption levels. In rank order from wealthy to poor if the fortieth person had two shillings to spend on bread and the thirty-nine above him had more and the ten below him had less than two shillings 'the actual price of the article, according to genuine principles of trade, will be two shillings'. If more than two shillings was asked then the dealers could not dispose of all the bread because fewer than forty people could afford it. To ask less than two shillings, humane though it may be in terms of rationing, the supply to allow all fifty people to get some, though insufficient, supply of bread, may produce a lower gross income for the dealer. Now suppose that a poor relief supplement of one shilling was given to each of the ten with less two shillings. Everyone could now afford to buy some bread. But there is still only enough bread fully to satisfy forty empty stomachs. 'According to every genuine principle of fair trading, the commodity must immediately rise.' A different ten people would now be excluded from purchasing bread, but in their turn they would receive a supplement of poor relief. Prices would rise, relief would be given again, and different people – though always the recipients of the smaller incomes – would pass in and out of the orbit of purchasing power, though nobody would be forever excluded.[36]

So Malthus saw the application of poor relief, a system he says he would otherwise condemn, as on this occasion an advantage.

> The principal benefit which they have produced is exactly that which is most bitterly complained of – the high price of all the necessaries of life. The poor cry out loudly at this price; but in so doing, they are very little aware of what they are about; for it has undoubtedly been owing to this price that a much greater number of them has not been starved.[37]

So, the higher prices had forced a greater number to suffer partial scarcity and a smaller number to face actual or potential famine than otherwise would have been in the case. Furthermore, it was Malthus's belief that the nature of corn was such that it was in so many hands that 'monopoly, to any pernicious extent, may safely be pronounced impossible'.[38] On this last point, however, we may respectfully suggest that Malthus was somewhat unrealistic of his own times and neglectful of the immobility of the market in national terms. It was evidently not a single market but many regional or local ones where indeed it is possible to imagine individual corn merchants, millers or bakers holding something approaching monopoly positions. For example, in Cheshire, the practice of wholesale trading in corn at local markets gave way towards the second half of the eighteenth century to private marketeering, to corn dealers and bakers buying secretly by sample, where 'bulk buyers, agreed to give artificially high prices to keep up the assize of bread'.[39] As Malthus admitted, people's perceptions of scarcity would not allow them to see a situation where 'you may get what quantity of corn you please if you have but money enough',[40] unless the scarcity was artificially created. So, whether we disbelieve the cry of artificial scarcity as Malthus disbelieved, nevertheless, if 'common people' did believe it then it becomes an important ingredient in the dearth and distress of the times. Perhaps it explains the types of riot and disturbances which took place, which very often were directed against middlemen. The general belief of monopoly practice is evident from the national archives and we may usefully conclude with some of this evidence.

Early examples of the actions taken against middlemen were threats by mobs to pull down mills and destroy flour if prices did not fall.[41] Pure theft was rarely resorted to, or at least where it did occur the mob seized the flour and dispersed it at prices which they regarded as equitable. This is the classic 'moral economy' at work. The breakdown of local public marketing to be replaced by private marketing institutions was the signal for the enactment of the moral economy, for the reimposition of legitimate marketing practices where 'the consumer was guaranteed pure food, honestly measured and at a fair price'.[42] This came about commonly by threats from the mobs to fix the prices of provisions to counteract the extortions of monopoly practice; a sort of monopolising in reverse. In a similar, though lawful way, local worthies sponsored charitable subscriptions in order to buy up provisions for resale to the poor at below cost price. This can be viewed as an alternative administration of poor relief. Whilst encouraging such local subscriptions for the relief of the poor, the government nevertheless positively discouraged selling corn below the market price lest it should occasion too great a consumption and thereby result in a greater future scarcity. If low prices were not to prevail therefore, then higher wages would be demanded, as they were by the journeymen fullers of Exeter in March 1795 and the townspeople of Hoddesdon in Hertfordshire in July of the same year. If neither poor relief nor higher wages were forthcoming then demands and threats would be made for lower prices; as demanded of the butchers and bakers of Portsmouth, or by implication when the farmers, butchers and bakers of Coventry were jostled by the mobs at market in April 1795. The provocation for such actions was invariably a suspicion of profiteering, almost of the institutionalising of an artificial scarcity by all suppliers of provisions.

The assize of bread was set at Lewes in Sussex at £17 per load but there were complaints that it was sold to Kentish millers at £20 per load, and in Oxfordshire came a similar report that 'foreign' dealers from Derbyshire, Staffordshire and Warwickshire attended the markets and were able to give the farmers whatever price they wanted to the detriment of the local inhabitants. This was a common practice and there were numerous and loud complaints at such exportation, even though it was exportation within Britain. All that people knew locally was that this was the loss of their grain – though not necessarily overseas – and therefore in this sense artificially causing a local scarcity by middlemen and speculators. Even the efforts of the government could not be appreciated. The minutes of the Privy Council indicate coastwise movements of imported grain and locally grown grain as the government attempted to relieve those areas where the scarcity was most acute, at the cost of those areas where 'relative' plenty existed. The local perception of this procedure in the absence of complete information was seen as the artificial creation of a scarcity. In addition, the example of Liverpool was common to other seaports; as imported grain was landed non-local agents congregated and succeeded in forcing prices up beyond the pockets of the local inhabitants. This was seen as another example of creating a local scarcity.

From Wheatley in Oxfordshire, in July 1795, came a report that between London and the Chilterns grain was in short supply but because it was at a lower price than elsewhere, dealers bought it up and exported it to places where the price was higher. The authorities were alive to the fact that forestalling and regrating occurred, and in some areas they promised to prosecute offenders, as at Gloucester in July 1795. In Buckinghamshire, at the Michaelmas Quarter Sessions in 1795, 'from rumours in circulation that such scarcity and dearness has been augmented by the interested endeavours of forestallers and persons of that description and their confederates', actions would be taken against those indicted on charges of forestalling, regrating and engrossing. The petty constables were asked to look out for and report any such incidents.[43] Elsewhere, in order to keep prices down, the government suggested that imported wheat should not be offered for sale on the open market where corn dealers would get it and resell it at higher prices, but instead it should be sold directly to the bakers.

Direct accusations against the hoarding practices of corn factors who subsequently sold at their own prices was common, as was the sort of report which came from Carlisle, in July 1795, where people from Lancaster bought up the wheat, barley and oats before it reached the market, forcing prices up from 32 to 45 shillings per Cumberland bushel. At the same market people were employed on commission by Liverpool corn dealers to buy up as much as they could. Near Whitehaven a 'Mr Brown of Tallantyne has wheat, but have given directions to his husbandmen not to thresh it out, expecting the price still higher'. In

Oxfordshire, there was a report of 'jobbing', that is, buying wheat from farmers before it ever reached the market, and similarly in Ormskirk in Lancashire two Yorkshiremen attempted to buy wheat and other grain as it grew. Millers sometimes bought wheat for retention until prices reached a peak, and millers, mealmen and maltsters were often accused together of causing the scarcity.

The people who transmit these reports of artificial scarcity to London are by no means the 'common people', but rather as Malthus put it 'men of sense' whose eleoquent turns of phrase betrayed their middle or upper class stations in life.[44] In 1800, the Duke of Bridgewater added his weight to the debate and was of the firm opinion that 'the evil of scarcity is aggravated by undue monopoly',[45] and many of the incumbents who acted as returning officers for the 1801 crop returns reported monopolising practices.[46]

IV

These have been examples taken mainly from the 1795 scarcity. Similar reports can be found for the crisis of 1799–1800, though on that occasion it appeared that the rioting became more violent, with actual damage, such as the burning down of property belonging to farmers, millers and other producers and distributors of food accompanying the threatening behaviour.[47] Three main conclusions emerge. The worst year for popular unrest was 1795, it became the shock year which set the pattern for subsequent crises of dearth and distress. It was the first crisis on such a scale, in most cases, within living memory, and in real money terms the inflation in food prices that year almost rivalled the worst inflation of the war period. Secondly, hunger was not always manifest by hunger riots. Wage and other riots and other examples of popular protest can surely be viewed sometimes as an expression of food scarcity. Finally, the middleman was believed at large to be the culprit for producing high prices and food shortages; the government blamed home supply through bad harvests; twentieth-century scholars are unsure of the causes but there is equal emphasis on inadequate foreign supplies and poor domestic harvests. As an alternative we should take very seriously the beliefs of the common people. Even if not nationally then perhaps locally the severity of the early crises as measured by inflationary prices was partly due to artificial means. Certainly local perceptions believed this to be the case, and it is an important aspect which Malthus for one underplayed, and perhaps we do also.

126   *Corn Crises in Britain in the Age of Malthus*

NOTES AND REFERENCES

1. My thanks to the Social Science Research Council for a Research
   Fellowship in Agrarian History in 1978 when most of the research on which
   this chapter is based was carried out, and to Professor F. M. L. Thompson,
   Director of the Institute of Historical Research where the Fellowship was
   held. My thanks also to the staff of the Public Record Office, Kew. Since the
   Malthus conference was held in May 1980 I have taken the opportunity to
   present my research findings at seminars in the Universities of Hull, East
   Anglia and Durham, and at Coleg Harlech. I would like to thank all those
   people who took part in discussions and generously offered their criticisms.
2. The following is but a small sample of the literature on food riots: A. Booth,
   'Food Riots in the North West of England 1790–1801', *Past and Present*, 77
   (1977) 84–107; J. Stevenson, 'Food Riots in England 1792–1818', in J.
   Stevenson and R. Quinault (eds), *Popular Protest and Public Order*
   (London, 1974) pp. 33–74; R. A. E. Wells, *Dearth and Distress in Yorkshire,
   1793–1802* (Borthwick Papers, 52, York, 1977); S. I. Mitchell, 'Food
   Shortages and Public Order in Cheshire, 1757–1812', *Transactions of the
   Lancashire and Cheshire Antiquarian Society*, 81 (1982) 42–66.
3. That is when harvest failures or market disruptions such as sharp rises in
   prices resulted in actions like the hoarding of food. This produced fear,
   panic and social disorder such as riots. But the general food shortage may
   have occasioned 'little, if any, change in nutritional status'. This recognises
   the difference between nutritional or true famine from psycho-social
   famine. 'True famine would emerge only when with food markets continuing in disequilibrium, public policy (if such existed) failed to provide for the
   at-risk groups in the community' – D. J. Oddy, 'Urban Famine in
   Nineteenth-Century Britain: The Effects of the Lancashire Cotton Famine
   on Working-Class Diet and Health', *Economic History Review*, 2nd series,
   XXXVI (1983) 68–86. especially 70–1.
4. For the geography of the crises *see* A. Charlesworth (ed.), *An Atlas of Rural
   Protest in Britain 1548–1900* (London, 1983) especially 96–108.
5. For which *see* R. A. E. Wells, *Insurrection: The British Experience
   1795–1803* (Gloucester, 1983); *see also* J. Bohstedt, *Riots and Community
   Politics in England and Wales 1790–1810* (Cambridge, Mass., 1983)
   especially chapters 1 and 2.
6. *See* W. E. Minchinton, 'Agricultural Returns and the Government During
   the Napoleonic Wars', *Agricultural History Review*, 1 (1953) 29–43; M. E.
   Turner, 'Agricultural Productivity in England in the Eighteenth Century:
   Evidence from Crop Yields', *Economic History Review*, 2nd series, XXXV
   (1982) 489–510.
7. Adapted from D. G. Barnes, *A History of the English Corn Laws* (London,
   1930) pp. 299–300.
8. J. D. Chambers and G. E. Mingay, *The Agricultural Revolution 1750–1880*
   (London, 1966) pp. 115–16; M. Olsen, *The Economics of the Wartime
   Shortage* (Durham, N. Carolina, 1963) p. 65.
9. Adapted from B. R. Mitchell and P. Deane, *Abstract of British Historical
   Statistics* (Cambridge, 1962) pp. 486–7.

10. Stevenson, loc. cit., 35–7; *see also* R. A. E. Wells, 'Counting Riots in Eighteenth-Century England', *Bulletin of the Society for the Study of Labour History*, 37 (1978) 68–72.
11. W. F. Galpin, *The Grain Supply of England during the Napoleonic Wars* (New York, 1925) pp. 79–80.
12. Mitchell and Deane, op. cit., pp. 468–9.
13. As Bernard Eccleston also demonstrates from his analysis of Corn Wages in Chapter 10.
14. Bohstedt, op. cit., pp. 16–17 also clearly demonstrates the shock of the first inflation peak of 1795 producing the greatest number of riots in a single year.
15. Stevenson, loc. cit., 52; the idea is strongly refuted, however, by Bohstedt, op. cit., pp. 16–21.
16. Galpin, op. cit., pp. 13–14.
17. For example, *see* G. Hueckel, 'War and the British Economy, 1793–1815: A General Equilibrium Analysis', *Explorations in Economic History*, 10 (1973) especially 367–70.
18. G. E. Mingay (ed.), *The Agricultural State of the Kingdom, 1816* (reprinted Bath, 1970) introduction p. viii.
19. T. Tooke, *A History of Prices*, vol. 6 (London, 1857) p. 476; Minchinton, loc. cit., 38.
20. Stevenson, loc. cit., 66.
21. Indeed, excess mortality in London in 1795 actually occurred in the winter months of 1794–5, before the period of high prices. Stevenson, ibid., 38–9; *see also* W. M. Stern, 'The Bread Crisis in Britain, 1795–6', *Economica*, XXXI (1964) 172–3.
22. E. A. Wrigley and R. S. Schofield, *The Population History of England, 1541–1871* (Cambridge, 1981) pp. 371–2.
23. Ibid., pp. 332–3.
24. Unless otherwise stated all of the evidence concerning 1795–6 is taken from P[ublic] R[ecord] O[ffice], Home Office Papers, HO/42, boxes 34–8 and PRO, Privy Council Minutes, PC 4/6–7.
25. For which *see* Turner, loc. cit., and Minchinton, loc. cit.
26. This last paragraph is based on PRO, HO/42/48–56, 61–2 and HO/67; *see also* S. Lambert (ed.), *House of Commons Sessional Papers of the Eighteenth Century* (Wilmington, Del., 1975), in which volume 99 reprints parliamentary papers of 1795–6 on the question of *Food Supply*, and volume 131 reprints those for 1799–1800; an edition of the 1801 crop returns has now been printed in M. E. Turner (ed.) *Home Office Acreage Returns*, in four volumes (London; List and Index Society, volumes 189–90 and 196–7, published in 1982 and 1983 respectively).
27. The productivity effects of enclosure are discussed in Turner, loc. cit., 497–501.
28. For which *see* M. E. Turner, *Enclosures in Britain 1750–1830* (London, 1984) pp. 46–52.
29. Lambert, op. cit., vol. 104, the *Committee on Waste Lands* of 1797; *see also* M. Williams, 'The Enclosure and Reclamation of Waste Land in England and Wales in the Eighteenth and Nineteenth Centuries', *Transactions of the*

Institute of British Geographers, 51 (1970) 55–69, and J. Billingsley, 'An Essay on the Best Method of Inclosing Dividing and Cultivating Waste-Lands', *Letters to the Bath and West of England Agricultural Society*, 11 (1807) 2.

30. Quoted in Williams, ibid., 57.
31. As indeed confirmed by Malthus himself in *The Grounds of an Opinion on the Policy of Restricting the Importation of Foreign Corn* (London, 1815) p. 6; subsequent information in this paragraph from Turner, op. cit., *Enclosures . . .* chapter 2.
32. On the 'moral economy' *see* E. P. Thompson, 'The Moral Economy of the English Crowd in the Eighteenth Century', *Past and Present*, 50 (1971) 76–136.
33. T. R. Malthus, *An Investigation of the Cause of the Present High Price of Provisions* (London, 1800) p. 2.
34. Ibid., p. 3.
35. My emphasis but based on ibid., pp. 6–10.
36. Freely adapted from ibid., pp. 5–7. Malthus does not make special mention of bread, harvest failure or established Poor Law practices in this, his theoretical explanation of distributing a scarce product, though he brings the discussion back to food and food prices immediately afterwards on p. 8,

> The rise in the price of corn, and of other provisions, in this country, has been effected exactly in the same manner, though the operation may be a little more complicated; and I am firmly convinced, that it never could have reached its present height, but from the system of poor laws and parish allowances which have operated precisely in the same mode as the donatives of a shilling in the instance I have just adduced.

37. Ibid., p. 19.
38. Ibid., p. 14.
39. S. I. Mitchell, loc. cit., 46–7.
40. Malthus, op. cit., *An Investigation . . .* p. 22.
41. As for note 24 above.
42. S. I. Mitchell, loc. cit., 51.
43. Buckinghamshire County Record Office, Quarter Sessions Records, vol. 24, Michaelmas 1795.
44. 'There must be some mode devised and enforced to check that intolerant spirit of many farmers and corn factors to extort extravagent prices under the specious pretence of a scarcity much more than really exists', PRO, HO/42/36, letter of 29 October 1795.
45. PRO, HO/42/50/folio 322, letter of 23 June 1800.
46. For two Essex examples of this *see* Turner, op. cit., *Home Office Acreage Returns*, vol. 189, p. 155 (Hatfield Broad Oak) and p. 160 (Moreton).
47. For which *see* PRO, HO/42/49–56 and 61.

9 Malthus and the Corn Laws[1]

WRAY VAMPLEW

1

In the last five years of the French Revolutionary and Napoleonic Wars the price of wheat in Britain averaged over 100 shillings a quarter as contrasted with an immediate pre-war quinquennial average of under 50 shillings. Aggregate demand, enlarged by the rise in population over two decades, had played a role, but probably more important was, in the face of restricted overseas trade, the domestic suppliers who could only respond to this demand stimulus by bringing marginal land into cultivation, a move which necessarily incurred increased unit costs of production. In fact it was this rise in the supply price which provided the empirical base for both Malthus's and Ricardo's theoretical exposition of the law of diminishing returns. Fears that such relatively less productive land would be rendered uneconomic by cheaper foreign corn supplies once peacetime trading resumed, led to a successful political campaign by the landed interest to impose a Corn Law which would restrict grain imports unless the domestic price was such as to offer adequate remuneration to the British cereal grower. Most political economists who entered the Corn Law debate opposed such a policy as being inimical to the tenets of free trade, but Malthus diverged from mainstream political economy on this issue and swam against current orthodoxy in recommending protection for the nation's grain producers.

Although he had commented previously on the utility of corn bounties and tariffs, his views are best expressed in detail in two pamphlets written in 1814 and 1815 at the time of the debate on the abolition of the bounty and the imposition of restrictive grain import legislation. He claimed that the earlier pamphlet, *Observations on the Effects of the Corn Laws*, was an unprejudiced consideration of the advantages and disadvantages of a protective policy for arable agriculture, but, to a later audience, it is apparent where his sympathies lay.[2] The second pamphlet, *The Grounds of an Opinion on the Policy of Restricting the Importation of Foreign Corn*, openly declared that he held 'a decided opinion in favour of some restrictions on the importation of foreign corn'.[3] Although most other political economists shared Ricardo's opinion that Malthus was preaching 'dangerous heresy',[4] he continued to hold his favourable view towards agricultural protection as can be seen from his *Essay on the Principle of Population* (1826) and the postumously published *Principles of Political Economy* (1836).

Malthus justified his belief on the grounds that particular countries, including Britain, might need to maintain an independent source of grain so as to ameliorate the supply and price problems caused by war and trading policies in an imperfect political and commercial world. Certainly he feared the danger of a dependence upon foreign nations for the feeding of Britain's population, a potential peril no doubt emphasised by the ongoing European conflict which had drawn attention to the precarious position of Britain, both geographically and agriculturally. Blockades threatened food shortages and national security. He maintained that free trade in corn would be detrimental to the agricultural sector and that, once capital and other resources had vacated that part of the economy, British agriculture could not be resurrected overnight.

Moreover, by undermining the incomes of those in the agricultural sector, particularly the landlords, the rest of the community would be likely to suffer either by having to make up the tax shortfall or by losing the markets for their goods and services. Only if demand overseas rose more than domestic demand fell would the manufacturers and other producers benefit from a reduction in British trade barriers and, in the political and economic circumstances of the time, he felt this could not be guaranteed.

Nor was Malthus happy that the manufacturing sector should become dominant in Britain. He believed that industrial labourers faced worse conditions of life and work than their counterparts in agriculture. Additionally, he maintained that too much of a concentration on industry could endanger the stability of both the economy and society because of the more violent fluctuations in demand and employment to which, he believed, industry was subject as opposed to a protected agriculture. Free trade promised the worst of all possible worlds: highly unstable corn prices and severe manufacturing fluctuations. Ideally he wished agriculture and industry to co-exist, but this would necessitate some form of agricultural protection: industry, of course, already received protection from foreign competition and thus an equity argument could be added to the others which Malthus put forward in support of an agricultural/industrial balance within the economy.

In the long run free trade might result in higher standards of living, but, to Malthus, it did not appear a practical proposition at the time at which he wrote his corn law pamphlets. Moreover, Malthus felt that during the necessarily long time period in which the economy would be restructured, there would be substantial social dislocation and he questioned whether such human costs could be justified.

II

Malthus said very little about the actual mechanism of protection. He recommended the imposition of a constant duty which would have offered protection without prohibition, thus combining the favourable features of simplicity of operation, protection to the farmer, and revenue to the government. The latter point was not an insignificant consideration: Malthus was well aware that subsidies or bounties could also have promoted domestic grain growing, but he was appreciative of the fact that they took money out of the exchequer whereas a well-devised tariff could contribute to the government's coffers. As it was, neither the 1815 legislation nor its major revision, the sliding scale of 1828, followed Malthus's dispositions.

The 1815 Corn Laws allowed foreign wheat to enter Britain duty free for the three months following any quarterday on which the national average price for the preceding six weeks had been at, or over, 80 shillings a quarter, the lowest price which, it was argued, would provide the British cereal farmer with adequate remuneration.[5] For barley and oats the threshold prices were 40 shillings and 27 shillings respectively. However, because of faults in the data collection and in the method of calculation, the official average price did not truly represent the actual average market price.

Between 1815 and 1821 the official national prices were based on returns made by inspectors in 139 towns in twelve maritime districts of England and Wales.[6] All dealers in corn were bound, under a £10 penalty, to supply these inspectors with weekly accounts of the price and quantity of all their transactions in British grain. At the end of each week the inspectors calculated market averages for their towns by dividing total receipts by total sales. This information was then used by the Central Receiver of the Corn Returns in London to compute district and national average prices. Unfortunately many of the inputs in the national calculation must be suspect because inertia and inefficiency on the part of the inspectorate meant that 'with the exceptions of the returns taken at the Corn exchange, the greatest neglect and inattention has universally prevailed'.[7]

Even if the town data had been perfect, the method of calculation would have produced a false national price as the district averages were simply the sum of the market prices in the district divided by the relevant number of towns and the national average was the sum of the district averages divided by twelve. A few examples will illustrate the absurdity of not weighting the prices according to sales volumes. Taking the week ending 30 January 1819 the Ninth District had registered wheat sales of 414 quarters 7 bushels at an official average price of 82s 7d a quarter. Yet Cardigan, with sales of 1 quarter 5 bushels at 93s 4d, had been allowed exactly the same influence on the district average as Pembroke with sales of 254 quarters 7 bushels at a price of 71s 0d. If proper weighting procedures had been adopted then the district price would have been 74s 2d. At the national level Lynn, whose 1949 quarters at 75s 9d were the largest sales that week outside London, had less influence than Cardigan's meagre transactions because Lynn was one of eleven towns in its district whilst Cardigan was one of nine. A recalculation of the national average with due weighting for sales figures reduces the official price of 77s 4d to 75s 1d.

The effect of the method of calculation was to raise the official national price above one produced by weighting prices according to sales in each market. Thus a Corn Law, which offered protection at a price determined by the official averages, in practice could cease that protection when the true price would still be below the protective level. Although the ports were never opened for wheat when they should have remained closed, this certainly happened for oats in February 1817, May 1819 and August 1820 and for barley in November 1817. In 1821, following a parliamentary investigation, the weighting system was altered to take due account of sales levels in each market and the number of towns was increased to 148. As there was no corresponding alteration in the Corn Laws, protection was now being offered at home prices more genuinely approaching the threshold levels of the original legislation.

With the introduction of the sliding scale Corn Law in 1828 the list of inspected markets was revised to include all major inland consumption centres, thus making the weekly national average even more reliable.

Unfortunately, a different weighting problem appeared as the calculation of the quarterday prices was abandoned and the duties were adjusted weekly on the basis of an average of the previous six weeks' prices. However, this was obtained by totalling the relevant national averages and dividing by six: no cognisance was taken of varying sales volumes in any of the weeks. As five of the six prices determining the average were known, there was a strong possibility of predicting whether the average, and hence the duty, would change, particularly as prices varied relatively little from week to week. Anyone with a knowledge of corn market trends could make a very good guess at what the duty was going to be. Holders, and potential holders, of foreign corn thus would be in a position to take any necessary action before the duty actually changed.

Their situation would be strengthened by time-lags in the regulatory process. Although for any particular week the data collection at each market ended on Saturday, the national average based on that data was not computed until the following Thursday and the six week average, which included that figure, would then regulate the corn duty for the succeeding week: in effect the average for weeks one to six was declared in week seven and controlled the duty for week eight. This worked to the corn dealers' advantage as it gave them time in which to make decisions. By the Saturday of any week their knowledge of the market-place would have given them a good idea as to what ruling local prices were. Additionally, in most cases a copy of the local return would have been exhibited in the market-place some time prior to the national calculation. If experience had demonstrated that a relationship existed between local and national prices, then they could make a reasonable guess as to the probable official average, especially in view of the relative price stability between weeks. They would then have until the Thursday to take action before the duty actually changed, a period in which, of course, further market information would become available.

The corn dealers also benefited from the bonded warehouse system, which allowed foreign grain to be stored in Britain without having to pay duty until the corn actually left the warehouse for domestic consumption. The intention was to isolate corn supplies from the influence of foreign politics and foreign commerce, but what it meant for the dealers was that when the duty changed, or threatened to change, they could respond immediately without having to wait for grain to cross the sea.

The possible influence of the time-lags and the bonded warehouses can be seen in Appendix 9.1 where details are given of wheat entering for home consumption between July 1830 and July 1831. In week 33 of 1830 the price of wheat began to fall. The continuation of the fall in weeks 34 and 35 would alert dealers to the fact that the six week average would be likely to fall and hence duties to rise. Most likely this explains the substantial increase in the volume of wheat entered for home consumption in week 36. The sharp fall of prices in that week – published towards the end of week 37, though the dealers would be aware of it during week 36 – meant that a rise in the rate of duty would be inevitable in week 38. The realisation of this led to a rapid emptying of the bonded warehouses in week 37 with 622 000 quarters of wheat being entered for home consumption. In the following two weeks dealers who had been slow off the mark pulled grain out of bond before duties rose to prohibitive heights, which they had done by week 41. As prices crawled back to higher levels relatively little wheat was entered for home consumption until week 10 of 1831 when the pattern began to repeat itself.[8].

Unfortunately, prior to 1842 weekly import data are not readily available. However, the use of the bonded warehouses in the manner described above is suggested, particularly for wheat and oats, by the monthly figures for imports and quantities entered for home consumption which are shown in Appendix 9.2.[9]

Clearly the predictability of the duty, the time-lags, which provided an early warning system of possible duty changes, and the bonded warehouses, which allowed stocks of foreign corn to be accumulated within Britain, gave dealers in foreign grain the opportunity to minimise the amount of duty which they had to pay within any cycle of duties. Thus in the short run the protective intentions of the Corn Laws could be mitigated. Even in periods where duties were high, it needed only one or two weeks of relatively low duties for warehouse stocks to be reduced rapidly. Only when duties were prohibitive even at their lowest level was there no response from stockholders, as in the period 1832–6 when practically no wheat came out of bond. Imports did not cease in these years, though they were reduced, and grain was accumulated in the bonded warehouses to await the eventual lowering of duties which came in 1838. Significantly, the one week in which the duty fell to a mere shilling saw over 1¼ million quarters of wheat entered for home consumption.[10]

III

Malthus believed that in restricting the entry of foreign grain the Corn Laws would raise the level of domestic cereal prices, which in turn would lead to investment in agriculture and a stimulation of home corn production. Table 9.1 assesses the validity of this view by showing the price levels and price fluctuations (as measured by standard deviations) for nine decades, divided into four sections approximating to pre-French wars, the wars, the years of Corn Law operation, and the post-Corn Law period. It would seem that the Corn Laws were partially successful in that mean prices remained higher during their years of operation than prior to the artificial wartime situation or the post-Repeal decades. It is less evident that price fluctuations were dampened, a secondary benefit of the Corn Laws anticipated by Malthus. Table 9.2, unfortunately for a more restricted time-period due to data deficiencies, supports Malthus in suggesting that even if home production was not stimulated at least protection helped maintain domestic output levels. Certainly when protection was lessened, and later abandoned, the impact on barley and oats production was significant.

TABLE 9.1 *Grain price levels and price fluctuations 1775–1864*

	Wheat		Barley		Oats	
	Mean	*Standard deviation*	*Mean*	*Standard deviation*	*Mean*	*Standard deviation*
1775–1784	45.06	6.14	23.03	4.36	16.06	2.08
1785–1794	47.26	4.79	26.14	3.10	18.19	1.64
1795–1804	75.26	22.31	38.31	13.59	25.19	7.13
1805–1814	83.51	28.91	46.58	8.86	31.38	5.61
1815–1824	68.75	14.98	36.26	9.76	25.33	4.58
1825–1834	60.07	6.46	33.74	3.71	23.53	2.90
1835–1844	56.82	9.23	32.39	3.35	22.28	2.32
1845–1854	51.52	11.17	31.36	5.65	21.58	3.94
1855–1864	53.72	10.62	35.76	3.38	23.73	2.00

SOURCE *London Gazette.*

NOTE All prices are in shillings per quarter. Some of the prices used in this analysis have been recalculated elsewhere using weighting procedures which allowed for differential weekly sales, but their application does not significantly alter the results shown here. See W. Vamplew, 'A Grain of Truth: The Nineteenth-Century Corn Averages', *Agricultural History Review*, XXVIII (1980) 1–17.

What can be suggested is that the actual mechanism of the Corn Laws offered less short-term protection than was envisaged by the legislators. Apart from a few periods when duties were absolutely prohibitive, generally within any cycle of duties there were one or two weeks at which

TABLE 9.2 *Index of cereal production*

	Wheat	Barley	Oats
1828/29–1834/35	100	100	100
1835/36–1841/42	120	116	99
1842/43–1848/49	117	87	66
1849/50–1858/59	104	81	31

SOURCE Public Record Office, Corn Office Papers, MAF 10/257, 298–301.

NOTE For details of the calculations which are based on sales being used as proxies for production see W. Vamplew, 'The Protection of English Cereal Producers: The Corn Laws Reassessed', *Economic History Review*, 2nd series, XXXIII (1980) 390–391.

the duty was sufficiently low to render it attractive to enter corn for home consumption. Moreover, the warehouse system enabled an immediate response to be taken by holders of foreign corn. Such short-term loopholes weakened the longer-term protective impact of the legislation and thus prevented the effects of the Corn Laws, as predicted by Malthus, from coming to full fruition.

APPENDIX 9.1 *The operation of the Corn Laws*

Week*	Domestic price of wheat (per quarter)		Price controlling the duty (per quarter)		Duty (per quarter)		Entered for home consumption '000 quarters
	s	d	s	d	s	d	
3028	69	6	66	0	20	8	3
3029	70	3	66	7	20	8	1
3030	72	8	67	2	18	8	1
3031	74	11	67	11	18	8	1
3032	74	11	69	1	13	8	6
3033	73	4	70	6	10	8	8
3034	71	4	71	9	6	8	13
3035	70	5	72	7	2	8	132
3036	66	7	72	10	2	8	319
3037	62	4	72	11	2	8	622
3038	60	2	71	11	6	8	98
3039	60	8	69	9	13	8	26
3040	62	0	67	4	18	8	9
3041	62	8	65	3	21	8	1
3042	62	6	63	8	23	8	1
3043	61	6	62	4	24	8	1
3044	61	3	61	8	25	8	0
3045	62	3	61	7	25	8	0

APPENDIX 9.1 *The operation of the Corn Laws (cont.)*

Week*	Domestic price of wheat (per quarter)		Price controlling the duty (per quarter)		Duty (per quarter)		Entered for home consumption '000 quarters
	s	d	s	d	s	d	
3046	63	9	61	9	25	8	0
3047	64	8	62	0	24	8	1
3048	64	8	62	3	24	8	1
3049	65	7	62	7	24	8	0
3050	66	1	63	0	23	8	0
3051	67	2	63	8	23	8	0
3052	67	7	64	6	22	8	0
3053	68	1	65	3	21	8	0
3101	68	3	65	11	21	8	0
3102	69	8	66	6	20	8	0
3103	70	6	67	1	18	8	0
3104	71	8	67	9	18	8	0
3105	73	3	68	6	16	8	0
3106	74	8	69	3	13	8	0
3107	75	1	70	2	10	8	0
3108	73	10	71	4	6	8	0
3109	72	4	72	5	2	8	1
3110	71	9	73	2	1	0	191
3111	71	8	73	5	1	0	38
3112	72	2	73	5	1	0	57
3113	72	4	73	2	1	0	73
3114	71	7	72	9	2	8	65
3115	70	8	72	4	2	8	116
3116	70	10	71	11	6	8	14
3117	70	5	71	8	6	8	62
3118	70	3	71	6	6	8	91
3119	66	11	72	4	6	8	183
3120	68	4	71	0	6	8	79
3121	65	5	70	5	10	8	41
3122	66	4	69	10	13	8	5
3123	66	10	69	0	13	8	43
3124	67	9	68	3	16	8	4
3125	68	1	67	8	18	8	1
3126	66	7	67	3	18	8	2
3127	65	9	67	1	18	8	6
3128	64	11	66	10	20	8	4

SOURCE *London Gazette.*

NOTES   *The first two digits give the year, the last two the week; thus 3028 is the twenty-eighth week of 1830.

      †The market price is for the week cited; the price regulating duty in that week was declared the previous Thursday.

138   *Malthus and the Corn Laws*

APPENDIX 9.2   *Corn imports, 1829–31*

	Month	Wheat and Wheat Flour		Barley		Oats and Oatmeal	
		I	EHC	I	EHC	I	EHC
1829	J	326	322	112	100	57	1
	F	140	142	15	17	20	
	M	117	133	7	2	13	
	A	95	11	12	1	5	
	M	159	23	41	1	27	
	J	162	81	30		34	
	J	277	474	17	1	70	112
	A	187	25	19	7	135	4
	S	141	179	16	5	120	15
	O	61	32	17	88	50	55
	N	26	1	13	6	11	
	D	25		6	1	7	1
1830	J	13		1			
	F	8					
	M	12					
	A	56	7	2			
	M	273	244	16		5	
	J	205	24	28	2	38	27
	J	198	11	15	1	73	56
	A	300	337	20	1	133	247
	S	360	1032	21	14	185	522
	O	74	8	16	4	65	50
	N	44	2	4	8	7	
	D	49		10	17	6	
1831	J	48		10	9	1	
	F	37	1	8	82		
	M	272	487	33	104	4	
	A	342	317	139	141	50	
	M	441	454	75	77	70	7
	J	205	80	31	31	83	45
	J	285	19	12	8	138	39
	A	196	9	5		134	62
	S	145	1	8		109	192
	O	36	1	1		14	1
	N	34		6	5	12	
	D	45	1	40	54		

SOURCE   'Returns Relative to the Importation and Exportation of Corn 1828–42', *British Parliamentary Papers*, LIII, no. 6 (1843) 34–42.

NOTES   I = Imports
EHC = Entered for Home Consumption
All measurements are to the nearest '000 quarters.
Foreign grain only has been considered as colonial imports were regulated by a different scale of duties.

NOTES AND REFERENCES

1. This revised paper has benefited from a reading of P. Boyce's unpublished Honours Thesis, *Malthus, Ricardo and the Corn Law Debates* (University of Melbourne, 1980).
2. T. R. Malthus, *Observations on the Effects of the Corn Laws*, in *The Pamphlets of Thomas Robert Malthus* (reprinted New York, 1970) pp. 95–131.
3. T. R. Malthus, *The Grounds of an Opinion on the Policy of Restricting the Importation of Foreign Corn*, in ibid., *The Pamphlets*, pp. 137–73.
4. M. Paglin, introduction to T. R. Malthus, *Principles of Political Economy* (reprinted New York, 1964) p. v.
5. 'Select Committee on Petitions Relating to Agricultural Distress', *British Parliamentary Papers*, 11 (1820) Report, 7.
6. For a detailed study of the corn returns *see* W. Vamplew, 'A Grain of Truth: The Nineteenth Century Corn Averages', *Agricultural History Review*, XXVIII (1980) 1–17
7. 'Select Committee on Petitions', loc. cit., Report, 5.
8. The existence of such a cycle for most of the period during which the sliding scale operated is demonstrated in W. Vamplew, 'The Protection of English Cereal Producers: The Corn Laws Reassessed', *Economic History Review*, 2nd series, XXXIII (1980) 382–95.
9. The data after 1842 confirms that this was happening, for which *see* ibid.
10. The 38th week of 1838, for which *see* Vamplew, loc. cit., 'The Protection of English Cereal Producers', 388.

Part III
Labour: From Wage Earning to Social Welfare

10 Malthus, Wages and the Labour Market in England 1790–1830

BERNARD ECCLESTON

'Mr Malthus . . . and . . . his usual and laudable habits of attending to facts and experience.'[1]

I

The approach of the classical economists to the determination of wages contains certain problems for the economic historian. Principally these concern the tension between their direct observations of wage patterns and their attempts to integrate these observations into a wider theoretical framework. In particular the links between the wage fund, the natural or subsistence wage and the labour theory of value, necessitated the simplification that labour was homogeneous so that 'labour could be evaluated in relation to the great mass of day labour'.[2] This simplification has left a legacy in later analysis of the wage structure which has tended to underemphasise the problems of relative wages.

Whenever occupational or geographical wage differentials were considered, classical analysis tended to follow Adam Smith in stressing supply side factors such as non-monetary influences (risk, esteem, disagreeable jobs, perquisites and so on) and mobility constraints related to the Settlement and Apprenticeship Laws. Policy proposals aimed at reducing labour market inequalities were then set in terms of reducing mobility obstructions.

Following this lead, many writers have concentrated their attention on *average* wages for occupations, regions or the whole country despite the work of later classical economists who introduced the notion of non-competing groups.[3] A. L. Bowley pioneered attempts to construct wage indices for the Malthusian period but his data was set within the classical framework by dwelling on *representative average* wage rates because 'wages throughout the country for equal degrees of skill are equal at any given time'.[4] T. S. Ashton summed up this approach when he concluded that by 1830

> instead of a number of local and imperfect markets for labour there was coming into being a single increasingly sensitive market for labour . . . Wages in one industry were linked with those in another and in particular the earnings of farm labourers and builders moved up and down with those of factory workers.[5]

However, other studies of the operation of labour markets have stressed continuing market imperfections by pointing out that mean wage rates to not take enough account of the *dispersion* of wages paid. Indeed, many classical economists made similar statements when referring to local variations in wages, yet they seem to have neglected these variations in developing more general theories.[6] This may be explained partly by their concern to comment on general or aggregate trends, but there were other factors involved which are related to their views on what wages *ought* to be paid. The philosophical assumption of people possessing equal talents was related to the need to see equality as a long-term goal to compensate for the short-term poverty associated with early industrialisation. Similarly the desire to remove obstacles to free market operations meant that wage differentials were said to be merely a temporary feature.[7]

Some economic historians have used historical evidence on the existence of wage differentials to stress a 'multitude of related markets, some only very tenuously related, rather than a single labour market'.[8] In so doing they reject the assumption that these differentials are a temporary phenomenon associated with a partially integrated national economy; rather they are essential elements in the labour market structure.[9] They are essential because they allow more weight to be given to demand side influences as they affected the local reaction of firms to wider market forces, such as changes in aggregate demand or inflationary pressures like those experienced during the Napoleonic wars. By relating external and internal influences on wage setting some room is created from managerial discretion in the wage bargaining process instead of assuming a passive response by firms to external pressures. It was precisely this sort of bargaining discretion that Adam Smith used to note the strength of masters' combinations, which Arthur Young meant by an employers' assessment of what was fair and what Malthus inferred in his references to trade unions.[10]

Therefore in considering the work of Malthus on labour and wages we need to recognise the existence of a segmented market for labour and to look at the differences within, and between, regions and occupations.

II

In the *Principles of Political Economy* (1820) Malthus sought to deal 'critically with certain economic principles which doctrinal controversy and current events have brought to the fore' (Introduction), and it has been suggested that his book was written to repudiate the abstract, deductive method of analysis which had been developed by Ricardo.[11] His style of appealing to 'facts and experience' is clearly evident in chapter IV, where Malthus reviewed the 'Corn Wage of Labour' over five centuries by relating money wages for 'standard labour' to wheat prices. Although this chapter concentrates on homogeneous units of labour, the analysis does offer some useful insights into wage adjustments during and after Napoleonic inflation.

There is some confusion about the precise meaning of 'corn wages' in his other works,[12] but in this particular chapter Malthus is clearly comparing wheat prices with wage rates. It is not accurate to use this concept as a proxy for real wages because we are saying nothing about levels of employment and therefore earnings. Equally it is important to recognise that bread took up only a part of household expenditure – Malthus himself quoted a weighting of two-fifths in the 1790s although this almost certainly rose during the war years. We also need to note that wheat prices both rose and fell faster than other price series between 1790 and 1830.

Notwithstanding these problems, Malthus did indicate two important trends: (a) that in 1810–11 wages could just about purchase the *same* amount of corn as they did in the early 1790s; and (b) that by 1821–3 a labourer's wage would allow the purchase of 40 per cent more corn than in the pre-war years. In Figures 10.1 to 10.3 I have deflated three established wage indices and four new series for the Midlands by London and Birmingham wheat prices to assess the trends that Malthus observed.[13] (In all cases 1790 equals 100.) These figures seem to indicate that his view was not inaccurate although there are regional and occupational differences, to which I will return later.

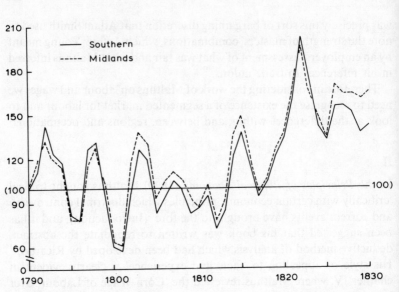

FIGURE 10.1 *Index of daily corn wages for building craftsmen, 1790–1830 (1790 = 100)*

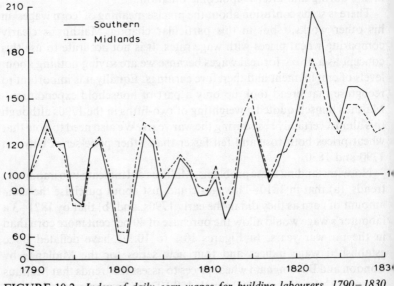

FIGURE 10.2 *Index of daily corn wages for building labourers, 1790–1830 (1790 = 100)*

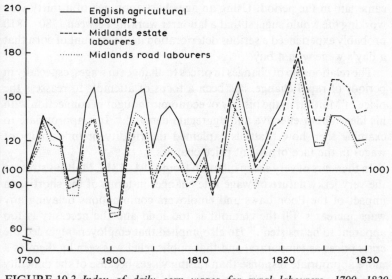

FIGURE 10.3 *Index of daily corn wages for rural labourers, 1790–1830 (1790 = 100)*

The most vivid characteristic of the figures is that 'the wages of labour have been subject to great fluctuations' and Malthus pointed to the social consequences in the resulting 'discontent and tumult'.[14] These fluctuations were obviously associated with soaring wheat prices in the years 1795–6, 1800–1 and 1812–13, followed by generally falling prices after 1814, except for the smaller rise in 1817. Trends in 'corn wages' appear to show at best fairly stable, and at worst falling, levels from 1790–1813 with a notable deterioration from 1805–13. After the war, the trend was clearly upwards apart from the two setbacks in 1817 and 1824–5. The wide fluctuations make it difficult to generalise, but the substantial rise in 'corn wages' after 1813 reflected the very sharp increase in money wage rates in the later years of the war. It is important though to locate this rise in the very late war period and it only produces a dramatic impact on 'corn wages' after 1814–15 when wheat prices fell quickly. This late surge in wages should serve as a warning to the dangers of using the later war years as end points in any trend analysis. If we look at the whole period from 1790 to 1815 then there does appear to have been a 50 per cent improvement in 'corn wages' but it is obviously wrong to express this as an annual rate of change when most of the increase came late in the period. Using an age-chart approach of a thirty year working life would suggest that a labourer working between 1780–1810 probably experienced a serious deterioration in the amount of corn that a day's wage would buy.

The relationship of changes in prices to changes in wages, especially in periods of rapid change, has been a focus of attempts to reassess the place of Malthus in the history of economic thought in connection with his ideas about effective and aggregate demand.[15] It is appropriate to examine then how Malthus explained the rigidity or inflexibility of wages in the face of violent price changes.

In the years of very sharp inflation from 1794–1813, Malthus stressed the very jerky nature of wage rate changes in terms of the short-term impact of the Poor Laws and employers combinations delaying any wage increases 'till the clamour is too loud and the necessity is too apparent to be resisted'.[16] He also implied that employers regarded the crisis prices as temporary, and that public relief was seen by them as a more appropriate response than raising wages because of the difficulty of reducing wages once the crisis passed.[17] We can see evidence of this sort of reaction in the lag of wages behind prices especially in the years of devastating harvest failures in 1795–6 and 1811–12. It is also clear that in the years of steadily rising prices which did not produce the 'clamour' of crisis harvest failure, 'corn wages' deteriorated over a number of years as they did for instance from 1805 to 1812. From this assessment of wage rigidity Malthus went on to question Adam Smith's assertion of corn prices as *the* influence on wage rates, suggesting instead that corn prices were only *one* factor involved, and pointing out the lags in the process of adjusting the subsistence wage.

Turning to the post-war deflation, Malthus again stressed the relative rigidity of wage rates in the short run by commenting on the lag of wage reduction behind corn price decline – 'the money price of labour never falls till many workmen have been for *some time* out to work'.[18] All of the series used in Figures 10.1 to 10.3 confirm this view of wage trends after 1815, when the wider deflationary forces were much more apparent in reductions in earnings through higher levels of unemployment than in wage rate reductions. However, even as late as 1830, there was little evidence that wage rates fell back to the levels of the 1790s, but there were differences between occupations and regions.

The data for the building trades, for example, show marked differences in the post-war behaviour of rates paid to labourers as opposed to skilled workers. Labourers' wages were adjusted downwards more quickly than their skilled colleagues so that the size of the premium for skilled workers widened through the 1820s, leaving labourers' rates at 30 per cent more than 1790 rates, while skilled builders received 50 per cent more. Although this trend is more obvious in the Midlands series than in the Phelps Brown data from southern England, there is reason to doubt the accuracy of the southern data because this relies too heavily on listed contract hire rates which do not reflect actual pay, and contract rates 'tend to drift along at unchanging customary rates'.[19]

Custom was important in determining rates and the speed of change, but it is all too easy to translate custom into a rigid, unchanging force in wage bargaining. For example, a common view of occupational differentials in building stresses their rigidity over long periods when a customary two-thirds of the skilled wage was paid to labourers.[20] This view tends to play down short-term reaction in the market for two different types of labour by paying too much attention to rates that were supposed to be paid rather than actual rates that we can discover in receipts and bills. Malthus noted that in the 1820s 'skilled men . . . were more prosperous than ever before'[21] and he attributed this to entry controls operated by trade unions. There is evidence from the Midlands that skilled unions were attempting to hold on to their wartime gains, but it is more likely that the skill differential widened because of surplus supplies of unskilled workers. In those Midland towns which saw increased speculative building in the 1820s, the pressure of large numbers of Irish labourers kept unskilled rates down compared to other areas.[22]

Those wage series which were representative of rural parts fell much faster in the later 1820s, but it is vital to distinguish different markets even here. Road labourers wages, for instance, fell back to 1790 levels in some cases, and their general index showed the smallest gains. But estate workers wages held firmer at 40 per cent more than 1790 rates because the estates offered better, more regular employment prospects in country parks, gardens and in land improvement schemes than for more casual agricultural or road workers.

Therefore we come back to the broader questions concerning the variations in wage rates paid and their relation to local labour markets.

III

One way of assessing the impact of these local variations in wages is to plot the *range* of wage rates as they are dispersed around the mean rate because, as Malthus noted, there were 'great differences in the price of labour in the different counties, and even in parishes not very distant from each other'.[23]

Unfortunately, only the Midlands data is suited to this cross-sectional approach as other series have concentrated exclusively on the behaviour of average wages. However, it is possible to analyse the dispersal of wages in the four main sources which underpin Bowley's agricultural wage index for Midland counties and then compare the extent of variation with my own Midlands data. Table 10.1 takes a measure of wage dispersion by expressing the standard deviation of all the observations in a given year as a percentage of the mean to give the coefficient variation. Although the number of observations does change

TABLE 10.1   *Dispersion of agricultural and rural wages in the Midlands (coefficient of variation per cent)**

	Bowley	Midland labourers	
	Agricultural labour	Estate	Road
1767–70	14.0	10.7	15.4
	(A. Young)		
1794–5	15.4	11.9	14.2
	(F. Eden)		
1823–4	15.0	14.7	14.3
	(S. C. Labourers Wages)		
1832–3	17.8	8.1	17.5
	(R. C. Poor Laws)		

* This is measured as the standard deviation of all the observations in a given year as a percentage of the mean to give coefficient variation.
SOURCES   Bowley, *JRSS* 1898; Eccleston Thesis, appendixes 2–3.

between the years it does seem that wage differences persisted through the 1830s and that there was little evidence of the emergence of a 'single increasingly sensitive market for labour'.[24]

The Midlands data allows us to examine the progress of the whole range of wages paid for the entire period from 1790 to 1830, and Figure 10.4 indicates the extent of wage differences for the same type of work, in this case clearing and maintaining parish roads. The upper path shows the highest wages paid and illustrates the problems of concentrating too much attention on mean rates. For example, in 1810 the mean rate of 25 old pence per day was part of a range which extended from 18d to 36d

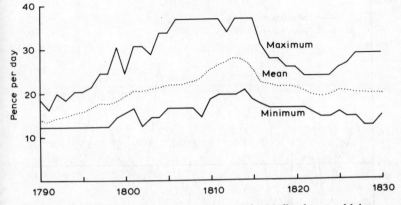

FIGURE 10.4   *Range of money wage rates in the Midlands – road labourers,*
1790–1830

and, as Malthus noted, these variations were evident in parishes which
were in the same area. At the end of the period, although some workers
were being paid well in excess of their 1790 rates, others had fallen back
to rates which showed little change over the forty years.

To illustrate the impact of this range on the movement of corn wages, I
have deflated money wages for the same series by Birmingham wheat
prices and the results in the form of index numbers (1790 equals 100) are
shown in Figure 10.5. This graph clearly shows the differing fortunes of
Midland road labourers and the lower path, in particular, reveals a
prolonged experience of wartime decline which is only relieved by very
short periods when their corn wages rise above the 1790 levels. The
deflated range does narrow markedly for a short time in the early 1820s,
but then it widens dramatically towards the end of that decade.

When the high and low wage observations are identified, however,
there is no consistent trend for individual parishes. Some parishes which
paid rates closest to the upper band before 1814 then slump to the lower
band in the 1820s, and this volatility is connected to the short-term
casual nature of the work. There were obvious problems for the
highways' surveyors in tight labour conditions when they had to
compete for labour with other employers. In the post-war years, pauper
labour was frequently forced on the surveyors, but this forced labour
was so unproductive that a pauper wage was paid at only 40 per cent of
the modal wage. (This pauper rate has not been included in the ranges
shown in Figures 10.4 and 10.5.)

Road wages were often dependent on the fortunes of local outworking

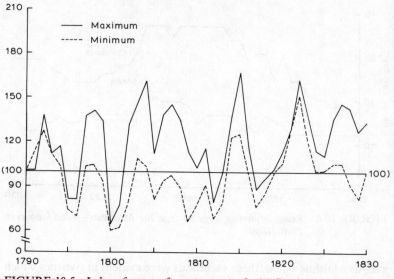

FIGURE 10.5   *Index of range of corn wages in the Midlands – road labourers, 1790–1830 (1790 = 100)*

industries. In the framework knitting areas of western Leicestershire (for example, in Kirby Muxlow or Stoke Golding) the movement from high to low wage paths after 1815 could be associated with the sharp decline of knitting. Similar trends can be seen in the ribbon weaving areas to the north of Coventry in the depression of the 1820s, and contrasted with the higher road wages in the expanding shoe making parishes around Northampton. Yet even in these local areas there were still quite remarkable wage differentials in related parishes.

The building trades also experienced substantial wage differences and for some landed estates it is possible to assess the pattern of wages paid to skilled builders, their labourers and agricultural workers employed on farms or in gardens. On the same site there were complex trends in the actual rates paid and in the changes to these rates. In two Northampton-shire estates at Milton and Grafton during the 1820s, the skill premium in building tended to narrow against the overall Midlands trend, but estate wages differed markedly with Milton employers paying estate workers a higher rate than building labourers. Neither was there any consistent patterns in the bigger towns where the skilled builders increased their craft differential in Nottingham and Leicester, but in Stratford and Stafford building labourers closed the gap in wage rates.

These examples should serve to illustrate the difficulties of aggregating even subregional wage data into representative averages. Although it might be possible to find higher wage path observations in the northern Midlands than in the depths of southern Warwickshire or Northamptonshire, it is vital to recognise that substantial wage differentials existed for the same type of work even within these local subregions. For this reason the points that Malthus made about local wage differences should serve as a warning to those who generalise about high or low wage counties or areas.

Given the complexity of the wage structure in a multiplicity of local labour markets, any analysis of trends in wages should take care in using the all-embracing notion of an average wage for homogeneous units of labour. It is equally unsatisfactory, though, to eschew the search for any general explanations of wage patterns as this results in 'halting agnosticism which can neither forecast nor understand'.[25] By stressing a *range* of wages paid for the same job in an area, we can relate the movements in the rates over time to external market factors yet allow the internal response of each firm to determine their position within the overall range. Thus actual rates paid will be explained by the combination of wider external forces and internal conditions 'decided by a conflict of wills between employers and labourers'.[26]

IV

In his work on the labour market in *The Principles*, Malthus provides us with some clues to the way external and internal factors can be used to explain wage determination. As prices moved sharply upwards during the Napoleonic wars, Malthus observed that the nominal price for labour frequently remained the *same*. This he attributed to various factors: the expansion of population and labour supply, Poor Law wage subsidies and employers' combination. (He might also have added the greater use of previously underemployed labour including family work.) But from the series used in this paper, we can see that money wages did not remain fixed although they frequently lagged behind changes in prices, so that in the years of rapidly rising prices a small change in nominal wages may have meant that workers were subject to a 'money illusion' until the real wage fall produced the clamour that raised wages to match the rising cost of living.

Each of these factors would have had a variable impact on local wage bargaining and would help to account for different responses to excess labour supplies and changes in employers' reactions to inflationary pressures. We have noted above the way some employers took a short-term view of increased living cost regarding them as a temporary phenomenon. At Packington near Coventry, the Earl of Aylesford paid a supplement to wages of about 10 per cent from 1795 to 1801, and it was only after six years that the changed living costs were considered to be sufficiently permanent to increase the basic daily rate from 15d to 18d.[27]

In the post-war years Malthus again noted nominal wage rigidity as prices fell faster than wages 'till many workmen have for some time been out of work'.[28] Quite clearly Malthus saw the trade-off between rigid money wages and unemployment in the post-war depression by emphasising the reduction in 'effectual demand' that would result from unemployment and cause further economic depression. We have so little data on unemployment for these years that it is difficult to form any definite impression on the impact for wage bargaining, but the wage series do show that even in the 1820s nominal wage rates remained inflexible.

More modern analysis of the same feature points to several possible explanations. Firstly, some workers have sufficient bargaining strength to be able to resist money wage reductions and we have seen that in building, at least, there is evidence that some skilled workers retained more wartime gains than their labourers. Secondly, many employers are thought unlikely to reduce wages in the short run to avoid alienating their workforce and to avoid the loss of efficient workers that may be difficult to re-employ when trade recovers. Historical evidence on why some employers resisted the opportunity to adjust rates downwards as prices fell is sparse, but in the West Midlands there was a feeling among some estate owners that maintaining wages and employment on land improvement schemes was one way to undermine the support for rural protest movements like the Swing disturbances.[29] Dr Collins has stressed the need of contemporary farmers to keep labour in the area for use in the peak weeks of harvest employment, thus to gain access to an adequate labour supply meant finding ways to halt the townward migration of workers and their families.[30]

There might also have been other social or paternal motives. David Ricardo, for instance, writing as the economist, said that money wages *must* fall as the price of corn falls because money wages always buy the same quantity of necessities. But Ricardo, the Gloucestershire employer, resisted cutting money wages:'I as a gentleman supposed always to pay the same.'[31]

These illustrations help to establish the place for an internal response within each firm to external labour market pressures. To focus too much on the general supply and demand for labour ignores the imperfect flows of information and assumes the operation of daily auctions to set spot wage rates. External factors such as changing levels of aggregate demand or rising population were clearly important constraints, but within these constraints there was room for local or internal bargaining. Where custom, continuity and local labour market rigidities were apparent the determination of wages was not simply a passive response to external forces.

The historian therefore has to exercise caution in the construction of wage series especially in the attempts to measure *mean* levels of wages, incomes or consumption. 'In so far as [this] concentrates on averages it neglects dispersion which may make the simple average virtually meaningless for many of our purposes.'[32] Although the general trends are important starting points, the particular place of different groups of workers doing the same jobs in different areas owes much to the peculiar circumstances of their local labour markets. To ignore the impact of these local peculiarities is to neglect the 'laudable habits of attending to facts and experience...' that Malthus championed in some parts of his writings at least!

NOTES AND REFERENCES

1. Quoted in W. D. Grampp, 'Malthus on Money Wages and Welfare', *American Economic Review*, XLVI (1956) 930.
2. P. James, *Population Malthus* (London, 1979) p. 298.
3. For an important review of the whole problem *see* T. W. Hutchinson, 'The Decline and Fall of English Classical Political Economy', in R. D. C. Black (ed.), *The Marginal Revolution in Economics* (University of N. Carolina, Durham, 1973) pp. 176–202.
4. A. L. Bowley, *Wages in the United Kingdom in the Nineteenth Century* (Cambridge, 1900) p. 18.
5. T. S. Ashton, *The Industrial Revolution 1760–1830* (Oxford, 1948) p. 126.
6. Adam Smith, *The Wealth of Nations* (London, 1776) chapter X.
7. J. R. Poynter, *Society and Pauperism* (London, 1969) p. 51.
8. S. Pollard, 'Labour in Great Britain', in P. Mathias and M. M. Postan (eds), *The Cambridge Economic History of Europe*, vol. VII (Cambridge, 1978) p. 105.
9. For a survey of the empirical research in this area *see* J. Corina, *Labour Market Economics* (London, 1973).
10. Poynter, op. cit., pp. 47–8.
11. J. J. O'Leary, 'Malthus's General Theory of Employment and the Post-Napoleonic Depressions', *Journal of Economic History*, II (1943) 190.
12. Grampp, passim.

13. The English agricultural series is taken from Bowley, passim; the southern builders from E. H. Phelps Brown and S. V. Hopkins, 'Seven Centuries of the Prices of Consumables Compared with Builders' Wage Rates', *Economica*, XXIII (1956) 296–314. For the Midlands, the wage data are taken from my unpublished thesis *A Survey of Wage Rates in Five Midland Counties* (Unpublished Ph.D. thesis, University of Leicester, 1976). Midland wages were taken from account books, receipts and bills from landed estates, highways surveyors and borough surveyors, and the rates are expressed in terms of a composite annual wage. Wheat prices were extracted from the *Staffordshire Advertiser* and B. R. Mitchell and P. Deane, *Abstract of British Historical Statistics* (Cambridge, 1962). A recent, if controversial, survey of wage data during the Industrial Revolution may be found in P. H. Lindert and J. G. Williamson, 'English Workers' Living Standards during the Industrial Revolution: A New Look', *Economic History Review*, 2nd series, XXXVI (1983) 1–25.
14. James, op. cit., p. 257. *See also* R. A. E. Wells, 'The Development of the English Proletariat and Social Protest 1700–1850', *Journal of Peasant Studies*, VI (1980) 172.
15. O'Leary, passim.
16. Quoted in L. A. Dow, 'Malthus on Sticky Wages', *History of Political Economy*, 9 (1977) 106.
17. Wells, loc. cit., 122.
18. T. R. Malthus, *Principles of Political Economy*, 2nd ed. (London, 1836) p. 249.
19. G. N. Von Tunzelmann, 'Trends in Real Wages 1750–1850 Revisited' *Economic History Review*, 2nd series, XXXII (1979) 36.
20. Phelps Brown and Hopkins, loc. cit.
21. James, op. cit., p. 299.
22. *See* Eccleston, op. cit., chapter VI.
23. Malthus, op. cit., p. 251.
24. Ashton, op. cit., p. 126.
25. M. Dobb, *Wages* (Cambridge, 1946) p. 144. On the wider uses of a range approach see J. M. Clarke, 'Zones of Indeterminacy', *Proceedings of the American Philosophical Society*, 99 (1955) 121–6.
26. J. S. Mill, 'Thornton on Labour and its Claims', *Fortnightly Review*, XXIX (June 1869) 680.
27. Aylesford Labour Books 1758–1814 retained by the Earl of Aylesford at Packington Hall, Warwickshire.
28. Malthus, op. cit., p. 249. See also S. Hollander, 'Malthus and the Post Napoleonic Depression', *History of Political Economy*, I (1969) 320.
29. E. S. Richards, 'Captain Swing in the West Midlands', *International Review of Social History*, VII (1974) 86–99.
30. E. J. T. Collins, 'Harvest Technology and Labour Supply in Britain 1790–1870', *Economic History Review*, 2nd series, XXII (1969) 453–73.
31. Quoted in Poynter, op. cit., p. 245.
32. E. J. Hobsbawm, 'The Standard of Living Debate', in A. J. Taylor (ed.), *The Standard of Living in Britain in the Industrial Revolution* (London, 1975) p. 184.

11 Malthus and Reform of the English Poor Law

ANNE DIGBY

> A pamphlet on the poor laws generally contains some little piece of
> favourite nonsense, by which we are gravely told this enormous evil
> may be perfectly cured . . . Every man rushes to the press with his
> small morsel of imbecility; and is not easy till he sees his impertinence
> stitched in blue covers.[1]

This apt comment by Sydney Smith applies to many of Malthus's
contemporaries but not, we are so often told, to Malthus himself.
Malthus's contribution is alleged to be the vigorous application of a
scientific principle in place of piecemeal, meliorist reform of the Poor
Law.[2] This interpretation is based on Malthus's *Essay on the Principle of
Population* of 1798, where the application of the Poor Law had led
Malthus to the conclusion that there should be a 'total abolition of all
the present parish-laws'.[3] Yet while this early abolitionist stance is well
known his later reformist views have received less attention. This
chapter suggests that it was as a reformer, as much as an abolitionist,
that Thomas Robert Malthus (1766–1834) was to influence the shaping
of the New Poor Law.

I

For contemporaries the Poor Law appeared to be one of the most
interesting of Malthus's applications of the principle of population. His
views on poor relief at this time had much in common with those of a
group who adhered to natural law principles in political economy. They
saw the Poor Law as a distortion of the free market, and the poor rates

157

(which financed relief) as an undesirable diversion of money from the wages fund which reduced the amount of employment and wages available for the poor.[4] In the *First Essay* of 1798 Malthus advocated the 'abolition of all the present parish laws' since, although they were instituted for 'the most benevolent purpose', they produced 'irremediable' evils.[5]

> Their first obvious tendency is to increase population without increasing the food for its support. A poor man may marry with little or no prospect of being able to support a family in independence. They may be said therefore in some measure to create the poor which they maintain.[6]

His objections to the Poor Laws were to be developed in the second *Essay* of 1803, and elaborated still further in the fifth edition of the *Essay* of 1817. In these and other writings he criticised the impact which the Poor Laws had on the labour market and on wages. Since poor relief encouraged the growth of population, it increased the supply of labour beyond demand, and hence lowered wages.[7] Malthus condemned a permanent system of allowances because they destroyed the 'necessary connexion between the apparent corn wages of day labour and the real means which the labouring classes possess of maintaining a family'.[8] The parish poor rate thus became a subsidy for labourers' wages; an accelerating process of ever increasing pauperism was set in motion which could end only in 'the great body of the community' becoming paupers.[9] His conclusion in 1827 was still that 'no essential improvement can take place without the denial of a legal claim' to poor relief to the unemployed able-bodied poor.[10]

It was not only poor law allowances that Malthus viewed with a critical eye. He had reservations about other public interventions into the labour market, although his opinions often changed on these issues. By 1827 he was opposing public schemes for employing the poor which he had supported ten years earlier. He concluded that the short-term gains were more than counterbalanced by bad long-term results, because labourers were encouraged to marry and have children, whom they were unable to support when the public works ceased.[11] The alarming propensity of the poor to marry and breed made Malthus excessively cautious about colonial emigration: another fashionable contemporary remedy for removing surplus population and reducing pauperism. He would concede that the emigration of redundant labourers would be advantageous, but only if the emigrants' houses were pulled down so that those left behind were not encouraged to marry early and set up home.[12]

A similar concern about the supply of cottages led to ambivalence in his later views on the settlement laws of the Poor Law. In this case, uncharacteristically, the principle of population made him prefer the retention of the laws of settlement to their abolition. Yet earlier, in 1798, he had felt that one of the principal gains in abolishing the Poor Laws would be to end the settlement laws. This would free the labour market, and so 'give liberty and freedom of action to the peasantry of England', thus finishing 'a most disgraceful and disgusting tyranny' of poor people by parochial officers. Also, in their obstruction of the labour market, the settlement laws were criticised because they had 'a constant tendency to add to the difficulties of those who are struggling to support themselves without assistance'.[13] Later, Malthus deviated from conventional economic thinking on this subject and declared: 'I think that anything like an abolition of the present laws of settlement would be accompanied with more evil than good'.[14] By this he meant that it was better to countenance an impediment to a free labour market than the increased cottage building and encouragement to marriage that abolition of the settlement laws might bring. For similar reasons he defended existing inequalities in the financial incidence of the burden of the poor rate because they encouraged ratepayers to be vigilant over the administration of poor relief.[15]

'I certainly am disposed to refer frequently to things as they are, as the only way of making one's writings practically useful to society.'[6] This personal observation by Malthus is valid in so far as it refers to the way in which he applied his principle of population to a central issue of social policy, the system of poor relief, and read contemporary publications in order to understand it. His interest in the day-to-day management of the Poor Law appears to have been rather limited and his failure to link systematically the application of his principle to poor law policy, with the actual operation of poor relief, helps to explain some lack of consistency in his writing on the subject. It also gives an insight into the reasons why Malthus periodically admitted that the theoretical tendency of the Poor Law to increase population and aggravate poverty was not actually happening in practice. For example, in 1807 he conceded that 'the operations of the Poor Laws are so complicated that it is almost impossible to take in at one view all their different bearings and relations . . . [and] that the Poor Laws do not encourage early marriage *so much* as might naturally be expected'.[17]

II

Malthus's advocacy of the abolition of the Poor Laws stemmed both from elements in his economic theorising, and from his first statement of the principle of population. However, the subtle evolution of his views led to a fundamental restatement of the principle of population and hence to a different emphasis when this was applied to the subject of poor relief. In his first version of the principle Malthus had stated that 'the power of population is indefinitely greater than the power in the earth to produce subsistence for man. Population, when unchecked increases in a geometrical ratio. Subsistence increases only in an arithmetical ratio.'[18] In 1798, Malthus had argued that population increase might be reduced by positive checks (of misery and disease) and preventive checks (of postponement of marriage with consequent vice), but by 1803 he had developed his thinking on preventive checks with the idea of moral restraint.[19] This preventive check was defined as 'the restraint from marriage which was not followed by irregular gratification'.[20] The introduction of this moral element made his principle of population an indeterminate one, which depended for its operation on individual character. Moral restraint, involving a prudential postponement of marriage, was thus dependent on educating the poor and inculcating habits of self-reliance and self-respect. Malthus's views on poor relief reflected this concern for the elevation of the labourer's moral character.

In his view – and those of several other classical economists – the distribution of poor relief involved profound moral issues. Probably their most influential legacy in shaping the New Poor Law was the theory of unstable moral equilibrium in the life of a poor man: he might be subverted into pauperism or encouraged to retain his independence.[21] The starting point for Malthus's thinking on poverty and its relief was: 'It is by no means to be wished that any dependent situation should be made so agreeable, as to tempt those who might otherwise support themselves in independence.'[22] Social policy should tip the balance in that it should create a situation in which 'dependent poverty ought to be held disgraceful'.[23] Yet the institutional framework of the Poor Law, or its alternatives, should only hold the ring in stimulating desirable virtues of prudence and thrift in the labourer. 'The very admission of the necessity of prudence, to prevent the misery from an overcharged population, removes the blame from public institutions to the conduct of individuals.'[24]

It was the superior virtues of voluntary charity over the forced public charity of the Poor Law that made it preferable in Malthus's view. Since the incidence of voluntary charity was uncertain, no poor man could depend on it, but must rely on his own industry and forethought. Voluntary charity was better than poor relief because it exercised moral discrimination in selecting deserving objects for assistance; these were industrious, prudent individuals who needed help to overcome un- merited misfortunes. These worthy labourers would show gratitude for the assistance, rather than the indifference which characterised the recipients at the parish pay table. The charitable donor would benefit from fulfilling his moral obligation to practise the virtue of charity. Society would be improved as well, since the rich would increase their personal knowledge of the poor and closer bonds would be forged between different social ranks.[25] While the objects of charity retained self-respect, pauperism involved subjection and the extinction of honourable feelings. Malthus argued that the Poor Law should be replaced because it 'powerfully contributed to generate . . . carelessness and want of frugality'; by diminishing the will to save it weakened 'incentives to sobriety and industry, and consequently to happiness'; and removed 'one of the strongest checks to idleness and dissipation'.[26] Abundant poor relief effectively tilted the moral scales in society tempting the poor man down into improvident dependence and making more difficult his assimilation of bourgeois virtues.

For Malthus (like the Revd Joseph Townsend before him) a very important objective of social policy was to 'draw a more marked line between the dependent and independent labourer'[27] and in consequence he opposed many of the reforms for assisting the poor put forward by his meliorist contemporaries. Even those which had as their avowed aim the immediate encouragement of self-help might encounter his hostility, because Malthus felt that their long-term effect would be increased dependence. Both Arthur Young's suggestion for a potato ground and a cow for the labourer, and Samuel Whitbread's proposed legislation on the parochial provision of cottages were rejected by Malthus, since in his view they encouraged marriage and procreation, while not increasing resources proportionately.[28] Townsend's plan for universal, compulsory subscriptions to Friendly Societies to replace the Poor Law brought the predictable response that this would have the same undesirable attributes as a compulsory poor rate, while even voluntary subscriptions to these societies were condemned by Malthus in his most pessimistic mood.[29] The same reasoning might possibly have been applied to Savings Banks, but Malthus retained his belief in these institutions in helping prudence and thrift, and indeed served as a 'manager' of the

Providident Institution for Savings in West London.[30]

Malthus believed fervently in the 'moral obligation imposed on every man by the commands of God and nature to support his own children'. Pauperism was thus a practical consequence of the failure to exercise moral restraint. Hence, it was upon the moral understanding and moral character of the labourer that he felt the most lasting causes of improvement in the labouring classes were to be found.[31] It is not surprising to find him pinning his hopes on educating the poor rather than relieving them. Even a modified Poor Law 'would have a tendency to depress the independent labourer, to weaken in some degree the springs of industry and good conduct, and to put virtue and vice more on a level than they would be in the natural course of things'.[32]

III

Malthus's views on the Poor Law were complex. They involved both theoretical and practical analyses of the administration of poor relief, and policy prescriptions which included long-term ideal solutions and short-term realistic ones. In the short term, Malthus had to concede the practical necessity for poor relief in times of social distress. 'I hardly see what else could have been done,' he commented on the allowances given to the poor by the magistrates during the time of very high bread prices from 1799 to 1800.[33] His admission that poor relief was necessary during times of social distress was not just expediency but also reflected his underlying humanitarianism. It appears that it was his concern for the poor that had set him thinking about population in the first place.[34] We can see from the surviving fragments of his unpublished work of 1796, entitled *The Crisis*, that his views were similar to those of a humanitarian group of reformers who sympathised with the poor.[35] At this time, Malthus wished to relieve the poor in their own homes since 'it is certainly desirable that the assistance in this case should be given in the way that is most agreeable to the persons who are to receive it'.[36] Malthus felt that in times of high bread prices, such as 1800 or 1817, allowances could be justified since in sharing hardship they averted starvation.[37] Here 'the great moral duty of assisting our fellow creatures in distress' triumphed over abolitionist principle.[38] It was in distressed years such as 1816–17 that Malthus's conscience was most sensitive; the employment of the poor on temporary public works was useful 'to avoid the bad moral effects of idleness'.[39] To a limited extent Malthus was able to justify his humanitarian policies by economic reasoning. For example, when prices were high, temporary poor relief avoided an increase in wages which would be difficult to take back when prices came down again.[40]

The years of distress after the Napoleonic wars gave a practical demonstration, in Malthus's opinion, of Sir Frederick Morton Eden's previous conclusion that the legal right to relief under the English Poor Law could not be fulfilled.[41] But if it could not fulfil its promises then Malthus argued, as had Townsend earlier, that voluntary charity should replace the forced 'charity' of the Poor Law. This was an ideal prescription, but Malthus recognised that immediate abolition was not realistic. He appreciated that 'the relief given by the Poor-Laws [is] so widely extended, that no man of humanity could venture to propose their immediate abolition'. From this came the view that legitimate children who were born a year after legislation (or two years, if illegitimate), should have no right to relief. Therefore, abolition would come about very gradually.[42] But on the level of short-term policy Malthus, as we have seen, conceded that allowances or employment schemes under the Poor Laws were justified in years of social distress, and that the settlement laws did more good than harm. He acknowledged that abolition must wait upon a changed public opinion, including that of the labouring poor, who should 'be made to understand that they had purchased their right to a provision by law, by too great and extensive a sacrifice of their liberty and happiness'.[43]

In advocating abolition as a long-term and ideal policy objective which would ensure the happiness of the labourer, Malthus was prepared to accept that the price that would have to be paid for this involved individual hardship.[44] This led to charges of inhumanity, and an understandable identification of an apparently harsh policy with the character of its author. Malthus himself commented: 'I feel that I have no occasion to defend my character from the imputation of hardness of heart.'[45] Also, that 'I am not conscious of ever having said anything to countenance calumnious reports against the poor, and most certainly I never intended to do so'.[46] Contemporary admirers were at pains to distinguish the man from popular misunderstandings of his work. Bishop Otter eulogised Malthus as 'the most humane and considerate of men' who aimed to increase the poor's 'comforts, and to raise their moral and intellectual condition'.[47] Yet Malthus's defenders conveniently forgot the large group of helpless poor on whose fate Malthus maintained a deafening silence in nearly all his testimony. In his earliest work he took a sympathetic line towards the relief of the aged, children, or widows who could not maintain themselves through no fault of their own. Thereafter, he implicitly included them with the able-bodied poor, for whom hardship was a necessary spur to industry. This was a harder line than that of admirers, including Ricardo, who, although in agreement with the main lines of Malthusian abolitionism, still felt that these helpless poor needed relief.[48] However, Malthus typically offered a concession on this issue in 1827, when testifying to the Select Committee on Emigration. He was asked if a Poor Law system restricted only to the aged, infirm, and children would still be prejudicial and replied, 'Perhaps not.'[49]

IV

Alternately reviled and praised, Malthus's views were of central intellectual significance in shaping the debate over poor law policy for nearly forty years before the decisive reform of 1834. Pitt's Bill of 1796–7, which would have given relief as of right to families with more than two children, had been criticised by Malthus and by Bentham; their views convinced Pitt, and he became an opponent of poor law allowances.[50] During the opening years of the nineteenth century his abolitionist views attracted widespread support, as the following accolade in the *Edinburgh Review* of 1807 suggests: 'While other writers busied themselves in criticizing and amending paltry details, Mr Malthus went to the bottom of the evil, and showed that the system was so vicious in its principle, that no amendments could render it beneficial.'[51] In the same year, Samuel Whitbread, in introducing his Bill on the Poor Laws in the Commons, paid tribute to Malthus in having argued from sound principles.[52] A decade later Malthus's influence was at its height, when the Select Committee on the Poor Laws of 1817, under its Malthusian Chairman, Sturges Bourne, accepted much of the abolitionist case. In 1826, Wilmot Horton, who had corresponded with Malthus for several years on emigration, chaired the Select Committee on this subject. Its *Third Report* spoke of the empirical testimony of other witnesses having 'been confirmed in the most absolute manner by that of Mr Malthus', and advocated emigration as a means of reducing redundant labour and decreasing pauperism.[53]

The narrow focus of Malthusian argument on the able-bodied poor – on their moral condition, and redundant numbers – was to be repeated by the Royal Commission on the Poor Laws of 1832–4 and in the legislation which followed it. In the *First Essay*, Malthus had contemplated providing deterrent workhouses in each county for the able-bodied where 'the fare should be hard, and those that were able obliged to work'.[54] Later, he abandoned this idea because he argued that the dependent poor in workhouses consumed provisions, and that this diminished the resources available to sustain the independent poor.[5] His opposition to workhouses was caricatured in 1818 by Thomas Love Peacock in his novel *Melincourt*, where Malthus, personified as Mr Fox, denounces the fact that paupers marry even in the workhouse so making of it 'a flourishing manufactory of beggars and vagabonds'. Yet the workhouses set up under the Poor Law Amendment Act of 1834 were identified in the popular mind as Malthusian instruments, in which the separation of members of the family under the workhouse classification scheme would restrain the poor from breeding.[56] This stemmed from radical opinion, shaped to a considerable extent by William Cobbett, whose attacks on Malthus over the years had culminated in 1831 in his satirical melodrama *Surplus Population*. Here the fanatical Malthusian, Peter Thimble, pens a 'Remedy Against Breeding' in which he argues against 'that great national scourge, the procreation of the human species'.[57]

For contemporaries there seemed no doubt of Malthus's influence on the New Poor Law, whether they were critics of the Poor Law Amendment Act of 1834[58] or admirers like Malthus's old friend Bishop Otter. In 1836, Otter wrote that 'the Essay on Population and the Poor Laws Amendment Bill, will stand or fall together'.[59] Yet recent writers have been less confident about the nature, or degree, of Malthus's influence on this decisive reform of the Poor Law. Patricia James's comment on Otter's statement was that 'nothing could be further from the truth', J. R. Poynter stated that 'the case describing the Amendment Act as Malthusian is weak', while W. Petersen referred to Malthus's 'indirect' influence and concluded that 'in some respects he left no doubt he was opposed to the 1834 Act'.[60]

It has been suggested in this chapter that Malthus's views on the Poor Law were complicated, and further that over a period of thirty-four years they changed on several important issues. Thus, if one wishes to ask to what extent the 1834 Act was influenced by Malthus, it is possible to make a case out of either the similarities or the divergences between his opinions and the provisions of the 1834 legislation. If the 1834 Act is defined by reference to its provision for emigration subsidies, its creation of a more complex administration of the Poor Law, and its failure to take radical measures to abolish poor relief, the New Poor Law cannot be termed Malthusian. In contrast, the New Poor Law might be thus characterised if the stringent reforms of the Poor Law Amendment Act are taken as a step towards abolition, which, as we have seen, tended to Malthus's later position. This is the case, too, if the bastardy clauses (penalising unmarried mothers), and the workhouse classification scheme of the Poor Law Commission (which separated husbands and wives), are taken as applications of the principle of population. Also, the ending of outdoor allowances to the able-bodied may be viewed in the Malthusian moral context of strengthening the labourers' independence and prudence. Thus, on balance, the Poor Law Amendment Act might be considered a Malthusian measure because it reflected moral and reformist elements that were central to Malthus's later prescriptions for a practicable social policy.

The Poor Law Amendment Act had followed many of the conclusions of the Royal Commission on the Poor Laws of 1832–4. In spite of the presence of abolitionists such as Sturges Bourne, Bishop Sumner, and Bishop Blomfield in the Commission, its *Report* had come out in favour of a reform of poor relief. The reformist ideas of the two authors of the *Report*, Nassau Senior and Edwin Chadwick, decisively shaped the legislation which followed. Nassau Senior was not an orthodox Malthusian: he did not believe that population was outstripping subsistence because he emphasised to a far greater extent than did Malthus the force of the desire to better oneself, and hence the psychological drives of ambition and the achievement of self-respect as key factors in keeping the growth of population and resources in step. Unlike Malthus, he did not think that increased population *necessarily* produced poverty. Moreover, he thought abolition of poor relief impracticable.[61] His fellow author, Chadwick, commented that the enquiries of the Poor Law Commissioners had disproved the pessimistic conclusions of the population principle as it had been applied to the Poor Law.[62] He thought that it was the application of relief under the Old Poor Law, and not the principle of relief, that was wrong. Hence, he advocated reforming the Poor Law in order to remove its pernicious tendency to seduce labourers into pauperism, and to create a positive framework of law which encouraged the labourer to choose moral and economic independence.[63]

Total abolition was rejected but the moral arguments of Malthus were to help fashion the mechanism of reform. The *Report* of the Royal Commission concluded that 'under strict regulations, adequately enforced, such relief may be afforded safely and even beneficially'. The essential precondition of reformed relief was to be that the pauper's situation 'on the whole shall not be made really or apparently so eligible as the situation of the independent labourer' and that 'every penny bestowed that tends to render the condition of the pauper more eligible than that of the independent labourer, is a bounty on indolence and vice'.[64] The workhouse test of the New Poor Law was designed as the practical application of this moral principle; those who from lack of prudence and forethought were forced to seek relief would receive assistance in the deterrent conditions of the union workhouse. This was in accord with Malthus's final views on the subject: 'If it be generally considered as so discreditable to receive parochial relief, that great exertions are made to avoid it . . . there is no doubt that those who were really in distress might be adequately assisted.'[65] Those who entered the new union workhouses after 1834 were imprinted with the moral stigma of pauperism; their misfortunes were their own responsibility since the better-off had fulfilled their responsibility to them in underlining the necessity for prudence and thrift. The abrasive class character of the New Poor Law was thus rooted in the moral sentiments of Malthus.

V

Malthus admitted that public opinion was not ready to embrace his ideal policy of abolishing the Poor Laws and that he would settle for their reform: 'Practically, therefore I am inclined to look forward to the first improvement as likely to come from an improved administration of our actual laws, together with a more general system of education and moral superintendence.'[66] This moral element gives us the key to much of Malthus's thinking on the Poor Law; he advocated the elevation of the labourer so that it would increase his moral restraint and hence reduce pauperism. In doing so Malthus posed the question (which is still with us today), of how far a collectivist system of social benefits would modify an individual's attitude to work. He concluded: 'To what extent assistance may be given, even by law, to the poorest classes of society when in distress . . . depends mainly upon the feelings and habits of the labouring classes of society and can only be determined by experience.'[67] Malthus's own experience gave him a view of pauperism as a moral disease whose contagious qualities provided a built-in multiplier to an ever increasing, dependent population. His pessimistic vision of expanding poor relief increasing moral and social degradation lent urgency to the discussion on a necessary reform of the Poor Law in the years before 1834, and influenced the reforms adopted in the New Poor Law. It was neither the originality nor the consistency of his views on social welfare which gave them such relevance. Rather they commanded support because of their apparent inevitability when linked to his principle of population.

NOTES AND REFERENCES

1. S. Smith, 'Poor Law', *Edinburgh Review*, 65 (1820) 91–2.
2. *See*, for example, S. and B. Webb, *English Poor Law History*, vol. I, part II (reprinted London, 1963) pp. 21–5; S. E. Finer, *The Life and Times of Sir Edwin Chadwick*, 2nd ed. (London, 1980) p. 44; R. G. Cowherd, *Political Economists and the English Poor Law* (Athens – USA, 1977) pp. 19–20, 23. *See also* the views of contemporaries cited in notes 51 and 59.
3. T. R. Malthus, *An Essay on the Principle of Population*, Royal Economic Society facsimile of the 1798 edition (London, 1926) p. 95. Hereafter, *First Essay* refers to this edition.
4. Cowherd, op. cit., pp. 19–20; R. G. Cowherd, 'The Humanitarian Reform of the English Poor Laws from 1782–1815', *Proceedings of the American Philosophical Society*, 104 (1960) 339–40.
5. *First Essay*, op. cit., pp. 93, 98.
6. Ibid., p. 83.
7. T. R. Malthus, *An Essay*... 5th ed., vol. II (London, 1817) p. 371.
8. T. R. Malthus, *Principles of Political Economy*, 2nd ed. (London, 1836) p. 232.
9. Malthus, op cit., *An Essay*... 5th ed., vol. II, p. 368.
10. 'Select Committee on Emigration', *British Parliamentary Papers*, V (1826–7) Q.3369.
11. Ibid., QQ. 3343–4.
12. Ibid., QQ. 3252–3.
13. *First Essay*, op. cit., p. 92.
14. T. R. Malthus to the Revd T. Chalmers, 21 July 1822, quoted in P. James, *Population Malthus* (London, 1979) p. 450.
15. Malthus, op. cit., *An Essay*... 5th ed., vol. III, pp. 265–7.
16. T. R. Malthus to D. Ricardo, 26 January 1817, quoted in G. F. McCleary, *The Malthusian Population Theory* (London, 1953) p. 167.
17. 'A Letter to Samuel Whitbread, Esq. M.P.', reprinted in D. V. Glass (ed.), *Introduction to Malthus* (London, 1959) pp. 192–3.
18. *First Essay*, op. cit., pp. 13–14.
19. Ibid., pp. 63–73.
20. Malthus, op. cit., *An Essay*... 2nd ed., p. 14.
21. A. W. Coats, 'The Classical Economists and the Labourer', in A. W. Coats (ed.), *The Classical Economists and Economic Policy* (London, 1971) pp. 156–7.
22. 'The Crisis, a View of the Present Interesting State of Great Britain by a Friend to the Constitution', Extract quoted in Bishop Otter, 'Memoir of Robert Malthus' appended to Malthus, op. cit., *Principles*, 2nd ed., p. xxxvi.
23. *First Essay*, op. cit., p. 85.
24. T. R. Malthus to W. Godwin (undated letter), quoted in James, op. cit., p. 69.
25. Malthus, op. cit., *An Essay*... 5th ed., vol. III, pp. 216–23.
26. *First Essay*, op. cit., pp. 86–7.
27. 'Letter to Samuel Whitbread', loc. cit., p. 191.
28. Ibid., pp. 192–3; Malthus, op. cit., *An Essay*... 5th ed., vol. III, pp. 238–50.
29. Ibid., *An Essay*, pp. 229–33, 270–2.
30. James, op. cit., p. 222; 'letter to Samuel Whitbread', loc. cit., p. 203.

31. Ibid., 'Letter', pp. 202–3; Malthus, op. cit., *An Essay . . .* 5th ed., vol. II, p. 277.
32. Ibid., 'Letter', p. 198.
33. T. R. Malthus, *An Investigation of the Causes of the Present High Price of Provisions*, 3rd ed. (London, 1800) p. 13.
34. W. Empson, 'Life, Writings and Character of Mr Malthus', *Edinburgh Review*, 64 (1837) 479–83.
35. Cowherd, op. cit., *Political Economists*, pp. 2–23.
36. Malthus, loc. cit., 'The Crisis', p. xxxvi.
37. Malthus, op. cit., *An Investigation*, p. 19.
38. Malthus, op. cit., *An Essay . . .* 5th ed., vol. II, pp. 354–5.
39. Ibid., p. 357, and vol. III, pp. 272–7.
40. Ibid., vol. II, p. 324.
41. Ibid., pp. 351–3.
42. Ibid., vol. III, pp. 176–9.
43. 'Letter to Samuel Whitbread', loc. cit., p. 188.
44. Malthus, op. cit., *An Essay . . .* 5th ed., vol. III, pp. 181–2.
45. 'Letter to Samuel Whitbread', loc. cit., pp. 189–90.
46. T. R. Malthus to D. Ricardo, 13 September 1821, in P. Sraffa (ed.), *Works of David Ricardo*, vol. IX (Cambridge, 1952) p. 64.
47. 'Memoir of Robert Malthus', loc. cit., p. xlv.
48. M. Blaug, *Ricardian Economics* (New Haven, 1958) p. 198.
49. 'Select Committee on Emigration', loc. cit., Q. 3255.
50. J. Bonar, *Malthus and His Work*, 2nd ed. (London, 1924) pp. 29–30, 43.
51. *Edinburgh Review*, 11 (1807) 111.
52. S. Whitbread, *Substance of a Speech on the Poor Laws* (London, 1807) pp. 10–11.
53. James, op. cit., pp. 388–96.
54. *First Essay*, op. cit., p. 97.
55. Malthus, op. cit., *An Essay . . .* 5th ed., vol. II, pp. 332–3.
56. For example, F. H. Maberley, *To the Poor and their Friends* (London, 1836); T. Marsters, *Reform and Workhouses*, 2nd ed, (Lynn, 1835).
57. Quoted in H. Ausubel, 'William Cobbett and Malthusianism', *Journal of the History of Ideas*, 13 (1952) 253–6.
58. For example, A Friend to the Poor, *The Malthusian Boon Unmasked* (Maidstone, 1835) p. 11.
59. 'Memoir of Robert Malthus', loc. cit., p. xix.
60. James, op. cit., p. 451; J. R. Poynter, *Society and Pauperism: English Ideas on Poor Relief, 1795–1834* (London, 1969) p. 325; W. Petersen, *Malthus* (London, 1979) p. 114.
61. M. Bowley, *Nassau Senior and Classical Economists* (London, 1937) p. 311; McCleary, op. cit., pp. 116, 129; Finer, op. cit., p. 23.
62. *Edinburgh Review*, 63 (1836) 491–2.
63. Finer, op. cit., pp. 22–3, 44–5.
64. S. G. and E. O. Checkland (eds), *The Poor Law Report of 1834* (Harmondsworth, 1974) pp. 334–5.
65. T. R. Malthus, *A Summary of the Principle of Population*, reprint of the 1st ed. of 1830 in A. Flew (ed.), *Malthus* (Harmondsworth, 1970) p. 269.
66. T. R. Malthus to the Revd T. Chalmers, loc. cit., p. 450.
67. Malthus, op. cit., *A Summary View*, p. 269.

12 Malthusian Ideology and the Crises of the Welfare State

ANNIE VINOKUR

In his introductory paper to the 1980 International Congress of Historical Demography of *Malthus, Yesterday and Today*, Nathan Keyfitz wrote:

> One hundred and eighty-one years have passed since Malthus anonymously published the first edition of his Essay on Population. If criticism could kill a book, this one would have been extinguished in its infancy, yet it remains vital; despite its age, we do not even call it a classic, but argue with it as with a contemporary. In sheer volume of criticism of Malthus, France exceeds any other country, but it is here that we are summoned to a colloquium on Malthus, to try to explain the longevity of his work.[1]

We do not, therefore, intend to add more pages to the already superabundant discussions for and against the arguments developed by Malthus in the *Essay*, but to try to contribute to the understanding of the longevity and present success of what can be called 'Malthusian ideology'.

Of course, a ready answer to this question lies at the core of Malthusian ideology as generally received by people outside the small circle of specialists. Common dictionaries, for example, usually retain two propositions from the *Essay*: (a) the cause of human woes is to be found in the comparison between the arithmetical power of production and the geometrical power of reproduction; (b) the remedy lies in the moral restraint of human reproduction. The contradiction being in

Nature itself, not in human society, the wealthy classes are thus exonerated from the responsibility of misery, which rests with the prolific poor themselves. This would be, in all times and places, a very convenient ideology for conservative politics.

This, however, is only part of the picture, as the ideological effectiveness of the argument presupposes that the poor are prolific. In our advanced economies, where birth rates have fallen near or under the threshold of stationary population, conservative forces are generally strongly anti-Malthusian in the demographic meaning of the word. Would that imply that Malthusian ideology is now but a panacea for external use only, in our relationships with underdeveloped, over-populated countries? We do not think so.

To account better for the present revival of interest for the ideas propounded in the *Essay* in industrialised societies, we must consider two aspects:

(a) the similarities of situations, beyond the huge differences of socio-economic backgrounds. We undergo here an investigation of what is generally called the 'crisis of the welfare state'. The *Essay* was written to find an answer to the crisis of the Poor Law system at the end of the eighteenth century, that is, to the crisis of the first historical system of social protection implemented in a capitalist society, and

(b) the proposition that, in the *Essay*, Malthus's main concern was with the supply of labour; demography as such was only second, in the sense that the passion between sexes was assumed by Malthus to be the prime determinant of labour supply. A trace of this is to be found in the common acceptance of 'Malthusianism' – at least in French ency-clopaedias – as 'all sorts of voluntary restraint of supply', whether of children (demographic Malthusianism) or of goods (economic Malth-usianism). It is therefore in the vision of the labour market, then and now, that we shall search for a constant of Malthusian ideology.

I

The Crises of Social Protection Systems, the English Poor Law

All societies, past and present, have developed various systems of solidarity to cover the needs of those among their members who are unable to secure their subsistence by themselves, either because of age, illness, or disability. The specific feature of capitalistic relations of production is that any able worker is a virtual pauper: being divorced from his means of production, his access to subsistence is subordinated to external social conditions, to the rhythm and forms of capital accumulation which command the levels of both employment and wages. Therefore, as soon as a sizeable part of the workforce has entered wage earning on a permanent, lifelong basis, some sort of social protection system must develop to compensate both for the loss of traditional solidarities and for the consequences of capital accumulation on social reproduction.

The history of the Old Poor Law follows this path. Designed at first to take the place of Church charity for the impotent, while the whip took care of the 'sturdy beggars' and the magistrates of apprenticeship regulations and wage levels, it had turned two centuries later into a system of social protection. Wage fixing had been abandoned early, repression had slowed down; Tudor England used local rates to provide work for the unemployed; from the early Stuarts access to parish assistance was a right, prescribed by a national legislation and paid for by the compulsory poor rates; by the end of the eighteenth century, under systems such as Speenhamland, outdoor relief was extended from the able-bodied unemployed to the 'industrious poor' and geared to the price of corn and the number of children in the family. Financed by compulsory levies, affording assistance as a right to the fraction of the labour force unable to make a livelihood – from disability, unemployment, family burden or insufficient wages – the Poor Law at that time presented the main features of the actual systems of social protection in a capitalist setting.

The crises of social protection systems first appear in the form of financial crises. In several advanced economies, social expenditures have grown nearly one and a half times faster than GDP since 1960, and their share in national product between 1960 and 1981 grew from 7.3 per cent to 15 per cent in the USA, from 10 per cent to 19 per cent in Great Britain and 18 per cent to 26.4 per cent in West Germany.[2] The idea runs that there is a ceiling to the socially acceptable level of compulsory levies for social expenditures, and that the limit has already been exceeded. However, this had already been said long ago of public expenditure, and the fact that the ratio of social expenditure to GDP is very different from one country to the other clearly shows that it is only a political symptom of the crisis, not the real problem.

At the end of the eighteenth century, in England, there is also the financial crisis of the Poor Law. Expenditure went up from £1 million in

1770 to nearly £4 million in 1800,[3] and the cry was that it could not go up further. However, it did keep on growing, to reach nearly £8 million in 1817.

In the case of the Poor Law, the historical distance of over 150 years may help us take a better view of the contradictions underlying the contemporary political outcry. What functions had the Poor Law performed in the regulation of British society, what were the new forces at work when Malthus wrote the *Essay* and where was the breaking point?

Through two centuries, enclosures gradually established in England a capitalist definition of ownership and capitalistic relationships in agricultural production: there was the concentration of control of the means of production in the hands of a small class of landlords and farmers and the freeing of a labour force, divorced from its traditional means of subsistence. The concomitant changes in agricultural productions and techniques were certainly labour saving in the long run, but above all their implementation required a differentiation of the labour force, mainly between (a) a regular labour force, more or less fully employed the year round and (b) casual labour, paid in cash or in kind by the day or piece rate.

The problem was to keep a sufficient reserve of workers, available at any time when needed (for seasonal labour-intensive tasks like haymaking or harvest, or for irregular tasks like the making or repairing of fences), but nevertheless paid under the minimum level of yearly subsistence. Could this have been provided by small farmers for labourers by making up their subsistence with a plot of land, a cow and with what the commons could provide, as in continental Europe? No, this would have contradicted the logics of land concentration.[4] Besides, even at the end of the eighteenth century when excessive poor rates were in question, the landed interests feared that even a small amount of economic independence for the labourers would mean a shortage of hands for seasonal work.[5]

Therefore, parish assistance, combined with the settlement law which discouraged geographical mobility, secured the maintenance and local permanent availability of a sufficient reserve for precarious employment. The Poor Law Commissioner's Report of 1836 quotes one of those labourers, 'the farmers keep us here [on the poor rates] like potatoes in a pit, and only take us out for use when they can no longer do without us'.[6]

The Poor Law also performed a function of differentiation between landowners. The poor rates were administered in a decentralised fashion, in each parish, by the Justices of the Peace. They were the King's servants, but not in his pay nor in his dependence, they were country landlords who combined judicial, political, economic and administrative power. The poor rates being laid on property, their enforcement contributed to the eviction of small landowners.[7] Besides, where the 'labour rate' was in use, a ratepayer who employed labourers was excused from the tax up to the amount of the wages paid. The independent owner therefore subsidised the employers, and the eviction effect grew with the weight of the rates. In turn, it encouraged the substitution of casual work for permanent employment.

The check on geographical mobility prevented employment migration from the south to the north of England, where landowners complained of the high wages they were compelled to pay to their labourers because of the competition from nearby industrial centres.

The social protection system of the Poor Law was a powerful instrument of compromise between the conflicting interests of the two dominant classes: landlords and merchant-entrepreneurs. The expansion of commercial capital required increased production of manufactured goods and lower purchase prices from the producers. Both were found in the development of the domestic system, which evaded the restrictive practices and price regulations of the urban guilds. However, if subsistence wages were to be paid by entrepreneurs to rural workers, they would have to be geared to the cost of living, of which the price of bread was the main determinant. Sheltered from foreign competition by the Corn Laws, corn prices are said to have doubled during the second half of the eighteenth century, and rents considerably expanded as well.

If the landed interests and the entrepreneurs were in full opposition on the question of corn prices, they coincided on two points: both groups (a) needed an excess of supply of docile rural labour and (b) they valued political stability. Parish outdoor relief administration favoured the political control of rural votes.[8]

The poor rates were but a small price to pay – out of growing rents – for the landed interest to buy the merchants' support of the Corn Laws. For the entrepreneurs, the link between corn prices and nominal wages was broken as long as the rural workers could turn to parish assistance whenever they had no work or insufficient wages. Besides, assistance could be favourable to an increase of birthrates; there was work for children in the domestic system and, along mercantilist lines, from an increased supply of workers could be expected more production and lower wages. This is why the Speenhamland magistrates, who met in

1795 to enforce a minimum wage legislation (which was what the workers were asking for), eventually chose to extend outdoor relief to the industrious poor along a scale designed to cover the minimum cost of reproduction of the family in a time of rising food prices.[9] Thence

> wages fell, poor relief increased. This pauperization of the working classes at a time when industrial conditions were undergoing revolutionary change was, from a social point of view, most unfortunate; from the business point of view, it was ideal. As the poor rate increased, wages decreased and manufacturing profits correspondingly increased. In its incidence, the poor rate amounted to a species of subsidy to the manufacturers. Those manufacturers who employed parish apprentices sometimes even received annual payments from the parish for keeping its paupers at work. The taxpayers were burdened for the benefit of the manufacturing classes rather than for the support of the unfortunate.[10]

This solution to the conflict could not but have inflationary consequences on the expenditures for assistance where it was implemented, for a growing part of the labour bill was to be met through the poor rates. The number of 'beneficiaries' sometimes exceeded 10 per cent of the population; by the end of the Old Poor Law, half the cases of poverty were due to casual or irregular work, and one-fifth of the aided able-bodied received assistance for insufficient wages.[11]

What were the forces at work to find a way out of the crisis? The labourers who fell to the parish rates strongly resented the humiliation of assistance and the ignominy of the control and harassment that came with it; but the working class was segmented, by status and location, and some believe that it is owing to the Poor Law system that England avoided the social outburst of the French Revolution. The most heavily burdened by the poor rates were the numerous independent farmers in the south who were forced to subsidise both the larger farmers who employed labour and the entrepreneurs. But land concentration, with the peak of enclosures around 1800, took care of their opposition even before the fall of corn prices in the beginning of the nineteenth century. In fact, a way out of this deadlock was found only with the implementation of the new regime of industrial capital accumulation, that is, with the necessity for a radical change in the social management of the labour force. After the peak of the enclosure movement, large-scale farming required a much reduced labour force, and very little casual work. Simultaneously industry needed a geographically concentrated labour force, mobile, permanent and disciplined by the total dependency for its living on direct wages, and in sufficient numbers to press down on wage levels.

Thence was born the New Poor Law, which sanctioned the temporary alliance of landed and industrial interests as far as the mobilisation of the labour force was concerned, and, later, the repeal of the Corn Laws which marked their conflict over its reproduction.

Cash allowances then dropped (at least for a time), while collective services in kind (schools, hospitals, workhouses) developed in answer to the needs of the new regime for accumulation as far as the reproduction, mobilisation and discipline of the labour force were concerned.

In today's crisis of social protection systems, some authors explain its uncontrolled growth by extra-economic factors, demographic (ageing populations) or psychological (excess demand of 'free' services like education or health, or preference for leisure); others point to the inner dynamics of Keynesian (or Fordist) growth driven by sustained aggregate demand, of which social protection has been a powerful regulator. Few authors point to the role of social protection systems in the social management of the labour force: of the regulation of the demographic flows in and out of the labour force; of differentiation by status (the development of precarious work in the recent period would have been impossible without social protection); of categorisation of segments of the labour force (the young, the women, the handicapped, the migrants) and their channelling into specific sectors, jobs, and types of firms. Therefore, they also perform a function of differentiation/ subsidisation between the different parts of capital.

Our contention is that the crisis of today's social protection system is, like the crisis of the Poor Law system, but a reflection of a crisis in the social management of the labour force, that is, of the economic crisis considered as a major change in the regime of accumulation. In the same way, it will not come to an end before a new regime of accumulation and regulation (yet unforeseen for us as it was for Malthus's contemporaries) is set up. It is in this perspective that we shall look for some ideological similarities between Malthus's times and ours.

II

Malthusian Ideology, Yesterday and Today

Malthus was a benevolent man, 'with the most anxious desire of extending the comforts and elevating the condition of the lower classes of society'.[12] A supporter at first of the Speenhamland system, he expressed in 1798 his apprehension 'that the attempt to sanction by law a *right* which in the *nature of things* cannot be adequately gratified, may terminate in disappointment, irritation, and aggravated poverty'.[13]

The fact is that, then and now, there is much disappointment and irritation at social protection systems, and aggravated poverty. This is the mould on which Malthusian ideology – the poor are responsible for their poverty – prospers. However, to be efficient, this ideology needs: (a) some kind of theoretical, scientific grounding; (b) a subtle shift from theoretical conclusions to common sense considerations of human nature; (c) that social institutions be taken for granted – and social expenditure at its face value, as a benevolent redistributive scheme exclusively; (d) a set of political recommendations for the improvement of the scheme, taking human nature into consideration for the good of the poor themselves; and (e) a specific, segmented, social structure to carry a large adhesion, even in the lower classes.

Malthus was certainly not unaware of some aspects of the Poor Laws as a stake between conflicting interests, particularly when the interests of his own social group were concerned.[14] But had he gone further in this direction, his pamphlet would not have been such a large success. To function as a dominant ideology, an argument must reconcile several contradictory points of view, and shift the explanation of the observed phenomena to some forces outside the fabric of society, where it should rest upon the *nature of things*. Therefore, whether the growth of the poor rates was but a consequence of growing poverty, or also the outcome of other factors was not in question; nor was the origin, logic and history of the institution of the Poor Law. Malthus endeavoured to establish the reason why there would be no satisfactory legal provision for the poor.

Three main propositions provided the structural and theoretical arguments of the *Essay*:

(a) there is an imperious, all pervading law of nature, which checks the constant tendency to increase all animated life within the bounds prescribed by the nourishment prepared for it;
(b) this natural law governs human populations, but its mode of operation is not the same in the different stages of human society;
(c) but the present stage of society, with a class of proprietors and a class of labourers, is itself the necessary result of nature's inevitable laws.

We are concerned here with the articulation between the first and the second proposition: how can the natural law of necessity – the constant tendency of population to increase beyond the means of subsistence –

explain the state of misery to be observed in the working class in the present stage of society? As the labourers have access to their subsistence through two markets (the labour market and the food market), the demonstration must show how the two natural opposing forces of population and subsistence can determine both the nominal and the real wage levels. To this central problem, recurrent all through the *Essay*, Malthus gave several, often contradictory answers. From these, we extract two main approaches.

The first and easiest concentrates exclusively on the market for subsistence. Supposing a constant nominal price of labour (which will generally by the case if the increase of manufactures and commerce be sufficient to employ the new labourers that are thrown into the market, and to prevent the increased supply from lowering the money price), then 'the increased number of labourers receiving the same money-wages will necessarily, by their competition, increase the money-price of corn. This is in fact a real fall in the price of labour'.[15]

But Malthus had to answer to the objection that 'many countries, at the period of their greatest degree of populousness, have lived in the greatest plenty, and have been able to export corn'.[16] There were two possibilities: one was to report in the distant future the effects of the law of necessity, 'but this increase, after a certain period, will be very different from the natural and unrestricted increase of population; it will merely follow the slow augmentation of produce from the gradual improvement of agriculture, and population will still be checked by the difficulty of procuring subsistence';[17] the second was to consider the labour market;

> the precise measure of the population in a country thus circumstan-ced will not indeed by the quantity of food, because part of it is exported, but the quantity of employment. The state of this employment however will necessarily regulate the wages of labour, on which the power of the lower classes to procure food depends . . . The quantity of employment in any country will not of course vary from year to year in the same manner as the quantity of produce must necessarily do, from the variations of the seasons; and consequently the check from want of employment will be much more steady in its operation, and much more favourable to the lower classes of people, than the check from the immediate want of food.[18]

In both cases the demand for labour is treated as an *exogenous variable*, as is the supply of food. So both money and real wages seem to depend only on the supply of labour which was the aim of the demonstration.

The second approach is a naive physiocratic theory of the wage fund, as exposed in his famous passage on the origins of wage earning:

> those who were born after the division of property would come in a world already possessed. The number of these persons would soon exceed the ability of the surplus produce to supply. Moral merit is a very difficult criterion, except in extreme cases. The owners of surplus produce would in general need some more obvious mark of distinction; and it seems to be both natural and just that, except upon particular occasions, their choice should fall upon those who were able, and professed themselves to be willing, to exert their strength in procuring a further surplus of produce, which would at once benefit the community and enable the proprietors to afford assistance in greater numbers. *The fund appropriated to the maintenance of labour would be the aggregate quantity of food possessed by the owners of land beyond their own consumption. When the demands upon this fund were great and numerous it would naturally be divided into very small shares. Labour would be ill-paid.*[19]

Of course, Malthus had some sound ideas about the relationships between wages, profits and capital accumulation, especially when he expressed the point of view of agricultural capital against manufactures and commerce, but had he gone further in this direction his natural theory of wages would have been thrown to pieces. He would, besides, have come to the problem of how to explain, by the contradictory general forces of population and subsistence, why only a specific part of the working class fell to misery and parish assistance.

Thus, the theoretical apparatus serves mainly as a (pseudo) scientific substratum for common preconceptions about human nature. We already find them in a letter of Malthus to Nassau Senior, where he gives another interpretation of the conflicting forces of population and subsistence: the growth of population is *instinctive*, while the increase of food presupposes work, which is *acquired*; 'a slight comparison will show the immensity of the first power over the second'.[20] The *Essay* is swarming with moral considerations of human nature: reluctance to effort, indolence, persevering idleness and misconduct, lack of prudence, foresight and virtue. Are the poor those who do not fight against these natural tendencies, and therefore do not fit both their number and their behaviour to the exogenous fluctuations of the demand for labour and the supply of food, on which human action has no power?

All policies which allow the free hands some amount of security can only, as a consequence, have perverse effects: 'it is only that kind of *systematic and certain* relief, on which the poor can confidently depend, whatever may be their conduct, that violates general principles in such a manner as to make it clear that the general consequence is worse than the particular evil'.[21] Nor is it only state assistance which Malthus opposes, he is equally opposed, on the same grounds, to Condorcet's proposition for the creation of an insurance fund supplied by the workers' own savings.[22]

By stressing the disciplinary effects of insecurity, Malthus certainly gives support to the 'less State' liberal outcry. However, he also calls for an alternative management of social expenditure, which should be distributed in kind and more discriminately. Social expenditure should 'attempt to better the condition of the labouring classes . . . by cultivating a spirit of independence, a decent pride, and a taste for cleanliness and comfort',[23] through the development of institutions like schools or savings banks, in the later case because 'By giving to each individual the full and entire benefit of his own industry and prudence, they are calculated greatly to strengthen the lessons of Nature and Providence.'[24] In as much as material help was necessary, he was not entirely against cheap soup, the general improvement of the cottages or the provision of a cow and a potato patch, as long as they did not result in (a) lower food prices and lower wages, (b) increased population, (c) indolence, for (even partial) economic independence has the same effects as parish assistance: 'it has always been observed that those who work chiefly on their own property, work very indolently and unwillingly when employed by others'.[25]

Assistance, therefore, whether in cash, in food, or in means of production, must be distributed discriminately, that is, neither generalised nor given to the poor who has 'involved himself in these difficulties by his indolence or imprudence'.[26] On these grounds, assistance must be administered on a decentralised basis.[27] Ricardo also saw in such a mode of collection and application of the Poor Law a mitigation of its pernicious effects.[28]

Nowadays, the main theoretical background of Malthusian ideology is a revised version of the neo-classical theory of wages. In traditional neo-classical theory, labour is a homogeneous factor of production, the price of which – in general equilibrium, that is, in pure competitive markets – equates its marginal productivity. In other words: (a) except for some differences in the relative toil of jobs, the price of labour tends to be uniform; (b) wage earners receive what – considering their number and willingness to work – they deserve, that is, what they contribute to total product; (c) there can be no involuntary unemployment, except if union or state intervention (through wage regulations) prevents the price of labour from falling to its natural, equilibrium level. Voluntary unemployment is, of course, possible if some labourers refuse to work for the current wage, an attitude greatly enhanced by the possibility to secure other means of subsistence, for example, through state assistance.

This theoretical construct – like Malthus's – largely occults the demand for labour and its determinants, and throws back on to the supply side of the labour market (the number and attitudes of the workers) the determinants of the wage level and the volume of unemployment. In addition, there is a moral justification for things as they are: everyone (wage earners as well as proprietors) receives what he deserves as long as there is no collective interference with the free play of the markets.

However, in the years following the Second World War, it appeared that poverty grew in the most prosperous economy, the United States, as it had grown at the end of the eighteenth century in the dominant economy which was then England. Thus appeared the analytically puzzling – and politically hot – question of why persistent poverty existed amidst plenty? It affected specific groups of the population (the young and the ageing, women, minority groups, unqualified and precarious workers, and so on) and at first a political solution was looked for by the development of social cash transfers, up to the point of negative income tax schemes. But there was much discontent: such schemes did not check the expansion of poverty; overburdened middle-class taxpayers, who already contributed to private insurance schemes, found it unjust; employers complained that it was a premium for idleness; the beneficiaries resented the social control and debasement that went with it.

A new, 'human capital' school of economic thought therefore endeavoured to account – within the general neo-classical framework – for the differentiation of wages which had been left unexplained by traditional theory. The complex hierarchical structure of earnings (and therefore the persistence of poverty at the bottom) in perfect competitive labour markets was theorised in the following manner. Wages have two components: one is the reward of simple labour; the other is the yield of investments in future productivity embodied by the individuals through a combination of personal effort and ability on the one side, and of costs (foregone earnings and direct expenditure) on the other. Formal education, on-the-job training, health, mobility, information, are such

182   *Malthusian Ideology and the Crises of the Welfare State*

investments in human capital. The rational individual invests in himself up to the point where the marginal yield expected (in terms of additional earnings) is equal to the opportunity return (the yield of alternative non-human investments). The model can also account for rational voluntary unemployment: the opportunity cost of being unemployed (loss of wages) is an investment in the search for a better job, so that the higher the unemployment allowances, the lower the cost of the investment and the longer the period of voluntary unemployment.

It was a very optimistic construct. Education, health, information, all good things and very much desired for themselves, would also promote individual economic betterment and aggregate economic growth (thence the international diffusion and enthusiastic adoption of the model). They would tend to equalise earnings and, by turning assisted population into more productive workers, be a positive alternative to passive cash transfer policies which maintain poverty instead of curing it. Social investment would replace social assistance with none of the perverse effects of the latter on labour supply.

Collective expenditure on education and health grew very rapidly during the 1960s and the beginning of the seventies (twice as fast as GNP in many countries), with seemingly no spectacular results on economic equality and on poverty. The 'segmented labour market' approach then tried empirically to explain the persistent differentiation and discrimination (both in work and unemployment) of the labour force by the complex interplay of socio-economic forces, in which labour demand – through the changing conditions of capital accumulation and the differentiated policies of employers and state – had a determinant role. But this, of course, is no satisfactory ground for ideology.

With the economic crisis and mounting unemployment, and the parallel growth of poverty and social expenditures (on social transfers, and education and health), the anti-welfare state liberal creed fed on both old and new Malthusian arguments:

(1) besides the ever present argument that taxes are levied on potentially productive capital (which goes for public expenditure in general), unemployment, precariousness and low wages are ascribed to excessive supply of labour. Demographic factors are seldom mentioned, though immigration or woman's foolish insistence on working is;

(2) the new arguments are easily derived from the modern neo-classical approach, as methodological individualism presupposes some kind of 'human nature', and therefore opens the door to moral considerations and prejudices. Those are the same under new words: irrationality has

replaced improvidence and lack of foresight, a preference for leisure has replaced indolence, undereducation has replaced lack of virtue, instability has replaced misconduct, and so on. In any system of thought which says that every one receives what he deserves – under the general constraint of scarcity – as long as no one interferes with the free play of natural laws, the persistence of misery amidst plenty can only be referred to the individual deficiency of the particular characteristics of the specific groups concerned.

As in Malthus's times, the liberal creed implies not only 'less State' but also fewer 'other state' policies. The policies advocated are similar. It is as impossible to abolish social protection immediately as it was to abolish the Poor Law. However, its vices could be mitigated by a better, more discriminate administration of social expenditure: more assistance and less insurance; aid should concentrate on the really needy and not be misallocated as a 'right' with its perverse effects on workers' willingness to work and exertion; aid should preferably be given in kind rather than in cash; the spirit of enterprise and independence should be enhanced (subsidies to the unemployed for the creation of private enterprises has replaced the acre and a cow approach), and so on. Therefore a decentralised collection and allocation of assistance is also advocated.

III

We have contended, so far, that there has been a powerful resurgence of Malthusian ideology, and tried to draw a parallel between the two crises of social protection systems, and the two intellectual constructs which support (or are consistent with) this ideology and its policy implications. But one could object that the ingredients were there before Malthus and have remained ever since; so how do we account for the fact that this ideology, at first sight fitted for the wealthy classes, could at times command an audience out of proportion?

Here we can only make a few tentative suppositions. The first one is that the cradle of Malthusian ideology is not a dominant or ascending social group, but a dying out middle class of independent workers, threatened by capital concentration and sticking to its only superiority over the wage earners, that of the country mouse over the town mouse. For example, what Malthus voiced was mainly the resentment of independent farmers, first crushed under the poor rate taxes for the benefit of agricultural and manufacturing employers, and then all the more threatened by enclosure and eviction.

184 Malthusian Ideology and the Crises of the Welfare State

Our second hypothesis is that it is adopted by employers as a convenient unifying ideology for a highly heterogeneous group when it comes to personnel management; for example (to oversimplify), from dominant, labour-saving fractions of capital – offering high wages, security of employment and good promotion perspectives – to declining or dominated sectors which could not survive but for low wages and precarious jobs – and therefore without the complex and costly apparatus of social protection systems which both compensate for insufficient wages and for periods of unemployment and channel into these jobs specific categories of the labour force. What they at least have in common, besides contributing (unequally) to social expenditure, is that they value general flexibility in the labour force (mobility and adaptation to changing working conditions) and resent infringements of their property rights over all factors of production.

Our third supposition is that the more finely segmented and differentiated is the wage earning force, the deeper can Malthusian ideology penetrate it. From the overtaxed salaried upper-middle and middle-class groups down to the smallest neo-corporatist vested interest, it is a suitable ideology to give vent to feelings of both resentment and superiority.

Lastly, if the 'moral hazard' ideas will be backed mainly by conservative forces, the eloquent Malthusian pleading against the humiliation, harassment and social control of bureaucratised assistance, and its praise of the spirits of independence and pride can appeal, then and now, to those who resent being kept 'like potatoes in a pit'.

Both in Malthus's and in our times, in widely different stages of development, we notice an apparent paradox: the crisis revives and creates numerous social protection devices, and simultaneously numerous dissertations against social protection. We have tried to support the proposition that these are not contradictory, but, on the contrary, indissoluble and complementary movements.

NOTES AND REFERENCES

1. But originally from N. Keyfitz, 'Passion and Reason in the Writings of Malthus', draft paper, Malthus Colloquium, 21 April 1979, p.1.
2. E. Andreani and others, 'Evolution et Perspectives de la Protection Sociale dans Cinq Economies Dominantes', Working Paper, Paris, 1984.
3. Cf. J. D. Marshall, *The Old Poor Law, 1795–1834* (London, 1968).
4. To the argument of greed a new argument was added for general enclosure – that of social discipline. The commons . . . were now seen as a

dangerous centre of indiscipline . . . It became a matter of public-spirited policy for the gentleman to remove cottagers from the commons, reduce his labourers to dependance, pare away at supplementary earnings, drive out the smallholder.

E. P. Thompson, *The Making of the English Working Class* (London, 1968) pp. 242–3.

5.   When a labourer becomes possessed of more land than he and his family can cultivate in the evenings . . . the farmer can no longer depend on him for constant work, and the hay making and harvest . . . must suffer to a degree which . . . would sometimes prove a national inconvenience.

Ibid., p. 243 quoting from the *Commercial and Agricultural Magazine* of 1800.

6. Ibid., p. 247.
7. Cf. L. M. Moreau-Christophe, *Du Problème de la Misère*, book 3, part 2 (Paris, 1951) chapter 1.
8. Cf. a letter from Bentham to Pitt in 1795 quoted in E. Halévy, *La Formation du Radicalisme Philosophique* (Paris, 1901) p. 328. We can also mention that a number of landlords had used part of their rents to enter manufacturing industry.
9. The demographic concern is clear in the Speenhamland provisions of 1795;

let us make relief a matter of right and honour, instead of a ground for opprobium and contempt. This will make a large family a blessing and not a curse; and this will draw a proper line of distinction between those who are to provide for themselves by their labour, and those who, after enriching their country with a number of children, have a claim upon its assistance for their support.

Quoted in J. Bonar, *Malthus and His Work* (London, 1966) p. 30.

10. B. Reuter, *Population Problems* (Chicago, 1923) p. 160.
11. M. Rose, *The Relief of Poverty: 1834–1914* (London, 1973).
12. T. R. Malthus, 'A Letter to Samuel Whitbread on his Proposed Bill for the Amendment of the Poor Laws', in *The Pamphlets of T. R. Malthus* (reprinted New York, 1970) p. 37.
13. Ibid.
14. For example, 'the funds for the maintenance of labour are thus turned from the support of a trade which yields a proper profit, to one which cannot maintain itself without a bounty'; 'the poor laws in England appear to have contributed to raise the price of provisions, and to lower the real price of labour', T. R. Malthus, *An Essay on Population*, Everyman edition, vol.II (London, 1927) pp. 55 and 49 respectively.
15. Ibid., vol. I, p. 17.
16. Ibid., vol. II, p. 137.
17. Ibid.
18. Ibid., pp. 137–40.
19. Ibid., pp. 20–1, my emphasis.
20. Quoted in Bonar, op. cit., p. 66.
21. Malthus, op. cit., *An Essay*, vol.II, p. 249.
22. Ibid., p. 3.

23. Ibid., p. 215.
24. Ibid., p. 243.
25. Ibid., p. 233.
26. Ibid., p. 221.
27. Ibid., p. 239.
28.   Each parish raises a separate fund for the support of its own poor. Hence it becomes an object of more interest and more practicability to keep the rates low than if one general fund were raised for the relief of the poor of the whole kingdom. A parish is much more interested in an economical collection of the rate, and a sparing distribution of relief, when the whole saving will be for its own benefit, than if hundreds of other parishes were to partake of it.

D. Ricardo, *The Principles of Political Economy and Taxation*, Everyman edition (London, 1965) p. 62.

Part IV
Capital: An Age of Commercial and Capital Expansion

13 The Growth of British Exports 1783–1820[1]

FRANÇOIS CROUZET

It can ... little be doubted that in this country, from 1783 to 1814, the whole exchangeable value of the produce, estimated either in domestic and foreign labour, or in bullion, was greatly augmented every year. In this increase of value, as well as riches, the extension of our foreign commerce has been considered, almost without a dissentient opinion, as a most powerful agent.

Thus wrote Malthus in his *Principles of Political Economy* (1820),[2] and several times in this work he stresses 'the general and powerful tendency of foreign commerce, to raise the value of the national income', as it increases 'immediately ... the value of that part of the national revenue which consists of profits ... and occasions [an] animated demand for labour, produce and capital'; 'if from the time of Edward I we had had no foreign commerce, our revenue from the land alone would not have approached to what it is at present, and still less our revenue from trade and manufactures', even 'if the same ingenuity had been exercised in the invention of machinery'.[3]

As a matter of fact, Malthus's formative years had seen in Britain both a 'rapid and astonishing increase in the value of national wealth', and an unprecedented upsurge of foreign trade, including domestic exports, which were massively made up of manufactured goods.

Moreover, in the late eighteenth and early nineteenth century, foreign trade was among the few sectors of the national economy about which detailed information was regularly available, as statistics extracted from the Customs accounts were published by government; they were also reproduced and discussed in various pamphlets and books. As a matter of fact, the bulk of those statistics were defective, and sometimes misleading: they were computed according to the system of so-called

189

official values (OV), which made them quite unreliable as 'values', though they were satisfactory as volume indicators. However, from 1796 onward, figures of *declared* or *real*, that is current values (CV) of total exports were computed and published.[4]

I

British exports had suffered a serious depression in the late 1760s and in the 1770s, mainly because of the conflict with the thirteen colonies and the American war. But, after a trough in 1781, they rose very fast and continuously until 1792; their official value increased by 141 per cent between these two dates, at a mean rate of growth of 7 per cent per annum.[5]

This upsurge was at first largely a rebound from the artificially low level to which exports had been forced by the war, a result from the backlog of orders which had accumulated in the markets which had been cut off from Britain. Nonetheless, the growth of exports during the 1780s and early 1790s had an unprecedented and spectacular character; their earlier rise in the mid-eighteenth century had been far less sharp. There was a decisive change of momentum in the course of exports, which entered an entirely new stage. After a setback at the beginning of the French wars, there was a new and very sharp upsurge of exports from 1797 to 1802, so that the rate of growth from 1792 to 1802 was 6 per cent, only one point lower than from 1781 to 1792; this difference cannot be interpreted as a sign of deceleration. The 1790s and early 1800s were prolongations of the 1780s as far as British exports were concerned and, taken together, those twenty years were one of the major leaps forward in their history. Moreover, owing to the rise in prices, the increase of export values was still sharper than that of volumes.

On the other hand, there was a definite turning point around 1802 in the progress of exports. Their volumes drifted downwards from 1802 to 1808 and, despite new peak figures in 1809, 1810 and 1814, recovery during the later part of the Napoleonic war was far less pronounced than the upsurge they had known around 1800. The rate of growth of United Kingdom exports from 1802 to 1814 was 3.2 per cent per year for official values, and 2 per cent only from Imlah's volume series. As for current values, their growth rate for those years was extremely low (0.7 per cent) and they suffered an actual fall from 1815 to the late 1820s. On the other hand, despite the post-war slumps of 1816 and 1819, the volume figures continued to rise in trend.

This difference in the behaviour of volumes and values results, of course, from the fall in the price of manufactured exports (and especially of cotton goods and yarn), which started at the turn of the century, thanks to technological progress. Imlah's index of average export prices falls by 5 per cent between 1800/2 and 1810/12 and by 38 per cent between 1810/12 and 1820/2. Malthus was too optimistic when he wrote in his *Principles*:

> A great fall in the price of particular commodities, either from improved machinery or foreign commerce, is perfectly compatible with a continued and great increase . . . in the exchangeable value of the whole produce of these particular articles themselves. It has been repeatedly stated that the whole value of the cottons produced in this country has been prodigiously increased, notwithstanding the great fall in their price'.[6]

On the whole, despite this slowing down after 1802, the period from 1781 to 1814 was marked by a fast increase in the volume of British exports, at a mean rate of 4.1 per cent per year. As for current values, as recalculated by Ralph Davis, their rate of growth between 1784/6 and 1814/16 was not less than 4.3 per cent.[7] However, there was a 'cyclical' pattern of long fluctuations in the rate of growth of exports in the eighteenth and nineteenth centuries, with, during the period under consideration, an upswing of fast growth from 1782 to 1802 followed by a phase of much slower growth, which extended astride the Napoleonic war and the post-war years. Malthus was too close to this change to discern it clearly and attempted to consider the war period as a whole; still, in the last pages of the *Principles*, he appears puzzled by the duration and seriousness of the post-war recession.[8]

II

In the preface to the 1817 edition of *An Essay on the Principle of Population*, Malthus reminded his readers that it had been 'first published at a period of extensive warfare, combined, from peculiar circumstances, with a most prosperous foreign commerce'.[9] Indeed, like many of his contemporaries, he marvelled at the 'increase in . . . national wealth, which had taken place during the last thirty or forty years', despite the wars: 'owing to the union of great powers of production with great consumption and demand, the prodigious destruction of capital by the government was much more than recovered'.[10]

On the other hand, many economic historians have thought that the

'Napoleonic' wars actually stimulated Britain's economic growth, and especially her exports, but the impact of the factors which are often quoted as stimuli must not be overestimated. The wars are thought to have crippled Britain's major continental competitors; indeed, the Revolution and warfare seriously harmed French industry and French exports during the 1790s.[11] But, as the rise of British exports in the 1790s and 1800s resulted mainly from the upsurge of cottons exports, the competition which was crippled to the advantage of Britain was a potential much more than an actual one, as the pre-1789 French cotton industry was not competitive with the British and did not export much. As for other continental cotton industries, they were actually saved from British competition by the protection they enjoyed under the continental blockade. Still, the fact that French manufactures, such as silks and linen, could not reach some of their former markets did help British cottons to replace them.

Britain's ascendancy at sea is also supposed to have favoured her trade by cutting off her competitors from overseas markets and giving her a monopoly of them. However, this did not happen before the Royal Navy was in absolute control of the seas, that is, in the later years of the Napoleonic war. But the great boon to British exports in these years came from the opening of Brazil and of the Spanish colonies, which was a consequence of political and military developments in the Peninsular in 1807 and 1808, much more than a benefit accruing directly from sea power. However, the latter made easy the conquest of enemy colonies and thus gave to Britain some new markets which, though not very large, were not insignificant.

On the whole, the wars brought about some trade diversion to the benefit of Britain, but it does not seem to have been very large, except the capture of Latin American markets from 1808 onward. As for the exports boom which developed from 1790 to 1802, it was mainly due to the fall in the prices of cotton goods. And the fast growth of exports to the United States, which was a major development during the 1790s, was only marginally stimulated by the war and resulted mainly from the increased demand by the fast growing and widening American home market.

On the other hand, the wars had a serious negative impact upon exports, through the closure of markets, when European countries joined France against England or were occupied by the French. The continental blockade, which, despite extensive smuggling, was pretty effective at times in closing most European markets to British goods, and the dispute with the United States, from 1807 onward, culminating in the war of 1812, were undoubtedly instrumental in the slowing down of the growth of British exports in the last years of the wars.

To sum up, the French wars – in the long run, as the influence of military and political development upon short-term fluctuations of trade was unquestionably very strong[12] – might have been either slightly unfavourable or neutral towards British exports.

III

'In carrying on the late war,' wrote Malthus in 1820, 'we were powerfully assisted by our steam-engines, which enabled us to command a prodigious quantity of foreign produce and foreign labour. But how would their efficacy have been if we could not have exported our cottons, cloths and hardware?' The choice of those articles was not accidental; Malthus had pointed out earlier that, in 1817, 'the exports of three articles alone in which machinery is used – cottons, woollen and hardware' made up a very large share of total British exports.[13]

If the goods which were responsible for the growth of British exports are considered, this growth during the war period appears very much 'unbalanced'. This had not been the case during the 1780s, when exports of all major commodities increased fast; if exports of cottons grew much faster than the rest, they had started from a low level and their contribution to the increase in the *official* value of total exports between 1780/2 and 1790/2 was only 16 per cent, much inferior to that of woollens and worsteds (36 per cent); the contribution of ironwares was small, just under 10 per cent. The leap forward of exports in the 1780s was not based on innovations in the cotton and iron industries, and the significance of these pioneers of the Industrial Revolution for the export trade must not be overestimated. Despite the spectacular rise in cottons exports, there was a general advance on a broad front, as earlier in the eighteenth century.

However, a different pattern emerged during the 1790s and 1800s. The growth of cotton exports by volume accelerated and, from 1792 to 1802, reached the amazing rate of 17.3 per cent per year; it was to go on during the next decade at a slower, but still impressive pace, of 8.4 per cent. As for woollens and worsted exports, they maintained up to 1802 the same relatively high rate of growth (nearly 5 per cent per annum) as from 1783 to 1792, but their volume reached a peak in 1801 and then fell markedly. For the other types of goods, the rates of growth were much lower after 1792 than in the preceeding decade and for silks and non-ferrous metals there was eventually a fall in the volume of exports.

As a consequence of these differentials in growth rates, cotton goods and yarns were responsible for 73 per cent of the increase in the *current* value of British exports between 1794/6 and 1804/6, and for the whole increase which took place from 1803 up to 1812. Altogether, from 1784/6 to 1814/16, exports of cotton goods and yarns, at *current* values, increased over twentyfold, while those of wool and other textiles, non-ferrous metals and 'other goods' increased three or fourfold only, and iron goods exports actually fell; cotton articles were responsible for 53 per cent of the increase in total exports against 14 per cent for woollens and worsteds, 7 per cent for the other textiles, 8 per cent for non-ferrous metals, 18 per cent for 'other goods'.

Malthus did not fail to discern the reasons for the enormous increase in cotton exports: 'The natural tendency of machinery is, by cheapening the commodity produced, so to extend the market for it, as to increase its whole value. This has been strikingly the case in the cotton trade; and when machinery has this effect, its enriching power is prodigious.'[14] Thanks to 'machinery', and to cheap cotton-wool from the United States, cottons enjoyed relative and increasing cheapness compared with other fabrics. So there was substitution of British cottons for other fabrics and for non-British cottons, but also creation of a new market through the overall expansion in volume of the demand for textiles. This trade creation effect of technological progress was stressed by Malthus: 'Facilities of production have the strongest tendency to open markets, both at home and abroad', he wrote, adding, about the 'introduction of machinery', that 'the presumption always is that it will lead to a great expansion of wealth and value'.[15]

The spectacular change in the commodity structure of British exports, which resulted from the rise of cotton articles, is well known. Their ratio to total exports at current values rose sharply: from 6 per cent in 1784/6 to 40 per cent in 1814/16; while the share of most other manufactures declined markedly – for instance woollen and worsted goods from 29 to 18 per cent. There was a reversal of the trend towards a broadening of the range of exports which had prevailed in the eighteenth century and their dramatic expansion was narrowly based, mainly, from the 1790s, on the upsurge of cotton exports. After 1815, however, there was a renewed diversification.

IV

As for changes in the geographical spread of British exports, they display an intricate and shifting pattern, especially during the French wars, when overseas markets were liable to close or to open suddenly, according to political and military developments; nonetheless, some broad trends can be isolated.

The conflict with the colonies and the American war had reversed the 'Americanisation' of British trade which had been an outstanding development of the previous decades. Even for a few years after the peace, exports to Europe progressed at the same pace as those to the United States and made a much larger contribution to the recovery of total exports. But they slowed down markedly after 1788, while shipments to the United States rose sharply and indeed more than doubled within four years; they played a decisive part in the exports boom which culminated in 1792 and which was America-based. There is no valid reason to speak, about the 1780s, of an 'invasion' of Europe by British manufactures, thanks to the recent technological breakthroughs, and to see such an invasion as a decisive factor in the upsurge of exports.

The shift towards America became more pronounced after the beginning of war with France. Exports to Europe fell sharply in 1793 and again in 1797, while exports to the United States also had a setback in 1793, but henceforth rose quite fast up to 1801; shipments to the British West Indies increased too and new markets were opened in the 'Conquered West Indies'. Thus exports to the New World rose by 50 per cent from 1788/92 to 1793/7, while those to Europe fell by 26 per cent.

However, there was a turning point in the very last years of the eighteenth century. The 'Americanisation' of British exports reached its maximum in 1798, when the New World absorbed 61 per cent of total exports. But exports to the West Indies and to the whole of America reached their peak in 1799 and then fell back. On the other hand, in 1798, exports to Europe (mostly to northern Europe) started an upward movement which went on strongly up to 1802. There was a 'return to Europe' and a partial reversal of the previous switch towards America. If one is to find an 'invasion' of Europe by British manufactures, it is during those few years from 1798 to 1802, but it was an invasion by cotton goods and yarns almost exclusively: exports of cotton to Europe rose amazingly from £0.7 million in 1797 to nearly £4.8 million in 1802 (OV).

Yet this movement was reversed as soon as war had broken out again in 1803. As French dominion over Europe extended and as Napoleon tried to close it to British trade, exports to the Continent declined up to 1807. On the other hand, shipments to the United States rose fast again to peaks in 1806 and 1807, and there was some progress in trade to other parts of America. Indeed, thanks to those increased exports to the New

World, losses of markets in Europe were nearly balanced. Still, the swing was not as pronounced as the earlier ones.

On the contrary, the next shift was quite clear-cut. The continental blockade nearly closed northern Europe to British goods during some years and, despite intensive smuggling in 1809 and 1810, average exports to that area for 1808/12 were 42 per cent lower than in 1803/7. Exports to the United States were also seriously reduced (by 36 per cent) by Jefferson's and Madison's policies. On the other hand, the Peninsular war opened widely to British exporters the markets of Portugal, Spain and their colonies. Exports to southern Europe increased more than threefold from 1803/7 to 1808/12, while those to the West Indies and Latin America more than doubled. These new markets more than made up for the lost outlets in northern Europe and in the United States. The collapse of Napoleon's Empire and the Peace of Ghent brought about a sharp recovery of exports to northern Europe and to the United States, but it was short-lived, and in the post-war years, there was a recession in trade with these two areas, while exports were expanding to 'new' markets, like India, Africa and Latin America.

From 1783 to the end of the Napoleonic wars, the increase of British exports was achieved through a succession of shifts between the main trading areas in Europe and America, one or two of them absorbing most of the additional exports for a few years – and also making good for the setbacks elsewhere. But a final balance sheet of those thirty years shows that America, and especially the United States, played a decisive part: it was responsible for 60 per cent of the total additional exports (OV) which were achieved between 1783 and 1812 (32 per cent for the United States alone).[16]

V

In the quotation which opens this paper, Malthus asserted that, from 1793 to 1814, foreign commerce had been for Britain 'a most powerful agent' of enrichment. Many writers have shared and generalised to other periods this view of trade as an 'engine of growth'. However, D. Eversley and P. Bairoch have claimed that exports played a marginal role only in British economic growth during most of the eighteenth century, up to *c*.1780. On the other hand, the position seems to have been different and the impact of foreign trade much stronger during the last twenty years of the century. Of course, national income estimates for this period are not too reliable, but if we use Deane and Cole's figures, the 'exports proportion' (or ratio of exports to national income, both at current prices), which had been quite low, 8 per cent, in 1783, rose very fast subsequently and *c*.1801 it had more than doubled, to reach 18 per cent; some additional evidence supports this estimate. As for the incremental ratio of exports to national income, between 1783 and 1801, it would have been as high as 40 per cent.

However, N.F.R. Crafts considers that the Deane and Cole figure for national income in 1783 is far too high; his own new estimates of national income give exports proportions of 10.5 per cent in 1780 and 15.3 per cent in 1801, and an incremental ratio of exports to national income between those two dates of 19.3 per cent, which is under one half of the percentage which this writer has suggested.[17] On the other hand, there is agreement on a very low incremental ratio for the earlier period 1760–80,[18] so that both calculations give to exports a more important role after the end of the American war than before it.

As British exports consisted mostly of manufactures, their increase must have had a relatively greater impact upon the growth of industry than upon national income. A recent calculation by W. A. Cole of the ratio of exports to final industrial output (gross value, at constant prices) shows an increase from 27.6 per cent *c*.1780 to 34.5 per cent *c*.1800.[19] From Cole's figures, the incremental ratio of exports to industrial production from 1780 to 1800 is 42 per cent, but Crafts maintains that the increase in output has been overestimated by Cole, and his own computations give therefore a higher ratio – 58 per cent.[20] Whichever of these guess-estimates is the best, there is no doubt that exports were a powerful engine of growth for British industry during the crucial twenty years of change at the end of the eighteenth century.

This is supported by the available data about the main industries. In the cotton industry, the ratio of exports to final output had been low, under 20 per cent, in the early 1780s, but rose dramatically in the 1790s; it may have reached two-thirds around 1805, and a highly conjectural calculation suggests that exports would have absorbed over 80 per cent of the additional output achieved by the cotton industry between 1784/6 and 1805/7. 'Are there any plausible grounds whatever', asked Malthus in 1820, 'for stating that, if the twenty millions worth of cottons which we now export, were entirely stopped ... we should have no difficulty in finding employment for our capital and labour equally advantageous to individuals ... and ... enriching to the country?'[21]

The incremental exports–output ratio was also high in the wool industry and the proportion of exports to output rose markedly; it might have reached 50 to 60 per cent at the close of the eighteenth century. But the case of the iron industry appears different. Exports grew fast in the 1780s, but this impetus was not maintained later on. Most of the additional output of pig and bar iron – which grew very fast – was absorbed by the home market and by the substitution of home-produced by imported bar. The contribution of foreign demand to the increase in output between 1788 and 1806 was modest, perhaps 20 per cent.

In our view, around 1800, Britain was becoming an 'export economy', with an exports proportion which was not much below the level it reached in the late nineteenth century. However, this development was interrupted, and for several decades. Using again Deane and Cole's series of national income, the exports proportion falls markedly from its peak in 1801 to 14 per cent in 1811 and 13 per cent in 1821. This fall, during the first decade, resulted from two factors: the war slowed down the growth of exports and their prices fell, absolutely, and still more relatively to agricultural prices which had risen; the current value of exports was not higher in 1810/12 than ten years earlier, while national income had undoubtedly progressed. Some diversion of resources from exports to domestic investment, mostly in agriculture, and to defence is likely during the war against Napoleon. In the post-war period, the exports proportion went on decreasing because of the rapid fall in the prices of manufactures and especially of cotton products, while the prices of many other goods and services did not come down as sharply, and because cotton made a far bigger share of exports than of national product. It is also likely that the share of industrial production which was exported fell back after 1802, and that the incremental ratio of exports to national product was slightly negative for the decade 1801 to 1811.[22] The export trade was not an engine of growth any more after 1802 (and up to the late 1840s), but it remained a major outlet for British industry and it was a vital factor in short-term fluctuations, as was shown by the severity of the economic crises which occurred in years like 1808 and 1811, when foreign trade was seriously depressed.

The main conclusion of this brief survey is the exceptional character of the twenty years 1782 to 1802 in the history of the British export trade and of its role in the economy, owing to the very high rate of growth of exports which was then achieved, to the 'leading' sector part which cotton played in this expansion, to the important role of American markets and to the strong impact of foreign demand on Britain's economic growth. On the other hand, the later years of the French wars are more akin to the post-war period, with exports growing more slowly, being diverted to Asian, African and Latin American markets, and making a very limited contribution to economic growth.

As for Malthus, though exports and even foreign trade were not among his major interests, most of his remarks about them appear quite sensible to the economic historian of his times (a proof of his pragmatism and of his interest in concrete data); this applies also to his remark, when returning from Paris in 1820: 'Generally speaking the French read but little political economy.'[23]

NOTES AND REFERENCES

1. This paper is derived from a longer study, 'Toward an Export Economy: British Exports during the Industrial Revolution', *Explorations in Economic History*, 17 (1980) 48–93, in which detailed references will be found. It deals with *domestic* exports only; re-exports are omitted.
2. Quoted in P. Sraffa (ed.), *The Works and Correspondence of David Ricardo*, vol. II, 'Notes on Malthus's Principles of Political Economy' (Cambridge, 1951), which reprints the *Principles*, p. 416.
3. Ibid., pp. 352, 355, 358–60, 366, 378, 388, 401, 404, 406–9, 414, 418. This was a major point of disagreement with Ricardo, who, in Malthus's view, tried 'to prove the unproductive nature of trade'. But it is never mentioned in the correspondence which the two men exchanged between 1811 and 1823.
4. In two passages of the *Principles* where Malthus quoted trade figures, he used official values, Sraffa, op. cit., vol. II, pp. 359, 363. However, in a review of T. Tooke, published in 1823, Malthus stressed the difference between official values, 'representing quantity', and declared or real values; B. Semmel (ed.), *Occasional Papers by T. R. Malthus* (New York, 1963) pp. 159–60.
5. All rates of growth quoted in this paper have been computed by exponential adjustment, except when expressly mentioned.
6. Sraffa, op. cit., vol. II, pp. 413–14. However, in 1823, Malthus observed, quite accurately, that current values had fallen much more from 1814/16 to 1819/21 than official values, Semmel, op. cit., p. 160.
7. R. Davis, *The Industrial Revolution and British Overseas Trade* (Leicester, 1978) tables 41 and 44, pp. 94, 97. In this case, of course, the rate of growth is calculated between two periods only.
8. Sraffa, op cit., vol. II, pp. 437–9, the 'excessive exportation' which 'glutted all the foreign markets' is mentioned as a cause of depression.
9. Quoted from the 6th ed., vol. I (London, 1826) p. xi.
10. Sraffa, op cit., vol. II, pp. 378, 438.
11. Ibid., vol. VIII, p. 108. Malthus mentions in 1809 'the destruction' of the French 'manufacturing population' during the Revolution.
12. They are mentioned occasionally by Malthus, *An Essay on the Principle of Population*, vol. II (London, 1798) p. 222; Semmel, op. cit., pp. 72, 92, 117, 157; P. James (ed.), *The Travel Diaries of Thomas Robert Malthus* (Cambridge, 1966) p. 224.
13. Sraffa, op. cit., vol. II, pp. 359, 361, 'The advantages from steam engines etc.

are in this instance I think exaggerated by Mr Malthus', observed Ricardo.
14. Ibid., p. 350.
15. Ibid., p. 366.
16. Ibid., pp. 383, 416, where Malthus writes that 'the annual increase of the produce of the United States . . . has been greater than that of any country we are acquainted with' and 'has undoubtedly been aided very greatly by foreign commerce'.
17. N. F. R. Crafts, 'British Economic Growth, 1700–1831: A Review of the Evidence', *Economic History Review*, 2nd series, XXXVI (1983) 197–9.
18. However, Crafts has an incremental ratio for 1700–60 which is high (21 per cent), so that his figure for 1700–80 is higher than both Bairoch's and mine.
19. In R. Floud and D. McCloskey (eds), *The Economic History of Britain since 1700. Volume I: 1700–1860* (Cambridge, 1981) pp. 40, table 3.1, and 39.
20. Crafts, loc. cit.
21. Sraffa, op. cit., vol. II, pp. 363–4, 'If we could not export our cottons, it is quite certain that . . . we should not have the will to consume them all in kind at home.' Compare with the statement by McCloskey:

> At first it seems odd to argue that without foreign markets for its output of cotton textiles . . . Britain would have been able to find markets at home. The result, it seems, would have been a land choked with cotton, from cotton nappies to cotton shrouds. In the long run, however, the men and money used to make the excess cotton could have been turned towards making beer, roads, houses, and other domestic things . . . The reasoning used here is characteristic of economics.

In Floud and McCloskey, op. cit., p. 100.
22. The values of both national income and exports were lower in 1821 than in 1811.
23. Sraffa, op. cit., vol. VIII, p. 225.

14 Trends in Capital Accumulation in the Age of Malthus

B. L. ANDERSON

I

The course and consequences of capital accumulation are key elements in the analysis of population growth and industrialisation of the kind that occurred in Britain over the lifetime of T. R. Malthus. He explicitly recognised that long-run trends in capital formation represented the outcome of many of the principal determinants of changes in output and population, when he wrote that 'The laws which regulate the rate of profits and the progress of capital, bear a very striking and singular resemblance to the laws which regulate the rate of wages and the progress of population'.[1] Indeed, one of the most arresting features of Malthus's work is his continuing preoccupation with the development of the British economy, especially in the period of trauma from the 1790s to the 1820s, which stimulated his overriding concern with the interconnections between supply and demand conditions over time and their effects in terms of price variations. These themes have been reiterated with considerable elaboration by economists and historians ever since, drawn to the central period of the Malthusian era because, on the one hand, it was marked by many of the features most recently summarised in the expression 'stagflation' and, on the other, because it witnessed the effective transition to an industrial economy in Britain.

Accordingly, before considering the evidence currently available on the level and structure of capital accumulation during the Industrial Revolution, a phenomenon which in retrospect appears to have been so closely coterminous with the life of Malthus, it is worthwhile recalling his own insights into the subject. These developed largely as a result of his debates with Ricardo, and can be seen in his two contributions to the *Quarterly Review* in April 1823 and January 1824. Following Adam Smith, Malthus regarded the main determinants of profits as the competition of capitals and the state of the capital market, that is not the absolute quantity of capital available for investment but the 'relative difficulty of finding *profitable* employment for it'.[2] Ricardo's error, he believed, lay in conceiving 'so confined a view of value as not to include the results of demand and supply, and of the relative abundance and competition of capital'.[3]

This disagreement can be traced back as early as 1813 and, as Ricardo made clear to Malthus in 1820, it was to be permanent.[4] Their divergent views on capital accumulation appear to have originated with their differences over the question of the role of effective demand in a period of high prices, which was ultimately founded on their fundamentally different conceptions of real wages. As Malthus saw it later, the vital distinction for him was as follows:

> If riches consist of the necessaries, conveniences, and luxuries of life, and the same quantity of labour will at different times, and under different circumstances, produce a very different quantity of the necessaries, conveniences, and luxuries of life, then it is quite clear that the power of commanding labour, and the power of commanding the necessaries, conveniences and luxuries of life are essentially distinct. One, in fact, is a description of value, and the other of wealth.[5]

Thus for Malthus real wages, rather than money wage-rates, was the key factor in population growth and, ultimately, in capital accumulation as well. Because, in his view, real wages were dependent primarily on the 'effectual demand' for labour which governed the level of employment, the latter was not automatically raised by increased capital formation. His concept of real wages included not merely food prices but the prices of all the items in the wage earner's budget. Capital formation and industrialisation would certainly have the effect of changing tastes and enlarging consumption. Indeed, Malthus saw the great benefits of these processes as bringing a wider range of consumer goods before larger sections of the population, and in breaking down traditional obstacles to increasing labour demand by setting up new institutional conditions of growth. As a growth economist, like Adam Smith, he was concerned with reconciling the problems of capital stock adjustment in a growing

economy, characterised by fluctuations of considerable amplitude, to
the maintenance of the real wages and, therefore, living standards of a
growing labour force. It was his observation of the effects of the trade
cycle on the growth process – particularly when it eroded the urge to
improvement on the part of labour beyond the point where real wages
could be maintained by increased effort and thrift, so that a reduction in
population growth became the final recourse – that led him to devote so
much attention to the maintenance of aggregate demand.[6]

It was partly his concern with the avoidance of deflation which led
Malthus to reassert the Smithian preconditions of growth – property
rights, incentives, inventions, the division of labour, the gains from trade
– and to carry this approach into his theories of profits and capital
accumulation. These were distinctly contrary to the Ricardian proposition that the general profit rate was governed by the level of money
wages, that it could only rise if wages fell, and that the level of wages
depended crucially on productivity in agriculture. Malthus's quite
different perception of the importance of the interrelations between
different sectors for understanding how the economy grows is, perhaps,
best illustrated in his debate with Ricardo on the theory of profits.[7]
Subsequently, in conjunction with the growing importance of his belief
in the interplay of supply and demand factors, Malthus's theory of
capital accumulation became an exposition of the way in which a
divergence between supply and demand could alter the conditions and
profitability of capital generally. This in turn led him to question
Ricardo's entire framework of long-run equilibrium, and to give more
emphasis to a view of the economy as imperfectly adjusting to exogenous
disruptions.

Thus Malthus's celebrated conclusion 'that no power of consumption
on the part of the labouring classes can ever, according to the common
motives which influence mankind, alone furnish an encouragement to
the employment of capital', led inexorably to the famous parting shot on
the last page of the *Principles*.

> Theoretical writers are too apt, in their calculations, to overlook these
> intervals; but eight or ten years, recurring not unfrequently, are
> serious spaces in human life. They amount to a serious sum of
> happiness or misery, according as they are prosperous or adverse, and
> leave the country in a very different state at their termination.[8]

It has been said that the legacy of Malthus to political economy lay in
the fields of applied economics and of economic history, rather than in

theory. It may be more accurate to say that his overall concern was with avoiding what he regarded as fundamental misconceptions in the New (Ricardian) Political Economy, by using the results of empirical analysis of the British economy in disequilibrium to inform and substantiate theoretical work.[9] This explains his great interest in and approval of Thomas Tooke's statistical investigations and the lessons for political economy which Malthus believed should be drawn from them.[10] In reviewing McCulloch's *Principles* the following year he took the opportunity to reassert his conviction that

> An average of ten or a dozen years, therefore, may fairly be considered as sufficient or more than sufficient to determine the ordinary rate of profits. But it is a matter of universal notoriety that, in the progress of a nation towards wealth, considerable fluctuations take place in the rate of profits for ten, twelve, or twenty years together out of one or two hundred: and the question is, to what cause or causes these fluctuations are mainly to be attributed.[11]

In a number of respects Malthus's approach to the role of capital accumulation in economic growth has found its fullest expression in the capital-stock-adjustment model of post-Keynesian economists.[12] At the same time, the great increase in the volume of empirical work on data collection and hypothesis testing produced by statisticians and development economists since the 1950s, has provided economic historians with some of the means to follow Malthus's own dictum, and to examine the historical problem of capital accumulation in his period by 'that constant reference to facts and experience on which alone it can be safely founded, or further improved'.[13]

II

Until very recently discussions of the subject have been conducted without benefit of any precise evidence as to numbers and causes and, as with other statistical lacunae of the period such as population growth, have generally been contradictory and inconclusive. Much of the data relating to British capital formation has been, and arguably still is, derived from very defective numerical sources and, where even these do not exist, from conjecture. Early modern administrators and political economists would have found the information costs of compiling raw data on a regular basis for an item so conceptually difficult to define and

measure as capital, quite disproportionate to their usefulness. Indeed,
down to the present day it has almost always been found easier to
construct estimates of the ways in which national income has been
earned or produced than of the ways in which it has been expended. Thus
even now any survey of trends in capital formation in the Industrial
Revolution has to be very provisional and, at every stage, the distinction
between taking figures seriously and taking them literally needs to be
made.[14]

With the exception of two pre-war articles which can be said to have
pioneered the subject in Britain, the first efforts to construct reasonably
comprehensive estimates were undertaken by Kuznets and Deane.[15]
These findings broadly indicated that net capital formation did not
achieve a level of twice its initial rate at any time during the eighteenth
and early nineteenth centuries in Britain. Instead, as with other
developing economies in the modern period, it increased more slowly
over a long period of time; this implied that while a higher investment
ratio did usually coincide with a faster growth of national income there
was by no means a direct relationship between the two. The conclusion
that capital growth may not have been the most powerful single
explanatory factor in the industrial revolution, and that an increased
savings ratio, far from being the prime stimulus may not even have been
a necessary condition, seemed to cast doubt on the most influential
working hypothesis among economic historians. The Lewis–Rostow
thesis had recently been developed around a major shift in the rate of
investment to around 10 per cent per annum or more of national income,
occurring as the central feature of a short period of accelerated,
irreversible economic growth located in the last twenty years of the
eighteenth century.

Thus even as post-war economists, increasingly preoccupied with the
problems of underdevelopment, were returning to the theory of
economic development and placing capital formation at the centre of
their growth models, the historical evidence for Britain seemed to rule
out the most striking feature of the 'take-off' concept. Instead of a sharp
acceleration in the investment proportion from 5 to over 10 per cent
during the period of the 'take-off', that is, at the onset of the Industrial
Revolution, the empirical evidence seemed to suggest an investment
proportion in the region of 5 per cent towards the end of the seventeenth
century, followed by a century and a half of small additions to savings
amounting to less than 1 per cent per annum of national income. Some
upward shift in the investment proportion appeared to have taken place
from the 1780s, but it was not until the peak of the railway construction

boom in the late 1840s that it reached 12 per cent, and certainly there seemed to be little evidence to suggest a doubling of the investment proportion in the period 1783–1802.[16] These findings, subsequently reiterated by Deane with only a few modifications and elaborated further by Kuznets, suggested that more emphasis needed to be given to the qualitative aspects of the inputs to the production process, that questions such as the degree of capital utilisation and the relative efficacy of the capital market required attention as well as the overall level of capital formation. Moreover, further studies in the field of national income for Britain and elsewhere tended to reinforce scepticism of the Rostowian climacteric. Historically, it would appear that quite long periods of income growth have often preceded a rise in the savings ratio; that raising the level of investment to a higher plane required a prior acceleration in the rate of growth generally.[17]

These early estimates of trends in capital formation were fragmentary and tentative, and invited further efforts to revise and improve them. One major weakness of Deane's figures, for example, was the heavy reliance placed on Gregory King's data to provide a starting-point estimate of 5 per cent for the late seventeenth and early eighteenth centuries. Even for the very prosperous years within that period so high an investment proportion, implying remarkably high incremental and average capital–output ratios, seemed at variance with comparable data for present-day undeveloped economies and for modern economies in their pre-industrial periods. On the other hand, though the net capital formation proportion may well have been below 5 per cent at the beginning of the eighteenth century and Deane herself mentions a long-term average of under 3 per cent, it is possible that the gross figure (to include current maintenance), and thus the incremental gross capital–output ratio, was very much higher. If before the Industrial Revolution a low rate of growth of product was allied to a high rate of fixed capital consumption, resulting from a short life for capital goods, it is possible that the gross capital formation proportion was high early on in the eighteenth century, and that as economic growth accelerated later much higher rates of net capital formation could have been sustained without anything like a corresponding increase in gross investment rates.[18]

This is an area in which little more than speculation is possible at present, however, and where the evidence is so circumstantial as to make an opposite interpretation at least as feasible. Non-reproducible capital items must have accounted for the major share of gross capital formation before and even during industrialisation, so that their greater durability would have lowered capital maintenance and replacement costs overall, even allowing for changes in the longevity of producers' equipment. At the same time, much depends on the rate of growth of product and this does seem to have been quite low, according to Deane and Cole no more than 0.3 per cent per annum between 1700 and the mid-1740s. Furthermore, given that repairs and maintenance of eighteenth-century capital equipment was a much larger item than new investment generally, the fact that obsolescence appears to have been quite high in the newer industries and that higher replacement rates were embodying considerable technical advance, almost certainly resulted in an appreciable rise in productivity growth. These conjectures pointed to the need for more reliable estimates of gross capital formation on a sectoral and aggregate basis in order to obtain a clearer picture of the reallocation of resources resulting from the onset of more rapid economic growth, and of the overall investment burden which the economy had to bear.[19]

This deficiency was even more marked for the later decades of the eighteenth century than for the earlier period. From the outset there had been considerable misgivings as to the accuracy of the Deane and Habakkuk critique of the initial timing and duration of the take-off, and its subsequent elaboration.[20] It was pointed out, for example, that if the empirical evidence suggested a net capital formation rate of 6 to 7 per cent around 1800 – a very marginal increase on the long-term average of 5 to 6 per cent established for the 1750s and 1760s – and a capital–output ratio of 3:1 at the same time then, even allowing for the increased rate of population growth at the end of the century, significant net growth per head was occurring. In other words, the take-off could have taken place at that period but at a much lower rate of net capital formation than seemed to be required by Rostow's analysis.[21]

More serious doubts were expressed regarding important omissions in the available estimates. It was noticed that the sectoral estimates of capital investment in industries such as cotton and iron were an inadequate basis for calculating the impact of industrial investment in the late eighteenth-century economy; not only did they leave out of account the capital needs of other important and rapidly growing sectors such as coal and shipbuilding, but estimates for circulating capital were lacking.[22] With the benefit of hindsight this last deficiency can be seen as a major source of underestimation in earlier calculations of capital accumulation, especially in industries such as cotton where the ratio of fixed to circulating capital was close to 1:3 before 1815.[23]

The first comprehensive attempt to calculate the magnitude of gross capital formation was made by Pollard in 1965.[24] These new and independent estimates were a landmark in the statistical study of the crucial period of British industrialisation. The principal conclusion drawn from them was that the proportion of gross national income going for investment was considerably higher at various benchmark dates between 1770 and the 1830s. As early as *c*.1770, according to Pollard, the gross investment rate was already 6.5 per cent, rose to 9 per cent by the early 1790s, fell back during the Napoleonic wars to peak at 8 per cent in 1813, and reached 11 per cent in the early 1830s before the railway construction boom began. The fact that Pollard's estimates were compiled in gross terms, the better to assess the true investment burden incurred, raised the question of whether they could be appropriately used to test the Lewis–Rostow hypothesis of a doubling of *net* capital formation as a proportion of *net* national income. This point acquired additional force from the results of a number of studies of the key areas of technical and structural transformation in the early industrialisation period. Evidence for the cotton and iron industries, in particular, suggested that rates of gross fixed capital formation embodying technical changes of high productivity potential, of perhaps as much as 12 per cent per annum on average in cotton and perhaps half that in iron, were being achieved in the two decades after 1783. Yet because the annual increment to total capital stock and the contribution to national income that can be attributed to these industries was relatively so small, even their combined impact on the growth of income per head and the investment proportion must have been slight, and quite possibly incremental capital–output ratios actually fell over this central period of industrialisation.[25]

The latest, and almost certainly definitive, estimates for capital accumulation by Feinstein are too recent for their full implications to have been worked through in the literature of the Industrial Revolution. Yet it is clear that a principal effect of their publication is to bring the process of aggregate re-estimation full circle and to refocus discussion on a clearly discernible period of 'take-off' by restoring considerable empirical support for the Lewis–Rostow hypothesis. In terms of broad comparison, Feinstein's new estimates of fixed capital formation are well below those of Pollard for *c*.1770 and much higher for *c*.1815. The greater divergence occurs in their estimates for manufacturing industry and trade, and the least for transport; indeed from Deane, through Pollard, to Feinstein there has been a progressive upward recalculation of the increase in the level of capital expenditure in the industrial and commercial sector of the British economy from the 1770s to the 1830s.

Feinstein's figures are close to those of Pollard for the early 1830s, so that his overall estimates show fixed capital formation increasing in the previous sixty years or so at a rate more than double the earlier estimates.[26] What is more, we now have something like a climacteric of the 1790s during which the 10 per cent per annum ratio was exceeded and beyond which it assumed a new long-term stability through the mid-nineteenth century.

III

Thus the latest estimates effectively recast the course of British capital accumulation during industrialisation along more traditional lines, familiar to readers of the classic works of Paul Mantoux and T. S. Ashton. Industry and commerce together are again the central feature of an upward shift of the investment ratio from an aggregate level already approximating 7 per cent per annum during the 1760s and 1770s, possibly representing a pre-industrial or 'preconditions' plateau, which was itself the product of a slow process of attainment dating from the beginning of the century or earlier. The decisive ten to twenty year period of transition appears once more as remarkably coincident with a Rostowian 'take-off' of 1783–1802, with the decennial investment cycle that came to a peak in 1792 reasserting itself as the critical one for raising domestic fixed capital formation in industry and trade to a permanently higher level (from 12 per cent per annum in 1771–80 to 30 in 1781–90.) At this stage net investment abroad and fixed capital formation in agriculture and social overheads remain relatively unmoved; but at the same time large reductions occur in the proportion of total domestic investment going to stockbuilding during and after the 1780s, and in fixed capital formation in transport, compared with the previous decade.[27]

The next major investment cycle exerted its strongest influence in the years 1799–1802; but though industry and trade took a rather lower proportion of total domestic fixed capital formation in the decades 1791–1800 and 1801–10 (23 and 24 per cent respectively) than in the 1780s (30 per cent), the resumption of war in 1803 does not appear to have depressed fixed capital creation in these sectors unduly. During 1801–10 Britain became a net capital importer for the first, and last, time in many decades; the share of agricultural capital formation continued to decline notwithstanding a switch of resources to that sector during the war; and the proportion of national wealth being devoted to residential and social overhead capital continued to increase up to the

1830s. But on the other hand, there was a very marked fall indeed in the relative importance of investment in stocks, work in progress, and so on. Overall, stockbuilding as a proportion of total fixed capital formation fell from around 20 per cent in 1761–1800 to about 9 per cent in 1801–60. In industry, commerce and agriculture this percentage fell from 40 per cent in 1791–1800 to 12 per cent in 1801–10.[28] The decennial estimates for such broad sectors mask, to some extent, what was happening there. But they do suggest that the heyday of rapid accumulation in industry and trade in the generation before 1815, accompanied for most of the period by heavy government borrowing for war purposes, was largely founded on a regional and sectoral complex of relations between merchants and manufacturers in the key industries – and between them and the contemporary capital market.

The fact that the transition occurred in the conditions of a war economy, undoubtedly points to a very temporary role for capital imports in easing the problem of capital allocation, by allowing the increased absolute level of total investment achieved in the 1790s to be sustained in the following decade. Furthermore, the fact that the institutional structure of the capital market had attained a high degree of flexibility, particularly in respect of remittance and discounting facilities, certainly provided a mechanism through which the economy as a whole could benefit from the funds released by the progressive reductions in the share of investment going to farm buildings and improvements over the period. But the latest estimates taken together with the considerable sectoral evidence, suggest that such considerations are of quite secondary importance. Granted that investment growth in industry and trade could on occasion be baulked by the bidding away of funds to meet government borrowing requirements.[29] Given, also, that the capital market was more than adequate for the task of reallocating the release of resources implied by the continuous downward trend in the relative importance of both fixed and circulating capital in agriculture.[30] It nonetheless seems clear that the complex of relations linking industry, trade and finance was largely self-contained – that this broad sector within which the essential transformations occurred, predominantly financed itself. The essence of the role of capital accumulation in the transition thus appears to lie with the capacity of those sectors, within which the key technical changes were taking place, to bring about a sharp rise in the ratio of fixed to circulating capital.

Following on some appreciable disinvestment in industry during the post-war depression, the third major investment cycle reached its height in the early 1820s: the upswing was marked, if short-lived, industrial investment being accompanied by considerable capital outflows abroad. The crisis of 1825–6 ushered in another period of lower industrial investment and considerable underemployment and, of course, throughout the twenties the share of fixed capital formation continued to fall, especially in agriculture, but also in transport compared with previous decades. The final spurt in industrial investment for the period came in 1832–6. Over the thirties as a whole a very considerable reduction in net investment took place, together with a substantial increase in capital formation in transport with the onset of the railway era, but the share of domestic fixed capital formation devoted to industry and commerce hardly altered from the previous decade. When taken together the four major investment booms, in which the growth of fixed capital in British industry before 1840 was largely concentrated, appear as intervals of great discontinuity. Prompted initially by new opportunities for exploiting manufacturing cost reductions, the precise timing of capital expansion outlays appears to have lagged behind gradual export growth which, in turn, had usually reinforced the effects of domestic income growth and lower grain prices. The investment bouts were, however, inherently unstable and their courses were sharply curtailed by crises in 1793, 1803, 1825 and 1836. They were, therefore, highly susceptible to changes in market prospects and credit conditions, to both of which profit expectations were closely tied.[31]

Whatever estimates are taken to illustrate the changing share of investment in industry and trade, it is clear that the bulk continued to go into areas other than manufacturing. The various estimates are not comparable but, according to Crouzet's reworking of Pollard's figures, the percentages of gross capital formation fell in agriculture from 28.6 in *c*.1770 to 11.5 by the early 1830s, rose gradually in transport (including shipping) from 14 to 16.8 and also in building from 24.5 to 28.8. Over the same period the proportions in manufactures and trade showed very little overall change, rising gradually from 24.5 to 26.3. The Feinstein decennial estimates are for domestic fixed capital formation and show greater variations in the proportions over time: for agriculture the percentage falls from 35 in 1761–80 to 14.5 in 1821–40, for transport it declines from 25.5 to 19 and for industry and commerce it rises from 16 to 34.5. In respect of the industry/trade sector Crouzet speaks of an 'almost constant' share over the period, whereas Feinstein shows a considerable rise, 'essentially due to the increased investment in machinery and equipment in manufacturing, mining, and the utilities'.[32]

The latest estimates point more strongly than ever to the crucial transformation in the composition of industrial and commercial capital in the Industrial Revolution, specifically, a sharp rise in the percentage of fixed investment in industry's capital goods (excluding buildings) from 4 in the 1760s to 9 in the 1830s, and from 2 in the 1770s to 10 in the 1780s. Yet it is difficult to avoid the conclusion that if the burden of increased capital accumulation during industrialisation had been merely confined to the industry/trade sector, it could not have been excessive at almost any stage. For all the evidence, aggregate and sectoral, suggests no overwhelming coincidence of capital requirements across a front so broad as to leave any significant gaps in capital provision. Indeed, the aggregate trends in British capital accumulation appear as the sum of many sectoral demands which, being of different intensity at different times, enabled available capital resources to flow in sequence to a large extent. In the last decades of the eighteenth century when the total investment rate rose from 10 to 14 per cent as the industry/trade sector effected major technical and structural changes, capital formation in agriculture and overseas investment were maintained at historically high levels. Later, the burden of railway construction appears to have been easily accommodated within an investment ratio that had hardly altered since 1815.

This flexibility of response on the part of the British economy to the changing emphases of capital accumulation over the period suggests that aggregate savings were adequate to meet new capital requirements from at least the early eighteenth century. By the later decades the distribution of such funds in terms of social group, geographical location and economic sector was sufficiently extensive to enable sectoral capital accumulation to occur in phase, and without more than temporary strains being exerted on the mechanisms and institutions of the capital market. The latest estimates confirm earlier impressions that the rate of growth of capital formation rarely surpassed that of incomes and that the British economy was already devoting perhaps 5 or 6 per cent of national income to investment in *c*.1688. An increase in the ratio to Feinstein's 7 or 8 per cent for the 1760s would have involved a very modest upward drift over three generations. Firm evidence is lacking but it seems a reasonable assumption that the ratio of fixed to circulating capital followed a similar course to achieve Feinstein's 1:1 relationship by the 1760s. It then rose to around 2.5:1 by the 1830s. A longer perspective is given by comparing Deane's 'estimate of a well-informed contemporary that what we might regard as an approximation to the "reproducible capital"' was growing at 1–1.5 per cent per annum during the whole of the seventeenth century, with Feinstein's rising growth rate for the same item from 1 per cent per annum in 1760–1800 to 1.5 in 1800–30.[33]

IV

Such estimates are extremely speculative, however, and leave untouched the important question of how, in a period of more rapid population growth, an expansion of aggregate productive capacity was financed. The answer seems to lie in the scale and timing of British industrialisation. The individual entrepreneur remained the principal vehicle of capital accumulation across the entire industry/trade sector throughout the period, and few enterprises were beyond the resources of the extended partnership to finance. The threshold of capital entry into the textile and iron industries, for example, was low and remained so until well into the nineteenth century. Technological change and capital growth in such areas did yield some economies of scale and size increases in production units; they extended division of labour and led to organisational change around a central power source. But even more characteristic of industrial expansion before the 1830s was the proliferation and dispersal of relatively small firms, few of which exceeded the optimal size for the market at any given time.[34] There is ample evidence to show that for long periods, before and during the Industrial Revolution, the limiting factors on increasing the rate of capital formation, especially in industry and trade, lay more with the slow growth of investment opportunities than with any scarcity of savings. The own funds of merchants and manufacturers *together*, arising from retained profits, kinship loans and even dishoarding, were crucial and closely intertwined – more so before 1815 than after.

The aggregate trends conceal extremely wide-ranging variations in the size and timing of capital inputs within and between firms and industries. Furthermore, because the business history of the Industrial Revolution has inevitably been concerned more with success than failure in enterprise, it is difficult to gauge the extent to which capital growth in successful firms was offset by retraction elsewhere. Since the aggregate estimates are available, at best, only at decennial intervals, short-term fluctuations of great absolute significance are unrecorded. Malthus himself frequently referred to the importance of such factors and recent authorities have concurred, remarking on the often considerable intersectoral differences in the duration of investment cycles and gestation periods.[35]

In some respects recent investigators of early British industrialisation have returned to the Malthusian theme of analysing the economy of his day as imperfectly adjusting to exogenous disruptions such as the impact of war, harvest failure and heavy government expenditure. Rostow's analysis of the transition in terms of unbalanced growth derived from discontinuous production functions and emphasising the importance of supply factors has also returned to favour.[36] He has reiterated that a doubling of the investment rate was an approximation, and that since the transition was essentially a process of disaggregated change it was not central to it; anyway he did not regard Deane and Cole's estimates as definitive. A rise in the ratio to *c*.5 per cent could even occur in the preconditions period, and the latest estimates indicate that this actually happened on the basis of increased capital formation in transport in the 1750s and 1760s. Indeed Rostow's original formulation had presupposed a considerable capacity to mobilise savings during the preconditions, and the evidence of the Bubble era suggests that productive outlets were exhausted long before investible funds.[37] Similarly during the transition, the latest estimates reveal a considerable growth of social as well as industrial fixed capital in the two decades after 1790. The evidence suggests that the same social groups carried both investment burdens simultaneously and that here were the 'lateral' linkages from the leading sectors to urbanisation.[38] Thus the balance of evidence on British capital accumulation in the Industrial Revolution has moved closer to an affirmative answer to the question of 'whether the acceleration is "surprising" enough to be called a "take-off"'.[39] At the time of writing, the latest reworking of the Feinstein estimates by Crafts broadly confirms this, although the jump in the investment ratio during the 1770s and 1780s becomes more moderate and the percentage rise in the earlier eighteenth century more remarkable.[40]

Finally, however, there is an important respect in which both the modern hypotheses concerning the transition in capital accumulation and the continuing efforts at refining the macroestimates of early British economic growth are far removed from the chief preoccupations of Malthus concerning the nature and role of capital in economic growth. Moreover, the position of Malthus on the questions of money and capital theory highlights the fact that there were always two distinct strands of thought at work in British classical economics that continue to haunt the debates on the sources of inflation and growth being conducted today. In classical thought Malthus stands with those who saw how monetary policy could have an influence not just on the general price level, but on relative prices; and through them exert changes in distribution and expectations that generate fluctuations in capital formation. In the crude, comparatively static, quantity theory of money originating in Locke and elaborated in Hume and Ricardo only the ultimate, equilibrium, macroeconomic effects of an increase of money on prices are seen as important; their concern was with the consequences of a period of increase in the quantity of money in *all* markets and on the *general* price level.

The approach of Malthus harked back to Richard Cantillon's criticism of Locke's formulation of the quantity theory; namely that 'he did not analyse how that takes place. The great difficulty of this analysis consists in discovering by what path and in what proportion the increase of money raises the price of things'.[41] In a remarkable anticipation of Wicksell's trade cycle theory, Malthus and his contemporary Henry Thornton, focused on the process of adjustment to changes in the quantity of money in a context of sharp fluctuations in output, employment and investment. Their analysis was concerned with the real consequences of a monetary phenomenon whose first impact was felt in the money market. In contemporary circumstances, a sequence of new money creation would destabilise the loan market through lower market interest rates. What Thornton saw as saving arising from 'defalcation of revenue', and Malthus called an 'Augmentation of capital through changed distribution of the circulating medium', offered the possibility of utilising investment funds that were not provided as a result of previous decisions of income earners to increase their savings. In short, a monetary expansion could lead to real investment exceeding intended or planned saving.

Of all the classical economists Malthus was perhaps the most sensitive to the importance of relative price changes in the allocation of resources. This awareness lay behind his criticism of Ricardo's use of the Corn model in the development of his theory of profit, and prompted the comment: 'It is not the *quantity* of produce compared with the expenses of production that determines profits (which I think is your position) but the exchangeable value or money price of that produce, compared with the money expense of production.'[42] In the same way, Malthus saw that the money aspect of the phenomenon, that is now called 'forced saving', was only the initial stage in a sequence of real consequences working through the economy which were difficult to determine and increased the uncertainty surrounding allocative decisions. In the circumstances of his own day this essentially monetary phenomenon could have its effects compounded by the fiscal forced saving taking place during wartime. Because Malthus understood that two distinct definitions of real wages are necessary for analysing the effects of monetary change on prices, investment and output, he was much more interested than Ricardo in the short-run effects of monetary disturbance and the microeconomic decisions which transmitted it through the economy.[43] It was his realisation that wages measured in units of output governed the demand for labour, and that wages measured in units of consumables governed its supply, which enabled Malthus to see how changes in relative prices alter the conditions of demand and supply in the factor markets and lead ultimately to changes in the structure of capital formation and the composition of output.[44] This is the first step to a theory of the business cycle.

APPENDIX 14.1 Selected estimates illustrating trends in capital formation in Great Britain, 1761–1840*

(1) Gross fixed capital formation, Great Britain, c.1770–1835 (£m. p.a. at current prices)

	c.1770	c.1790–3	c.1815	c.1830–5
From Pollard	7.2	13.3	21.9	31.0
From Feinstein	4.0	11.4	26.5	28.2

(2) Investment ratios

	1761–70	1771–80	1781–90	1791–1800	1801–10	1811–20	1821–30
Gross DFCF as a % of GDP	7	7	10	11	10	10	10
Total domestic investment as a % of GDP	8	9	12	13	11	11	12
Total Investment as a % of GDP	8	10	13	14	10	14	14

(3) Gross capital formation by sector as a percentage of aggregate gross capital formation

	c.1770	c.1790–3	c.1815	c.1830–5
Agriculture	28.6	22.5	21.1	11.5
Transport	14.0	15.0	15.5	16.8
Building	24.5	31.9	33.8	28.8
Manufacturing and Trade:				
Machinery	8.5	12.5	15.8	20.0
Stocks	16.0	12.5	10.1	6.3
Subtotal	24.5	25.0	25.9	26.3
Miscellaneous	8.5	5.6	3.6	16.8

APPENDIX 14.1 Selected estimates illustrating trends in capital formation in Great Britain, 1761–1840* (cont.)

(4) Structure of investment, 1761–1840 (in percentages)

	1761–70	1771–80	1781–90	1791–1800	1801–10	1811–20	1821–30	1831–40
DFCF								
Residential and Social	25	22	21	26	30	31	35	30
Agricultural	33	37	30	30	25	22	16	13
Industrial and Commercial	20	12	30	23	24	29	35	34
Transport	22	29	19	22	21	18	15	23
Stockbuilding as a % of FCF	15	28	18	21	6	10	14	9
Net investment from abroad as a % of total domestic investment	7	11	11	9	– 11	22	23	11

* Abbreviations used   DFCF = Domestic Fixed Capital Formation
       FCF = Fixed Capital Formation
       GDP = Gross Domestic Product

SOURCES   Tables 1, 2, and 4 from Feinstein, loc. cit., 'Capital Formation in Great Britain', 74, 91 and 93.
       Tables 1 and 3 from Pollard, loc. cit., 'Growth and Distribution', 362, and Crouzet (ed.), op. cit., *Capital Formation*, p. 33.

NOTES AND REFERENCES

1. T. R. Malthus, *Principles of Political Economy*, 2nd ed. (London, 1836) p. 327.
2. C. Renwick (ed.), *Five Papers on Political Economy by T. R. Malthus* (Sydney, 1953) p. 94.
3. Ibid., p. 106.
4. 'I differ as much as I ever had done with you, in your chapter on the effects of the accumulation of capital', P. Sraffa (ed.), *Works and Correspondence of David Ricardo*, vol. VIII (Cambridge, 1951–73) p. 185.
5. T. R. Malthus, *Definitions in Political Economy* (London, 1827) p. 25.
6. For further discussion *see* J. J. Spengler, 'Malthus's Total Population Theory: A Restatement and Reappraisal', *Canadian Journal of Economics and Political Science*, II (1945) in two parts, 83–110 and 234–64; and D. P. O'Brien, *The Classical Economists* (Oxford, 1975) chapter 8 and references cited there.
7. S. Hollander, 'Ricardo's Analysis of the Profit Rate, 1813–15', *Economica*, 40 (1973) 260–82.
8. Malthus, op. cit., *Principles*, pp. 404, 437.
9. Renwick, op. cit., p. 3.
10. *Quarterly Review*, XXIX (1823).
11. Ibid. XXX (1824) 315.
12. See K. Kurihara (ed.), *Post-Keynesian Economics* (London, 1955) chapter 7; and B. A. Corry, *Money, Saving and Investment in English Economics, 1800–1850* (London, 1962).
13. *Quarterly Review*, XXIX (1823) 214.
14. On the conceptual and estimation problems see E. F. Denison, 'Theoretical Aspects of Quality Change, Capital Consumption and Net Capital Formation', in NBER, *Problems of Capital Formation. Studies in Income and Wealth*, vol. XIX (Princeton, 1957) pp. 215–84; C. H. Feinstein, *Domestic Capital Formation in the United Kingdom 1920–38* (Cambridge, 1965); CSO, *National Accounts Statistics: Sources and Methods* (London, 1968); and J. P. P. Higgins and S. Pollard (eds), *Aspects of Capital Investment in Great Britain, 1750–1850. A Preliminary Survey* (London, 1971).
15. S. Kuznets, 'Quantitative Aspects of the Economic Growth of Nations: 5. Capital Formation Proportions', *Economic Development and Cultural Change*, VIII, number 4, (1960) 1–96 and '6. Long-term Trends in Capital Formation Proportions', idem., IX, number 4, (1961) 3–124; and P. Deane, 'Capital Formation in Britain before the Railway Age', *Economic Development and Cultural Change*, IX, Number 3, (1961) 352–68. The important early contributions are M. M. Postan, 'Recent Trends in the Accumulation of Capital', *Economic History Review*, 1st series, VI (1935) 1–12, and H. Heaton, 'Financing the Industrial Revolution', *Bulletin of the Business Historical Society*, XI (1937) 1–10.
16. W. A. Lewis, 'Economic Development with Unlimited Supplies of Labour', *The Manchester School*, XXII (1954) 139–90, and *The Theory of Economic Growth* (London, 1955) pp. 225–6; W. W. Rostow, 'The Take-Off into Self-Sustained Growth', *Economic Journal*, LXVI (1956) 25–48, and *The Stages*

220   *Trends in Capital Accumulation in the Age of Malthus*

of Economic Growth (Cambridge, 1960) pp. 41–5. On the criticism of the thesis *see* P. Deane and H. J. Habakkuk, 'The Take-Off in Britain', in W. W. W. Rostow (ed.), *The Economics of Take-Off into Sustained Growth* (London, 1963) pp. 63–82.

17. Deane, loc. cit.; and P. Deane and W. A. Cole, *British Economic Growth 1688–1959: Trends and Structure* (Cambridge, 1962) chapter 8. *See also* A. K. Cairncross, 'Capital Formation in the Take-Off', in Rostow (ed.), ibid., pp. 240–60; S. Kuznets, 'Capital Formation in Modern Economic Growth', *Third International Conference of Economic History*, Munich, 1965, vol. 1 (Paris – The Hague, 1968) pp. 15–53, and *Modern Economic Growth. Rate, Structure and Spread* (London, 1966).

18. Kuznets, loc. cit., 'Capital Formation'.

19. Higgins and Pollard, op. cit., pp. 6–7; and S. Kuznets, 'Population, Income and Capital', in L. H. Dupriez and D. C. Hague (eds), *Economic Progress* (Louvain, 1955) pp. 27–46.

20. Deane and Habakkuk, op. cit., pp. 73–7; Deane, loc. cit.; Deane and Cole, op. cit., pp. 260–3; and the discussion of these estimates in F. Crouzet (ed.), *Capital Formation in the Industrial Revolution* (London, 1972) pp. 14–18.

21. J. R. T. Hughes, 'Measuring British Economic Growth', *Journal of Economic History*, XXIV (1964) 60–82.

22. M. W. Flinn, *Origins of the Industrial Revolution* (London, 1966) pp. 38–44; P. Mathias, 'Capital, Credit and Enterprise in the Industrial Revolution', *Journal of European Economic History*, II (1973) 121–43.

23. S. D. Chapman, *The Cotton Industry in the Industrial Revolution* (London, 1972) chapter 3.

24. S. Pollard, 'The Growth and Distribution of Capital in Great Britain c.1770–1870', *Third International Conference*, op. cit., pp. 335–65.

25. Deane and Cole, op. cit., pp. 185 and 262; B. R. Mitchell and P. Deane, *Abstract of British Historical Statistics* (Cambridge, 1962) p. 131; Crouzet (ed.), op. cit., pp. 198–9. On capital–output ratios compare Cairncross, op. cit., pp. 252–5 with Rostow, op. cit., *The Stages*, p. 37; and C. H. Feinstein, 'Capital Formation in Great Britain', in P. Mathias and M. M. Postan (eds), *The Cambridge Economic History of Europe*, vol. VII (Cambridge, 1978) p. 84.

26. Feinstein, ibid., pp. 29–33, 73–82.

27. Ibid., pp. 89–91, and Crouzet (ed.), op. cit., pp. 203–10.

28. Feinstein, ibid., p. 93.

29. P. G. M. Dickson, *The Financial Revolution in England. A Study in the Development of Public Credit, 1688–1756* (London, 1967) p. 245; and Flinn, op. cit., p. 42.

30. P. Mathias, *The First Industrial Nation* (London, 1969) pp. 144, 175–7; Flinn, op. cit., pp. 51–2; H. J. Habakkuk, 'The Historical Experience on the Basic Conditions of Economic Progress', in Dupriez and Hague (eds), op. cit., and articles by S. Pollard and B. L. Anderson reprinted in Crouzet (ed.), op. cit.

31. F. Crouzet, 'Capital Formation in Great Britain during the Industrial Revolution', in Crouzet (ed.), op. cit., pp. 162–222.

32. Crouzet, editor's introduction in ibid., pp. 33–4; Feinstein, loc. cit., 92–4.

33. Deane, loc. cit.; Deane and Cole, op. cit., chapter 8; Feinstein, loc. cit., 85–7. Feinstein confirms earlier impressions of a slowly falling capital–out-

put ratio during the second half of the eighteenth century, followed by a more pronounced fall from 7.1 in 1800 to 4.9 in 1830.

34. S. D. Chapman, 'Fixed Capital Formation in the British Cotton Manufacturing Industry', in Higgins and Pollard (eds), op. cit.; V. A. C. Gatrell, 'Labour, Power, and the Size of Firms in Lancashire Cotton in the Second Quarter of the Nineteenth Century', *Economic History Review*, 2nd series, XXX (1977) 95–139; and A. Birch, *The Economic History of the British Iron and Steel Industry, 1784–1879* (London, 1967) pp. 197–8; C. K. Hyde, 'The Adoption of the Hot Blast by the British Iron Industry. A Reinterpretation', *Explorations in Economic History*, X (1972–3) 281–93; P. Riden, 'The Output of the British Iron Industry before 1870', *Economic History Review*, 2nd series, XXX (1977) 442–59.

35. Mathias, op. cit., pp. 44–7, 146–7, 234–7; A. Gayer, W. W. Rostow and A. J. Schwartz, *Growth and Fluctuations of the British Economy, 1790–1850* (Oxford, 1953); Higgins and Pollard, op. cit., pp. 9–10. *See also* S. D. Chapman, 'Financial Restraints on the Growth of Firms in the Cotton Industry, 1790–1850', *Economic History Review*, 2nd series, XXXII (1979) 50–69.

36. J. Mokyr and N. E. Savin, 'Stagflation in Historical Perspective: The Napoleonic Wars Revisited', in P. Uselding (ed.), *Research in Economic History*, I (1976) 198–259; J. Mokyr, 'Demand vs. Supply in the Industrial Revolution', *Journal of Economic History*, XXXVII (1977) 981–1008.

37. Rostow, loc. cit., 'The Take-Off', 32–3, and idem., op. cit., *The Stages*, 2nd ed. (1971) appendix B.

38. Ibid., *The Stages*, p. 206 and C. W. Chalklin, 'Capital Expenditure on Building for Cultural Purposes in Provincial England, 1730–1830', *Business History*, XXII (1980) 51–70.

39. Rostow, op. cit., *The Stages*, p. 200. For a more recent reassertion of his supply-side case *see* W. W, Rostow, *How it all Began. Origins of the Modern Economy* (London, 1975) pp. 171–189.

40. N. F. R. Crafts, 'British Economic Growth, 1700–1831: A Review of the Evidence', *Economic History Review*, 2nd series, XXXVI (1983) 177–99.

41. Cited in F. A. Hayek, *Prices and Production* (London, 1935) p. 1.

42. Sraffa (ed.), op. cit., VI, pp. 140–1.

43. Malthus, op. cit., *Definitions*.

44. For further references and discussion *see* F. A. Hayek, 'A Note on the Development of the Doctrine of "Forced Saving"', in *Profits, Interest, and Investment* (New York, 1970) p. 190; F. Machlup, 'Friedrich von Hayek's Contribution to Economics', *Swedish Journal of Economics*, 76 (1974) 498–531; T. Sowell, *Classical Economics Reconsidered* (Princeton, 1974) pp. 52–66; G. P. O'Driscoll, *Economics as a Co-ordination Problem* (Kansas City, 1977) chapters 3 and 5.

15 Malthus on Population in a War-Based Industrial Economy

EDMOND COCKS

Thomas Robert Malthus, an amiable man with more than the average talent for making mortal enemies, compounded this trait with a habit of inflicting wounds on himself. The result was to place Malthus in the centre of economic controversies in which his special talent was said to be the conducting of skilful retreats from untenable positions.

This being the case, it is not surprising that during his lifetime he lost his leadership of the English community of economists to David Ricardo, who was striving to raise economics to an exact science. It was a science looking for mathematical precision, and the don's shifts of position on major issues cost him the support of his colleagues and his leading position in the academic community.

In adversity, Malthus remained serenely unrepentant. He loved controversy; all his major works were inspired by his disagreements with the works of others. Although a cleric, he preferred the role of Devil's Advocate. (We tend to overlook the fact that the office of Devil's Advocate *is* a clerical office.) At a time when British economists were shaping a school of *laissez-faire* economics that was gaining worldwide recognition as the hope of progressive mankind, Malthus's views regarding international trade, taxes and government intervention in the economic process made him the odd man out among his fellows. Therefore, he was cast flaming from the pages of the *Edinburgh Review* into the outer world reserved for lapsed heretics.

Heresy proved to be his natural condition. In an age marked by buoyant optimism, his ability to see the darker side of the picture made him the Frederick Nietzsche of the age. Yet even as a Devil's Advocate, his second thoughts were always on the side of the angels. That was his

222

undoing. Denounced in his youth as the 'enemy of all reform' for his criticism of Godwin's ideas by liberals, he was, in later life, scourged by established economists for his support of reforms on behalf of the working classes.

His most famous 'orderly retreat with the artillery lost'[1] occurred in the 1803 edition (his second) of his *Essay on Population*, in which he conceded that moral self-restraint could play a significant role in population control. This was a concession to the importance of human reason in mankind's struggle with blind nature and was a triumph for the ideologists who had been the target of his original *Essay*. Characteristically, this concession opened so many controversies over what were reasonable and/or moral methods of controlling conception that the gains to his opponents were more apparent than real.

So much attention has been paid to this revision found in the second edition that little attention has been paid to a second and more significant shift away from the moralistic simplicity of the first *Essay*. In this work he had listed war[2] as one of the factors that limited population, along with hunger, disease, vice and misery. In his second edition (reversing his original position), he concluded that nearly a decade of general war in Europe had not only not reduced population but was in fact stimulating population growth in the combatant nations.

On the face of it, the finding seemed to contradict not only the first *Essay* but common sense itself. War obviously destroyed life and property, disrupted the economy and separated the sexes. Further, Malthus had argued in his first publication that it was the result of social breakdown, with consequent disease and famine, more than battle casualties, that caused depopulation during wars. In 1798, years of revolution and war in enemy territory seemed to have created such conditions, but the evidence he gathered in France in 1802 showed that the 'Four Horsemen of the Apocalypse' had failed in their historic mission. Adding to his embarrassment was the fact the Prime Minister William Pitt, to whom Malthus was sometimes an advisor on economic questions, believed that the Horsemen, urged on by his war policies, were trampling France into the dust.

Pitt's views on war were similar to those of Malthus. War was a struggle of competing economies, with bankruptcy, inflation, riot and starvation the fate of the loser. In a speech before Parliament in 1800, he explained why, in spite of continued French military victories, he expected final victory for England,

I will not dwell on the improved state of public credit, on the continually increased amount, in spite of extraordinary temporary burdens, of our permanent revenue, on the yearly accession of wealth to an extent unprecedented even in the most flourishing times of peace, which we are deriving, in the midst of war, from our extended and flourishing commerce; on the progressive improvement and growth of our manufactures; on the proofs which we see on all sides of the uninterrupted accumulation of productive capital; and on the active exertion of every branch of national industry which can tend to support and augment the population, the riches, and the power of the country.[3]

On the other hand, Pitt thought he saw the French economy buckling and her manpower diminishing,

If we compare this view of our own situation with everything we can observe of the state and condition of our enemy – we can trace him labouring under the equal difficulty of finding men to recruit his army, or money to pay it – if we know that in the course of the last year the most rigorous efforts of military conscription were scarcely sufficient to replace to the French armies at the end of the campaign, the numbers which they had lost in the course of it.[4]

By the time Malthus was involved in the research and writing of the second edition of his *Essay* he had reason to doubt Pitt's evidence and, by implication, some of his own views on population phenomena.

He explained his reasons in his second edition:

I should not have made this country [France] the subject of a distinct chapter but for the circumstance attending the revolution which has excited considerable surprise. This is the undiminished state of the population in spite of the losses sustained during so long and destructive a contest.[5]

Not only in the chapter on France (later expanded to two chapters) but in other chapters later dropped from post-war editions and no longer found in Malthusian works, *The Definitions of Wealth – Agricultural and Commercial Systems* and *Different Effects of the Agricultural and Commercial Systems*, Malthus compared the wartime economies of France and England. In these new sections he attempted to answer the question why many years of warfare had not produced the usual French economic débâcle, and the usual depletion of military manpower and food which had occurred during the previous eighteenth-century wars with France.

In his 1806 edition, with the war resumed in full fury and Napoleon's supposedly understrength and underpaid armies sweeping across Europe, Malthus went even further. He warned against putting reliance upon the widely shared view of Sir Francis d'Ivernois that 1½ million war deaths among the French up to 1799 had reduced the total population of that nation.

> We shall not therefore be inclined to agree with Sir Francis d'Ivernois in his conjecture that the annual births in France have diminished by one-seventh during the revolution. On the contrary, it is more probable that they have increased by this number.[6]

Although he recognised some distortion in the sex and age patterns of the French nation, he said that the social and economic breakdown which was confidently expected and hoped for by the British government was not occurring. Farmers called to arms were replaced by women in the fields: the nation was being fed and the young cared for. Although British blockades had distorted the French industrial economy, those thrown out of work readily found it again in the small farms newly created from the great estates of the Old Regime. War industries boomed.

Pitt was no less misled in his analysis of the French economy of the time than was Napoleon in his evaluation of the English commercial economy, which he expected to collapse into bankruptcy and revolution because its economy 'depended on credit and export and was therefore vulnerable'.[7]

Bonaparte and Pitt were both misled by common sense and the experience of history. Neither nation would suffer social or economic collapse, and the pale horsemen of famine and epidemic would not ride through war-torn Europe. But they were both right in sensing that the possibility was very real. The population of Europe had been growing from about 1400 but since the mid-1700s there had been a significant surge of growth that had taxed the food-producing capacity of that continent. The monarchial governments of the time had responded to the crisis with some intelligence, enriching their food environment by importing and disseminating new food plant varieties such as the potato and attempting, with less success, to remove internal barriers to free grain trade (as in France). Food imports from America increased. Such efforts had been only partly successful, and bad harvest years and/or wartime blockades of overseas grain often brought nations such as France close to starvation.

However, this would not happen during the war years, 1800–15. Both nations were headed by organisational geniuses who were between them hammering out the structure of the modern nation-state. It was an era of expanding governmental powers, not of political breakdown.

It was also an era of commercial and industrial expansion, activities now free of medieval restrictions by the state were encouraged to grow, often for the specific purpose of employing the unemployed. During the war, France and England greatly expanded their military establishments, often by compulsory enlistments, but made little attempt to subordinate the economy to the war effort. The consumer economy was not restricted in order to allow the expansion of war production, as in later wars, but encouraged to expand in order to supply tax funds for the war effort. The butter of the growing civilian economy was not seen as competing with the production of guns, but as a means of paying for guns.

According to his memoirs, Napoleon's problem had not been one of finding manpower for his armies but of finding work for his overflowing population. Fear of hungry Frenchmen was the one fear that he confessed. He showed little interest in improving his weapons, rejecting Fulton's steam boat, the submarine and balloon, but spent great sums to encourage the growth of consumer industries and especially food industries. (The British were quicker to adopt military innovations.)

Malthus was quick to recognise the importance of steam powered energy in the British war effort, but Napoleon stressed the mobilisation and feeding of the vast quantities of human energy released by the Revolution.

Peace at home and victory for his armies famous for 'marching on their stomachs' depended upon his ability to solve the problems of feeding both his troops and a growing population. He subsidised low bread prices and maintained the free movement of grain in France. To solve the food spoilage problem for his armies he created the canning industry (and the British adopted it for their navy). To replace blockaded cane sugar from the Indies he created the beet sugar industry. He was able to import enough rice to supply his troops. To replace coffeee he produced chicory. These substitutes for cane sugar and coffee did not prevent widespread discontent in central Europe.

His programme of road building did him no good in roadless Russia, where his new system of supply depots collapsed with the discipline of his Grande Armée. It was only relatively better with his improvised army of 1813, for by then he was running out of horsepower to move not only his cannon and cavalrymen but his supply wagons as well. The potato was certainly the reason for the French army's ability to live off the land.

Without this new vegetable from America, readily available to the troops from millions of peasant gardens during much of the year, the campaigns of 1813–14 would have resembled those of the closing years of the Thirty Years War.

Yet, for all the loss of this second army in central Europe, Napoleon was able to draft another army in France during the winter of 1813–14. Lefèbvre tells us that, in this final struggle in 1814, Napoleon's problem was not manpower but financing. He ran out of horsepower and financial credit before he ran out of men able to fight.

With industrial leadership, steam engines and access to the world's markets, the British did best in the economic competition with France; nevertheless, Napoleon's Continental System earned respectable attention. Although it may be true that the organisation of a continental economy was beyond his resources, his efforts won the admiration of Americans like Henry Clay and the German, Freidrich List, and strongly influenced the policies of their nations.

England, having survived the threats of wartime bankruptcy and flourished, now faced the disasters of peace. Unemployment on a massive scale followed the closing of war industries and the demobilisation of the armed forces. Trade languished, wholesale prices dropped about a third and capital investment in private industry, when it was most needed, declined abruptly. Tax money went to pay the government's creditors. William Cobbett used the sight of every ruined rural cottage as an occasion to lash out at the 'tax eaters'[8] made prosperous by the war and to renew his proposal to repudiate the ruinous national debt.

Cobbett had authority on his side. Adam Smith had predicted national bankruptcy if the national debt of his time was allowed to increase. David Hume, while granting that war served as 'a temporary encouragement to industry'[9] warned against wars on credit which 'mortgage the public revenues'[10] and 'trust posterity to pay'.[11] He further challenged the 'new doctrine that debts are a public good'.[12]

David Hume's argument against the deficit financing of the victorious Seven Years War had been challenged by George Chalmers near the end of the disastrous 1776–83 war (which had begun because the home government wanted the colonies to help pay the war debt of the previous war). Chalmers argued in his 'Estimate of the Comparative Strength of Britain During the Present and Four Preceding Reigns; and of the Losses of Her Trade From Every War Since the Revolution' that England could bear the economic burden of her war with the servicing of her debt as long as her commerce remained free.

Chalmers' arguments proved to be true for the war years ending in

1783 and again for the wars of 1792 to 1815 but failed to address the old problem of peacetime war debt payments. This problem had brought on the war between Britain and America in 1776 and the French Revolution in 1789. Again, the British had to make the transition from the feverish energy of war with an economy fuelled by borrowed money, to the convalescence of peace, chilled by heavy taxation.

David Ricardo, in his 1817 publication, *The Principles of Political Economy and Taxation*, turned to the same theme.

> Notwithstanding the immense expenditure of the English government during the last twenty years, there can be little doubt that the increased production on the part of the people has more than compensated for it. The national capital has not merely been unimpaired, it has been greatly increased, and the annual revenue of the people, even after the payment of their taxes, is probably greater at the present time than in any former period in our history.
>
> For proof of this, we might refer to the increase of population – to the extension of agriculture – to the increase of shipping and manufactures – to the building of docks – to the opening of numerous canals, as well as to many other expensive undertakings; all denoting an increase both of capital and of annual production.
>
> Still, however, it is certain that, but for taxation, this increase of capital would have been much greater. There are no taxes which have not a tendency to lessen the power to accumulate. All taxes must either fall on capital or revenue.[13]

He argued that, since wages are paid from capital which is saved from revenue, high taxes tended to increase the current problems of unemployment.

Malthus, in his *Principles of Political Economy* (1820), found a flaw in Ricardo's economic psychology. He agreed with all of Ricardo's above statements except the one dealing with taxation. It was clear to him that high taxes were part of the price that had to be paid for the kind of prosperity Britain had enjoyed during the preceding generation,

> It has been said that distresses of the labouring classes since 1815 are owing to a deficient capital, which is evidently unable to employ all that are in want of work.
>
> But it is a very different thing to allow that the capital is deficient compared with the population; and to allow that it is deficient compared with the demand for it and the demand for the commodities procured by it.[14]

Capital saved from taxes would not mean increased investment as long as prices and demand remained low: 'During nearly the whole of the war, owing to the union of great powers of production with a great effectual consumption and demand, the prodigious destruction of capital by the government was much more than recovered.'[15]

Most significantly of all, the war, far from decimating the population, carried it to a new level of growth, which continued after the war was over – 'the powerful stimulus which had been given to population during the war, occasioned the pouring in of fresh supplies of labour'.[16]

This disagreement with Ricardo regarding a tax policy to deal with the post-war depression induced him to make a more detailed analysis of the phenomena of their previous wartime prosperity. That experience had moved him further from the mechanistic view of the economics of scarcity found in his own first *Essay* and brought him closer to the Godwin–Condorcet view that economics was responsive to the human will and public policy.

During the war years, England's command of the sea meant that the persistent problem of high food prices never reached a crisis level. Increased domestic production and imports kept the growing nation fed, although meat prices soared. With high food prices, investment in agriculture increased, but with the return of peace, food prices plunged. In spite of drastically lower prices, hunger reappeared among the English unemployed.

Malthus resisted the idea of developing a two-track system of an industrial economy tending towards surpluses alongside an agricultural economy tending towards shortages. The post-war depression had injured both sectors of the economy. Adam Smith's rule that industrial labour gains its food at the expense of agricultural labour was changing as industry continued to produce more horse-powered farm machinery such as seed drills, harrows, self-sharpening steel ploughs, horse-hoes and threshing machines. William Cobbett, who held to the old views, hated the sight of such equipment in farm yards, seeing in them further evidence of the capitalisation of agriculture.

The collapse of farm prices after the war meant that the burden of heavy taxes was ruinous to thousands of once prosperous farmers and landlords.

David Ricardo urged that the taxes be reduced to relieve owners of capital and increase the funds available to pay idle labour:

The desire which every man has to keep his station in life, and to maintain his wealth at the height which it has once attained, occasions most taxes, whether laid on capital or on income, to be paid from income; and, therefore, as taxation proceeds, or as government increases its expenditure, the annual enjoyments of the people must be diminished, unless they are enabled proportionally to increase their capitals and income. It should be the policy of governments to encourage a disposition to do this in the people, and never to lay such taxes as will inevitably fall on capital; since, by so doing, they impair the funds for the maintenance of labour, and thereby diminish the future production of the country.[17]

Malthus pointed out the inconsistency of applauding a wartime prosperity while deploring the tax expenditures that helped generate that prosperity. He was convinced that less government taxing and spending would increase their problems. 'The evil imposed by a tax is rarely compensated by taking it off.'[18] He challenged Ricardo's idea, common at the time, that it was the expenditures of the capital-owning classes which drove the economy. Malthus argued that it was the growing middle classes and wage earners who generated effective demand in the market. Further, he defended the class denounced by Cobbett as 'tax eaters'.

With regard to these latter classes, such as statesmen, soldiers, sailors, and those who live upon the interest of a national debt, it cannot be denied that they contribute powerfully to distribution and demand; they frequently occasion a division of property more favorable to the progress of wealth than would otherwise have taken place; they insure that effective consumption which is necessary to give the proper stimulus to production; and the desire to pay a tax, and yet enjoy the same means of gratification, must often operate to excite the exertions of industry quite as effectually as the desire to pay a lawyer or physician.[19]

Malthus's proposed solutions to the post-war depression outraged both economists and moralists alike. To his morally impermissible idea of assigning to war the blessings traditionally associated with peace he added a defence of the 'unproductive consumer'. The phrase displayed his genius for putting his ideas into their most unpalatable form. In the language of the economists of the time, this simply meant that the work of such people did not result in the creation of a product or commodity. With his keen eye for social change, he had noticed the rapid increase of service workers during the war years. In this class he included doctors, government officials, dancing masters, menial servants, parsons, armed forces personnel and, presumably, professors of economics.

However offensive the name, 'unproductive consumers' played a key role in Malthus's political economy, both as consumers and performers of often essential or vital services. But Malthus could find no way to calculate the value of services in the summation of national wealth. (How do you compare the services of a dancing master with those of a surgeon?)

Ricardo found it impossible to accept the idea in this form, especially since he regarded the landlord class as the very model of the unproductive consumer.

When his colleague, J. R. McCulloch, attempted to come to Malthus's rescue on this point by insisting that services valued at their market price should be included in the listing of the nation's total production of wealth, he rejected the idea on technical grounds, thereby adding that able economist to the list of his enemies. (McCulloch became editor of the *Edinburgh Review* and henceforth barred Malthus from its influential pages.)

For all the value of these 'unproductive consumers', Malthus found that they were not able to create sufficient effective demand to match the productivity created during the war years. Hesitantly, for he was a Radical Whig with a long record of opposing the expansion of government authority, he recommended the old mercantilist device of government deficit spending on roads, harbours, public buildings, bridges and other public works as a means of reviving the effective demand for the nation's produce. In one of his last works he added railway construction to this list.

Correlated with this new understanding was his realisation that the worker was no longer motivated simply by the need to work enough to survive and maintain his family at the 'customary' level of existence, a concept that formed the base line for the then established labour theory of value which Malthus had expressed in his first *Essay*. Scarcity could no longer assure the worker's labour nor guarantee his purchases. If a few days labour could satisfy his usual needs, he must be offered goods more desirable than simple necessities to induce him to work the rest of the week. Malthus rejected the idea popular in upper-class England that the best solution to this problem was to cut wages. He argued that, while an agricultural society may create its own customers, this was not the case in an industrial economy. In this new age the desire to consume must be created before production could be made effective by consumption. He agreed with Say that wealth produces want but insisted that want also produces wealth, reflecting the growth of the psychological element as compared to the physical element in his thought. He pointed out that goods are not always exchanged for goods but increasingly for services.

The prevailing thought of the time held that capital, freed by low taxation from investment, would automatically generate prosperity. This was consistent with Jean Baptist Say's argument in his 1803 *Traité d'Economie Politique* that all economic production created an equal amount of consumption.

Malthus denied it. For one thing, the profit added to the labour cost of production assured that the workers could not consume all that they produced. (In at least one instance, Malthus stated that profits were taken from the labourer's 'produce', thus supplying Ricardo and Marx with this labour theory of value, but, for the most part, he employed the profit-added concept.) While the conditions of rising market prices prevailed, the needed consumption and investment were assured. Such conditions prevailed in times of massive government deficit spending, as in periods of war. In peacetime the process was reversed, bringing on depression.

The habits of investors compounded the problem.

> But it has already been shown that the consumption and demand occasioned by the workmen employed in productive labour can never *alone* furnish a motive to the accumulation and employment of capital; and with regard to the capitalists themselves, together with the landlords and other rich persons, they have, by the supposition, agreed to be parsimonious, and by depriving themselves of their usual conveniences and luxuries to save from their revenue and add to their capital. Under these circumstances, it is impossible that the increased number of productive labourers, should find purchasers, without such a fall of price as would probably sink their value below that of the outlay, or, at least, so reduce profits as very greatly to diminish both the power and the will to save.[20]

Malthus's belief that underconsumption was a characteristic of the peacetime industrial economy made him a champion of unpopular causes, especially among his fellow economists. This was most obvious in his defence of the Corn Laws and the interests of the landlords who benefited most directly from them. He denied that such government-sponsored benefits to one class violated the 'survival of the morally fit' ideas found in his first *Essay*. His aim was to maintain a viable balance between the growing industrial economy and the agricultural food supply of the country. He regarded industry as the ascendant economy of England at that time and likely to remain so for some time in the future. This fact should be recognised and accommodated in public policy, but it should not be seen as an eternal law. It should be realised that English industrial pre-eminence which gave her a claim upon the food supplies of the world would not last forever. He foresaw the days when cotton mills and foundries would be established everywhere in the world, and the English must look to their own food-producing capacity for survival. Also, now there was the possibility of a naval blockade to be considered. Therefore, the Corn Laws supporting English agricultural production were justified. English industrial leadership would end someday, but the population generated in an era of government-fostered expansion would still exist and would have to be fed from mainly national food sources.

Malthus agreed that this policy would deny cheap imported food to workers, but insisted that such a diet was not in their best interest, pointing to the cheap Irish subsistence diet of potatoes and the banana diet popular in Central America. In those areas, cheap food was associated with extreme poverty.

His defence in his later works was that he had produced not one but a number of laws of population; some applying to primitive mankind, others to classical and to modern agricultural societies. Emerging industrial societies had different demographic characteristics. In his *Principles of Political Economy* he dealt with an industrial–commercial society with its increasing ability to manipulate nature and man's economy to a degree that was not true in an agricultural age. Under this new system the government must take responsibility for the results of government action. When a generation (1793–1815) of expanding prosperity related to government wartime measures produced an extra 4 million British people, the government could not escape responsibility of their continued employment in peacetime. In an industrial society oriented towards war, Malthus's early ideas about the individual's responsibility for his employment did not apply, or applied only with important adjustments. The popular, reasonable and seemingly scientific idea that nature (or God) supplied some automatic balance wheel to keep mankind's numbers within his niche of nature had to be abandoned. The Ricardian idea that available capital regulated the size of population within the limits of exploitable soils was consistent with early Malthusian thought, but it ignored the fact that the wartime government had demonstrated its ability to generate capital at will. Therefore, the moral responsibility for population growth had been transferred to the government that incited and sustained this growth.

At the same time, he rejected the habit of considering rents and profits as the main concern of economic study. He would move the wage-earning classes and their economic well-being to the centre of the study of economics:

> In every point of view therefore, both in reference to that art of the annual produce which falls to their share, and the means of health and happiness which it may be presumed to communicate, those who live on the wages of labour must be considered as the most important portion of the society.[21]

This recognition of the interests of the wage-earning class as paramount in national policy represents a milestone in English economic theory. It induced Malthus to make important changes in his image of the worker, his attitudes, his life and the changes that were taking place in his life. Malthus had always argued that the limitations of the environment inspired the will to improvement and success, 'evil seems to be necessary to create exertion, and exertion seems evidently necessary to create mind'.[22] In his *Essay on the Principle of Population* he had stressed the role of the loser with Calvanistic fervour. Now, aware of the possibilities of the industrial age, he shifted the focus of his interests to the increasing opportunities for workers to break out of the drudgery of subsistence living. He foresaw that England's 1821 population (14 391 631) could triple and then level off with a higher standard of living.

During the century of peace following the Napoleonic wars, Malthus's thought survived outside the mainstream of economic doctrine. It required another post-World war depression to bring him back to popularity in the form of Keynesian economics; as he might have feared, popular to an excess. Programmes to increase the exchangeable value of the whole mass of the national product have been popular with governments to a fault. The inflation of currencies has progressed from a cure of depressions to a major malaise of industrial societies. Too soon the World has forgotten the Malthusian rule that the problems of economics are problems of proportion.

The problems of overpopulation, seen in his time as one for crowded little Europe, have now taken on the proportions of a worldwide crisis, more serious because the empty spaces are filled.

Malthus's original Law of Population seemed to assure that such a problem could not develop. The laws of economics seemed to operate in

harmony with the laws of nature to assure that mankind would continue
to function within the parameters of his niche in nature, in harmony with
eternal laws. Malthus's later revisions to meet the economy of the
industrial age denied this comfortable idea and presented mankind with
the problem of determining population levels in new and constantly
changing environments. It was his last service in his office of Devil's
Advocate.

NOTES AND REFERENCES

1. J. Schumpeter, *Economic Analyses* (New York, 1960) p. 16.
2. T. R. Malthus, *An Essay on the Principle of Population*, 1st ed. of 1798
(reprinted New York, 1954) p. 580.
3. W. Pitt, 'Address to the Throne', 3 February 1800, in C. Goodrich (ed.),
Select British Eloquence (New York, 1867) p. 628. *The Preliminary Observations to the Population Abstracts*, printed in 1811, gave the population of
England in 1790 as 8.675 million and in 1800 as 9.168 million.
4. Ibid., Pitt, p. 628.
5. Malthus, op. cit., *An Essay . . .* 2nd ed. of 1802 (reprinted New York, 1960)
p. 253.
6. Ibid., p. 258.
7. Napoleon Bonaparte, quoted by G. Lefêbvre, *From Tilsit to Waterloo* (New
York, 1969) p. 108.
8. W. Cobbett, *Rural Rides* (London, 1821) p. 30.
9. D. Hume, *Writings* (University of Wisconsin, 1955 ed.) p. 91.
10. Ibid., p. 90.
11. Ibid., p. 90.
12. Ibid., p. 92.
13. D. Ricardo, *Political Economy and Taxation*, in *Master Works of Economics*
(New York, 1948) p. 334.
14. T. R. Malthus, *Principles of Political Economy*, 2nd ed. of 1836 (reprinted
New York, 1964) p. 414.
15. Ibid., p. 416.
16. Ibid., p. 417.
17. Ricardo, op. cit., p. 335.
18. Malthus, op. cit., *Principles . . .* Boston ed. of 1821, p. 388.
19. Ibid., 2nd ed. of 1836, p. 409.
20. Ibid., p. 315.
21. Ibid., p. 368.
22. Malthus, op. cit., *An Essay . . .* 1st ed., p. 130.

Index

The references to the name 'Malthus' are too numerous to index with any satisfaction, and so under the entry Malthus an indication is given of the various subjects on which he made observations and for which there is some comment in this book. This book is primarily set in Britain, and so unless otherwise indicated entries in this index refer to England, Britain, United Kingdom, etc.

Index

working classes   *see* labouring classes
Wotton (Surrey)   20–2, 27–32, 38n
Wrigley, E. A. and R. S. Schofield   9, 11,
   13–15, 118
Wrotham (Kent)   58n

Yorkshire   125
Young, Arthur   88, 145, 150, 161